UNIVERSAL AUNTS

Kate Herbert-Hunting

UNIVERSAL AUNTS

Constable · London

First published in Great Britain 1986
by Constable and Company Limited
10 Orange Street London WC2H 7EG
Copyright © 1986 by Kate Herbert-Hunting
Set in Linotron Ehrhardt 10pt by
Rowland Phototypesetting Limited
Bury St Edmunds, Suffolk
Printed in Great Britain by
St Edmundsbury Press
Bury St Edmunds, Suffolk

British Library CIP Data
Herbert-Hunting, Kate
Universal Aunts
1. Visiting housekeepers – Great Britain
I. Title
362.1′4′0941   HV687.5.G7

ISBN 0 09 467170 2

I dedicate this book to
MARGARET FRY
and all the Universal Aunts, past and present,
who have made this story

CONTENTS

ILLUSTRATIONS

ACKNOWLEDGEMENTS

With acknowledgement and thanks for their kind help in my research:

Sir Fitzroy Maclean, Bt, CBE, MP (Fitzroy); Mrs Guy Mullens (Jane); Mrs Margot Alston (Miss Mouse); the late Miss Frances Blackett; the late The Hon Mildred Leith; Mr and Mrs John Faulder; Mrs Leila Faulder; Mrs Sheila du Pré; Mr Michael Turton; Mr Frank Wilby; Dr Raymond V. Turley; Miss Margaret Fry. I am grateful to the B.B.C. for permission to quote part of a script from *Mrs Dale's Diary*.

Carol Burns guided my first steps in writing; Joy Lee, Patsy Wright and Susan Palmer-Jones all spent patient hours typing; Jenny Ridley helped with spelling; and Angie Montfort Bebb provided 'The Duke of Clarence'. Special thanks to all the Aunts in the office who gave help when it was needed, particularly Marion Berlyn; and to Jo St Clair and Sue Brown who were so often 'the runners'.

My nearest and dearest have for so long boosted me along the writing way, I'm sure to their relief I can now say thank you – parents, husband, children: William and Mary Fry; Leonard; Anthony, Angie, Nicco, Jane, Jamie, Vanessa.

And to my partner, Penelope Henshaw, thank you for your support.

Kate Herbert-Hunting
1986

FOREWORD

In the winter of 1972 I walked into the office of Universal Aunts with no thought of a career and no talents to offer other than the happy experience of life as a wife and mother. Margaret Fry, the formidable but fair Managing Director, said that those assets could be put to good use outside one's own family. She knew, but I did not, the disciplines to be learned in order to do just that! Otherwise, would I have dared so confidently to accept the offer of £30 per week from 21 February 1972 to become head of the Special Services department and a working woman?

At the same time, the Managing Director was seeking another member of staff as head of the Meetings department, which took charge of travelling children and students. Penelope Henshaw was the choice and on 8 May she also changed her life and became a Universal Aunt. Her task was deemed more arduous than mine, her previous office experience more worthy and her remuneration, I seem to remember, was therefore slightly higher, but we have decided not to check back!

The standard three months' trial period hung over us both. We survived that; in 1974 we were invited on to the Board, and this led to our becoming joint owners of the Company ten years later.

Universal Aunts came into being on 21 February 1921, so a lot had happened before we arrived. Everyone knew Universal Aunts and we found that many people had their own versions of its history and were sure that they owned a great-aunt who had been its founder.

One day a letter arrived on my desk:

Mrs John H. Weinberg
Baton Rouge

31 June 1977

Dear Ladies,

The name of your organization and some of the work you do has been
known to me for a long time, by word and through 'In Britain'. I would
like to have some more information and history. For instance, do you
have a branch in New York?

Mr Weinberg and I will be visiting London in the Fall and would
very much like to call and see such an old British institution.

Yours very truly,
Clare H. Weinberg.

Not an unusual enquiry. Tourists often drop in to see if we really exist,
calling us 'Aunties' and remarking that we are 'younger than we
imagined'. I began to think up my usual one-page version of fifty-six
years of Aunts at work for Mrs Weinberg. 'Why this potted version?' I
thought. 'Why not really tell the story of this group of British women,
and give our Founder her due?'

There were piles of dusty books in cupboards, musty brown newspaper reports, sepia photographs. Valuable records had been put together
by former directors; immaculately kept Minute Books were handwritten
in the style of each decade. There were letters with crumbling edges and
smart, engraved addresses, and some famous signatures. There was, in
its secret dusty place in the locked stationery cupboard, an item of past
and present Company history to which we, in our turn, now had access.
Lifted out of a battered brown cardboard box, the great black-
lacquered, lead Company Seal came to light. It takes two separate
people to unlock its authority: the Managing Director holds one small,
craggy key, threaded through with a scrap of the *real* Founder's
pink-and-white spotted silk dress; the Company Secretary holds the
other, dangling from an old piece of pink legal tape. It takes the force of
both hands pressing down the handle, with its delicate worn gilt
scrolling, to imprint the round embossed seal on to a document and
complete the business of the day. The sight and feel of so old an
inanimate object excites the imagination of a less durable human being
to wonder what has gone before.

There were also those delightful and generous people who willingly gave me their time and were happy to reminisce. Through all of this, the true story has come together, and the gaps in the years and generations before my time have hopefully been filled as fittingly as they would all have wished.

K.H.-H.

ODE TO THE AUNTS

If the Duke of Clarence had not needed to look for his own Malmsey (for
  where was his butler?),
If King Alfred had had a cook,
If Anne of Cleves had taken some advice on prevailing English fashion
  and customs,
And if only the Princes in the Tower had been left with a proper
  babysitter . . .
If only there had been an institution offering help and advice . . .
If only there had been Universal Aunts.

Angela Montfort Bebb

It was in 1921 that Gertrude Eliza Maclean had her 'good idea' and
solved these problems.

PART I

1921

GERTIE

*Childhood – The General – Family aunt –
The idea – Joshua Steed*

Three years after World War I ended, many women were restless; Gertrude Eliza Maclean was one of them. Now well into her thirties, she sought a future. The past had not been uneventful and Gertie had a good few assets in hand.

She had been born before the turn of the century into a privileged class. When grown up and telling to children the story of 'when I was little', Gertie, as we all do, liked to recall the happy, sunny, holiday times. Sand and sun and ponies and cake for tea. There was Mama, soft and scented in big, floppy hats with roses, but often not well and not to be jumped upon; Papa sometimes in uniform, with shiny buttons that hurt when he hugged you, but he was strong, and played all the games, and rode the ponies when he came home from the Regiment; Grandmama in lace; Grandpapa with hidden pockets full of sweeties – mint imperials for him, but soft pastilles for you because once Aunt Elisabeth had choked on an imperial and had to be held upside down by her legs to get it out. This was the stuff of Gertie's life in the days when such a background merged the child almost into young woman-hood without much change, and cocooned her through the difficult times.

Soft wool rugs were spread on pink sand, a white tablecloth was unfolded and picnic baskets were unpacked for tea. There were little sandwiches and spongy buns and silvery milk cans wrapped in cool, wet napkins. For a treat, there were sweet biscuits with coloured icing packed in tins, decorated with flowers and cats and smiling children. A very typical figure presided; spry and forty-ish with thick, pale brown hair looped and pinned under a sedate cream straw boater with a grey ribbon round it and streamers down the back. A high-necked grey cotton frock, tucked, ankle-length, long-sleeved and with a tiny white edge to neck and cuff. Always the same, cushioning, cool, dependable and much-loved Nanny.

Summoned by her to 'come for tea', with a rush of shoves and squeals Gertie's brothers and sisters instantly obeyed: Elsie and Somerset, Henry, Adrian, Charles and George (who were older) and Minnie and Marguerite (younger). The call reached Gertie but only disturbed her quiet play and her thoughts. She scrambled on top of the boys' sandcastle and surveyed them all.

'I know what we can do, let's –'

They all drowned what she was going to say. 'Oh Gertie, not another good idea!'

Nanny got on with pouring milk and muttered to the skinny nursery maid, 'One day that seventh child is going to have a good idea that comes to something, I shouldn't wonder.' It was only a passing thought.

Within such sheltered unconcern the first sixteen years of Gertie's life passed. At that point, in 1900, she lost her father. Lt Colonel Allan Henry Maclean of the Royal Artillery died with his regiment in early middle age, leaving his beautiful wife Lucy finally unpregnant but also unequipped to cope alone with the legacy of nine children.

Grandfather Maclean became the central figure in all their lives. Five words adequately described the General – 'twenty-fifth Chief of Clan Maclean'. This spendidly ageing man, broad, upright, ruddy, white-whiskered, kept his heart in his ancestral and spiritual place, Duart Castle on the Isle of Mull. Resources did not match the needs of the gale-battered, leaking castle, so while things were at such a low ebb the General out of practical necessity had made a small and comfortable gentleman's residence in the southern counties of England his stronghold.

Lucy thankfully accepted her father-in-law as a watchful, resilient guardian of her younger girls, Gertie, Min and Daisy. Subtle, and to her incomprehensible, changes were happening. Her married daughters not only heard of but practised the previously unmentionable 'birth control', by which they were deciding how many children they had, and when. It was apparent in their blooming health and their ability to be free to join their husbands in other sports, whirling off into the country on a bicycle, playing tennis or swimming. Gentlemen were less abstemious, having their cake, etc. . . .

On the fringe of the world of the Macleans and their ilk were the working-class families who served their needs, or tenants to whom they had responsibilities by reason of status. These women could not afford the cost of, nor were they emotionally equipped for, such new methods. They went on increasing their brood in cottages and slums.

Divorce had existed for some time as a fact of life. Its basic purpose, however, was to act as a deterrent to a wife from engaging in adultery. She could be divorced for that alone, by which she forfeited her husband's support, her children and her home. A husband's adultery did not count, unless 'aggravated by another matrimonial offence'. Into this cosy legislation, initiated by men for the benefit of men, glided one Mrs Stark in 1910. This adventurous, bored, or otherwise dissatisfied lady overstepped the mark with a Mr Hitchins, and she and he were caught in bed together. The furious Mr Stark divorced his wife and kept their daughter. Mr Hitchins made an honest woman of the ex-Mrs Stark and the child ran away from Papa to join Mama. The mother went to jail for refusing to hand her back.

Their Lordships sat, and the Court of Appeal freed her, pronouncing that: 'the benefit and interest of the infant is the paramount consideration, and not the punishment of the guilty party.'

Their ruling did not, however, become law; the Church and the public at large were not ready for such a meddlesome influence within the institution of marriage. It was to take another twenty-seven years before lawyer, writer and wit, Sir Alan Herbert, managed to get these and further reforms passed in the Herbert Act.

On the political scene, Mrs Pankhurst and her followers were battering on the doors of every male stronghold in their fight for votes for women.

These, then, were the social influences shaping the role of women as Gertie grew up. Her mother, weakened in health and depleted by early widowhood, succumbed to the pressures of her loneliness and died. Grandfather's house remained Gertie's permanent haven.

Gertie had a delicate, elusive beauty. She was petite and immaculate, with tawny silk hair fashionably bobbed, large blue eyes, and a particularly attractive voice. Her character was diverse, darting and plunging into every idea that took hold. Between times she hibernated, reflective and remote, while she dreamed up the next idea; but never for long.

Gertie had many close friends and acquaintances. Together they engaged in the charitable works expected of them. She danced through the night and enjoyed the high flings and pranks of the hectic socializing of the day. Three times Gertie was engaged, and twice called off the marriage. On the third occasion, the cad, Wildbore-Smith, told her that he had promised to marry another girl (when he was very young) and felt 'in honour bound' to keep his promise when this girl objected to his engagement to Gertie. Gertie went on to dally with a noble Russian prince who threatened suicide if he lost her. She kept the affair thrillingly alive long enough to supply her nephew, Fitzroy, with a fine collection of Russian stamps and anecdotes with which he made his mark at school.

She spent any little money that came her way on the clothes she loved so much more than men. Slim wool and velour coats with fur and velvet collars and cuffs. Slender pastel chemise dresses for evening, short and beaded and hanging from narrow shoulder straps, designed to avoid any curve. Pale silk stockings, soft kid shoes, and slippers with little heels, strapped over the instep. Often, inside the neck, was stitched a small silk label, 'Jane'. Gertie was quite vain.

When not so occupied, she had in fact two more serious and fulfilling loves; her fantasies and the children in her life. She wrote romantic plays and stories. She roped in the family to act in the former, called on her young niece Jane, already a talented dress designer, for superb costumes, and produced them for after-dinner entertainment or charity in the homes of family and friends. Her stories were often illustrated and bound and donated as gifts. One such, about a fairy called Wavy Wind, had pictures drawn by the portrait painter Sybil Tawes. This she gave to her little niece and godchild, Margot, whose son Richard Alston has it to this day.

Gertie's first love and affinity was for her nephews and nieces, and children generally. It was curious that, not lacking in offers, she did not set her sights on a family of her own. This feeling, however, to the benefit of many, led her into her life's work.

Of the nine children of Allan and Lucy Maclean, all married except for Gertie and Min, who were the closest. Some died young, like George who drowned during his honeymoon in India. Min, following the family tradition of service, became a Queen Alexandra's nursing sister. She distinguished herself in India and took high rank when war broke out.

The family travelled widely, serving abroad in the navy or rusticating in the shires. Mama's place was always beside Papa, wherever he was, regulating or governing our affairs, but the children could not, of course, be kept from a proper English upbringing and their father's schools.

'Little Aunt', as the children knew her, was the one who was always on hand. She was a rock and a sport. Gertie met their trains and boats, gave them hugs and kisses and tucked them safely up in bed. She told them her stories and they confided to her about home, school and pets. She took them to Daniel Neal or Harrods for school clothes and into the animal department to see the puppies, little monkeys and minute baby alligators, then to tea at Gunter's. At packing a tuck box 'Little Aunt' was an expert, filling the corners with hidden treasures. The children loved it that she looked and smelt delicious. She was the perfect 'all an aunt should be'.

After the convulsions of the First World War, tours of duty came to an end. The Englishman abroad had prepared the ground in the pink areas of the world map, which began to need him in lesser numbers. Parents were coming home to settle and take up their own duties, and children were growing up. Gertie found her brood had flown.

It dawned upon her and her family that she was faced with less useful days ahead. Grandfather called them together to dine. They met before dinner, talked and giggled at the men's antics with their new toy, the cocktail shaker. The ladies were slender and pretty with fragrant pansy faces, powdered, lipsticked, with thin, surprised eyebrows; the gentlemen were immaculate as black-and-white penguins. The General joined them in full fig, a Highland chief, to sit at the head of his table.

Cook had excelled with the Scotch beef. The black, freezing night was shut away outside; inside was the blazing warmth of great logs and the soft glow of candlelight on silver and glass. Velvet hangings and oil paintings, and the sheen of wood, were in aged and muted colours of chestnut brown, greens, blues, ivory and mulberry. In the shadows the servants glided, their sleek darkness pin-pointed by the whiteness of gloves and silver buttons.

The matter of Gertie's future was discussed. Old Uncle Admiral Whitworth listened a while and came straight to the point. 'Why not, my darling gel, do for others what you have been doing for your own family?'

Gertie gave a quick reply.

'And be a Universal Aunt?'

Second thoughts and maybes were not part of Gertie's nature. She stayed up late, composing her letter to the family solicitor. Before putting it into the morning post, she read it through and realized she had found her need and her answer.

Joshua Owen Steed Esq,
Solicitor,
Long Melford,
Suffolk.

My dear Mr Steed,
Close to my family as you are, you will no doubt receive what I have to say with no great surprise.

I plan a venture which will, I hope, fulfil my search for an opportunity to use my time and intelligence.

I would hope, too, that other like-minded ladies can become involved. Since the war forced open the drawing-room doors, so many women with the advantage of background, commonsense and family experience have found it difficult to return therein.

There is now a yearning for a continued independence and, in many cases, a need for extra income. One sees that there are those small commissions and odds and ends of human need which no-one else seems to find it profitable to meet.

My proposed undertaking would bring the two together to the advantage of both. ANYTHING FOR ANYONE AT ANYTIME.

I would welcome an appointment to see you so that I may, once again, have your wise counsel as well as requesting your legal services for setting up my business.

In the expectation that you will, as usual, be in London on Tuesday or Wednesday of next week, I wonder if you might be free for luncheon with me at 1 Cromwell Place on one of those days at mid-day? Otherwise, perhaps you would suggest an appointment.

In anticipation of our meeting, when I hope to learn that you may share my enthusiasm and optimism for the future of the business which, by the way, I intend to call 'UNIVERSAL AUNTS'.

Yours most sincerely,
Gertrude Maclean.

Miss Gertrude Maclean
1 Cromwell Place
SW 7

My dear Miss Maclean,
It is with great interest that I read your letter of yesterday's date. I do indeed share both your enthusiasm and optimism, for it seems to me

that there has been such a reversal of circumstances brought about by the war that I have no doubt you will find no difficulty in procuring both workers and clients.

Gone are the days when the only women who may look to employ themselves outside the house were Girton girls or a 'blue stocking'. Certain lady pioneers and a world war forced upon us the fact that women can be gainfully, satisfyingly and attractively employed in the outside world. It has also been only too frequently proved that an amateur is not necessarily just a dabbler.

At most levels finances are strained. A daughter's allowance, for instance; an income earned by her would surely be encouraged.

Many have cut corners, but their lack of experience in household economy has produced ineffectual results.

Stringencies are being practised above stairs; below stairs, the staff and tradesmen continue their usual 'arrangements' so that no benefit is being felt by the master.

Your proposed service might do well to include a discreet household management course, ladies who could act as short term stewardesses. A sorting-out on a professional basis, preventing loss of face downstairs.

There is, too, the new money. Are those newly rich not likely to see you as an answer to their prayers for guidance through the minefields of society, more hazardous to them than those they faced in the war?

The possibilities are so endless that they have carried me into a letter of some length, so I must reserve further pleasure in discussion until our meeting.

I thank you for your most kind invitation which I am delighted to accept and I look forward with pleasure to luncheon at 12 o'clock in Kensington on Tuesday next.

Yours sincerely,
Joshua Steed.

Joshua Steed arrived on the dot. He was a man to whom one would certainly give a second glance, tall and powerful, with deep copper hair closely cut to the head to control the exuberant curling, kind eyes and a fine, aquiline nose. Handsome in early middle-age, he would become a distinguished 'old gentleman'. He walked, with rhythmic swings of his rolled umbrella, very upright to his full six foot three inches, from whence he always seemed to be enjoying the view. The perfect lawyer on duty, he wore black jacket, striped trousers, snowy, stiff-collared shirt; on his small estate, ancient soft Lovat tweeds.

Gertie, like every other woman client of Joshua Steed, felt prettier, more intelligent, confident and utterly secure in his presence. He was a good lawyer and an astute man with great charm. He knew that this scheme would restrain Gertie from frippering about looking for a cause. He also knew that any initial investment would be small and fairly secure and, if handled well, it was potentially a money-making project.

So to a light luncheon of cutlets, good hock and excellent cheese, which delighted without demanding attention. They talked. They enlarged upon the ideas expressed in the letters and found no obstacle to delay the project.

As usual, finance had not entered Gertie's head. She had very little to draw upon anyway. Joshua Steed had taken the precaution of checking the point with the General and been told that the family would rally round to find the initial outgoings. Their meeting ended with his suggestion that Gertie must seek an office from which to conduct her business. Returning to Suffolk, he would await instructions to secure such a place, arrange finance, advise and safeguard her in her role as employer and business woman.

1921

EMMIE

*The Universal Aunt – The blue office – The lady of
refinement and common sense – Post-war women –
The first Aunts – The first clients*

It was Grandfather, the General, who came by chance upon a workroom. While visiting his bootmaker, he heard that there was at 181,
Sloane Street, a little, unused room at the rear. The following morning
Gertie was on her way to view it. That evening at dinner she regaled
the family with her description of her first visit to a gentleman's
establishment.

She mounted shallow steps off Sloane Street and entered through the
door which said *'W. H. Smith. Bespoke Bootmaker.'* A small, smiling,
pink-faced man hurried forward to be of service in this important
matter. Mr Smith led Gertie through reception, a brown room with
military and sporting engravings, upright leather chairs and footstools.
Gertie found the smell of leather overpowering. She was to become so
accustomed to it as not to notice it.

Passing the door of the workroom, she glimpsed neat shelves of
wooden lasts like skeleton feet, labelled for identification. Several men
in huge aprons were bent over central benches. Mr Smith explained that
the men were 'clinking' with their small knives, slicing into the fine, soft
leathers, hammering and moulding the shoes and boots that would be
worn and cherished for a lifetime.

Mr Smith opened the next door and they entered a tiny square
room. The walls were clean and freshly painted blue. The window
on the far wall looked on to the backs of buildings and several huge,
gnarled trees with February's bare branches. It was not the Ritz, but
Gertie was thrilled. This would be her office. The rent of 10s a
week was agreed, the hours 9.0 a.m. to mid-day, and immediate
occupation.

Gertie decided that she needed a table and chair, a notebook and
pencil, someone to help her, and another chair for the 'someone'. She

borrowed the furniture from home, bought the writing materials, and advertised for the help:

A lady of refinement and common sense, tact and discretion needed to join other ladies in Britain's first Personal Service Bureau.

An elderly widow sitting in her drawing-room in Boundary Road, St John's Wood, turned the pages of her *Times*, snipped out the advertisement and passed it to her daughter with the unflattering comment, 'Why don't you apply? After all, you are not fitted for anything else.'

So it was that Emily Story Faulder, a spinster in her mid-thirties, replied and was invited for an interview at Gertie's new office. Gertie opened the door to a large, upright lady with a tendency to lean forward, the whole body supported on such slender legs that Gertie feared for her balance. Flaxen hair was turning to grey, she had a strong, rather severe face and voice, and the eyes behind rimless spectacles were authoritative. Emmie Faulder's manner was matter-of-fact but interested. She radiated goodwill and eagerness to be helpful. Her hat, coat and skirt were of good material and sombre colour, her matching black shoes, bag and gloves of excellent quality.

Gertie posed the questions and led Emmie to reveal her background. The family of her late father, Joseph Sewell Faulder, who had died in 1902, were the Faulders of Moor House Hall, Wetherall on the Eden, Cumbria, from where they had hailed for centuries, gentlemen of the parish and wool merchants. Emmie had recently returned from a spell in India, where she had acted as hostess to her brother Lt Colonel George Bertram Faulder, DSC Indian Army XIX Hyderabad. Her tact had been tested in negotiating the social intricacies of service life, and proved by the warm and enduring friends she had left behind.

Good humour had been instilled into Emmie's character as a necessity in taking charge, with her mother, of five younger brothers and sisters since the death of her father. She was obviously strong and healthy, and expressed a delight in children and animals. Since she was unmarried, the war had left her, like thousands of other women of her generation, a permanent spinster.

Emmie became Number Two to Gertie's directorship of the venture. From first to last, they referred to one another as 'Miss Maclean' and 'Miss Faulder'.

The scene was ready. Gertie set about putting it into action, offering to do the things that she knew how to do and roping in others who would also know or soon learn what was needed. She and Emmie plotted and planned and could be seen, with fear of failure looming before them, hatted and gloved and heading by trundling motor-bus to the offices of *The Times*. Their effort in advertising was designed to bring a response from both workers and wanters. It read:

UNIVERSAL AUNTS

(LADIES OF IRREPROACHABLE BACKGROUND)

CARE OF CHILDREN

CHAPERONAGE

HOUSE FURNISHING

SHOPPING FOR THE COLONIES

RESEARCH WORK

There it was in black and white, with a box number for replies. The answers came: suspicious, curious, interested. There was a number of 'irreproachable ladies' who longed to join the ranks if the ranks were really 'irreproachable' too. There were potential clients wanting fuller information, unable to believe that there were safe and reliable hands into which they might place their little problems.

Without a doubt there is a right moment for everything, and Gertie hit hers. *'Anything on a business basis'* was a most appealing notion. The idea germinated and the grapevine buzzed. There were increasing numbers of women at university or entering the professions, but a great many more with just intelligence, common sense, and new-found time to spare.

When the Great War had come, the women of Britain had been left in no doubt as to their DUTY: to tell their men to GO and to replace them on the land, in the factories, working in the hospitals and canteens, driving ambulances, on the buses and emptying the dustbins. Also, of course, keeping the children fed and safe and the home ready. National feeling was stirred up by great posters on every wall and hoarding – a buxom grey-haired mother with one arm round her son's shoulder, the other pointing to the word 'GO'; the slight figure of a wife at a window, with a small boy clutching her skirt, looking out at a departing band of soldiers. 'GO' was, as always, the biggest word in the caption, and all the messages urged the men to answer Kitchener's call and all the women looked brave and proud.

Lloyd George, as Minister for Munitions, fought for improved conditions for working-class women, for limited working hours and crêches for children, for hot meals in the factories, rest-rooms, washrooms with soap, towels and clean lavatories. In 1917 his Land Girls were recruited, trained, given working outfits of breeches, jackets and boots, and free railway passes. A number of them had worked on crops on the General's bit of land, so Gertie knew them well.

She had rolled bandages and packed parcels for the troops overseas, had read to the blinded and written letters to their loved ones.

The VADs, being the young women of the landed families, Lloyd George had left to fend for themselves. This they had done and had proved that they were not the joke of the war effort, as depicted by *Punch*. When the wounded men were shipped home, they were greatly needed. They learned to cut abscesses, give injections, cope with bedpans, scrub floors and, not least, to survive the scorn of the trained hospital sisters and nurses who accused them of playing nurses, looking pretty and wheedling postings from the right quarters.

In January 1918 the Bill had been passed which gave votes to women: to householders and their wives who were over the age of thirty-five. This gave the franchise to just six million out of thirteen million women and made it, for the time being, the prerogative of the better-class woman. Universal suffrage, it was thought, would have been cata-strophic, for with the colossal loss of men at the front a women's Parliament would have ensued. Panic later subsided as the young boys reached voting age, and full suffrage came.

Emmeline Pankhurst had been followed by a new generation of less violent and more persuasive emancipators. Maybe they could afford to be so; she had done the tough groundwork. On 1 December 1919, the rich, gay, elegant little figure of Lady Astor entered the House, the first woman to place her foot on the floor as an elected representative of the people.

Mrs Pankhurst was still battling. In an exchange with Mr Lloyd George, she enquired whether he thought that with the war over, women would again be persuaded to be cooped up in their nurseries or kitchens? Mr Lloyd George replied that he had 'never managed to keep a woman five minutes where she didn't want to be!' How right he was. The need for women outside the home, the praise, adulation and consideration that had been heaped upon them, had waned; but their taste for it had not.

Not surprisingly, therefore, there was quite a variety of women who wanted to work in 1921, to fulfil more than their homemaking talents. Hopeful Universal Aunt applicants wrote or called in. All were interviewed and the successful ones had then to produce two written references – a process that has never changed. Emmie's box of card-indexed workers made interesting reading; she had accurate judgement and a sense of humour about her fellow beings. A random selection follows:

No. 5   MRS ELIZABETH PRATT-STEED
        Disciplinarian. Firm without being brutal.
        Can converse on physics, spiritualism or foreign missions.
        Not a time-watcher, good cheap Aunt.

No. 9   MISS PHYLLIS BECKETT
        Age 30.
        Young and sporty. Knows all about 'footer' and white mice.
        Guaranteed not to nag. Can slide down banisters at a push.
        This lady will be one of our most popular Aunts and be in
        great demand.

No. 10 MISS PANSY TRUBSHAWE
        Age 32 (verging middle)
        Understands cricket and foreign stamps as she has five
        brothers. Not much else. There will be a waiting list of
        preparatory school boys.

No. 11 MRS MARTHA COKER
        Couldn't guess age. Grey ringlets and cap type. Thinks little
        boys should be seen and not heard. Speciality, reading to
        little girls *Little Women* and *The Book of Golden Deeds*.

No. 12 MISS HYACINTH PLUMMER
        Thirties (late)
        Can play Halma, Snakes & Ladders and tell moral stories.
        No doubt has a selection of modesty vests or chiffon roses
        for the front of her lower necklines.

No. 15   MRS CHARLOTTE HEDGECOMBE
          Age 55
          Hefty, stern, stand no nonsense. Stickler etiquette and
          deportment. On Borstal Board of Governors. Zoological
          Society's certificate. Cope older boys, any number.

No. 20   MRS KITTY PENDLEBURY
          Age 25. War widow.
          Young and jolly. A recognized authority on tuck shops and
          chocolate éclairs. First Aid certificate, good on accidents.
          An Aunt for all.

No. 21   MRS VIOLET RUMPTON
          Age 30
          Fully informed on circuses, pantomime and *Toad of Toad
          Hall*. Endless sewer of doll's clothes.

No. 30   MRS FLORENCE BARTON-HOWARD
          Age 40
          Knows everything about anything. Will have her uses.

Apart from those with attributes to appeal to children, there were 'good
shoppers', 'compassionate with the elderly', 'husband-seekers but not
dangerous'. The 1920s overall model Aunt emerged and was seen
about, the typical, mature, Englishwoman of her kind and easily identifiable on sight.

Wrapped in fine tweed. In winter, a coat with a wealth of fur on neck
and cuffs; in autumn, an excellent coat and skirt reaching slightly lower
than mid-calf. Hat, a cloche of velvety felt; gloves and bag of expensive
skin. On spring and summer days, a loose chemise frock of darkish
colour and long sleeves topped by a neat hat of soft straw. Round the
shoulders a fur, clasped to one side by its fox mask; the ensemble
finished with strapped shoes with low heels and white kid gloves.
Beneath this, the corset was gone; a lady was now clad in the lightest of
undergarments. Next to the skin, a silk item known as a camisole,
bloomers and petticoat, silk or lisle stockings according to time of day,
held up by garters.

The little band of workers began to be busy. One would be despatched
to escort a dog to the vet or collect an order for tapestry wools. Another

might be needed to stand in line for half an hour for tickets to Shaw's *Saint Joan*, to take oranges to an ex-charwoman in hospital, or try to get Evelyn Waugh's *Decline and Fall* from the library. 'I'm a complete "Universal Aunt" now,' she would think as she dropped *en route* into her club near Berkeley Square, because a rainy day necessitated a pause for a cup of tea.

It was usual now to see the Aunts at work at the main railway stations, escorting children on and off trains. It was a good sight. The beaming lady, oozing dedication, clutched the hand of a tiny boy whose eyes rolled upwards to peer from under the peak of his vast flannel cap. The boy bore a label in orange and black which was tied with non-perishable string to his jacket button. If he was lost, this label informed the rescuer that he must be instantly returned to the care of his UNI-AUNT. His neat case was similarly labelled.

The travelling children were usually *en route* by steam train from or back to their boarding schools. These always seemed to be located at the opposite end of Britain from their homes, the distance not having influenced father's choice. At last, however, a safe escort service was available to take his child across London and save him the tedious task. Northern lawyers, land-owners and businessmen rejoiced. So did southern ones if their sons were at Radley or Rossall; girls seldom went north.

Parents from overseas often wanted their children taken all the way to Grandmamma's home, wherever it might be; and if father were an ambassador or 'something in Europe', the Aunt would have the added pleasure of a boat trip.

The fond, waiting fathers were amazed and impressed by the Aunts' knowledge of suitable travelling snacks – buns, bananas, butterscotch – and literature – the *Boys* or *Girls Own Paper*, *Rainbow* and *Tiger Tim's Weekly*, which were acceptable reading at twopence. They wrote thank-you letters: 'He travelled happily and hopes to come again.' The regular children loved their Aunts and were docile in their care. The Aunts appreciated a nice tribute. Lady X wrote:

> I must thank you for the excellent Aunt you sent to take Geoffrey out last week. He seems to have had a splendid time and is still under the doctor.

Gertie and Emmie sat on either side of the table in the blue office and made their daily placings, Gertie with her basket tray of incoming requests and Emmie with her box of cards. Postcards were sent off with penny stamps to summon the chosen workers to attend the office for briefing. Commissions of every conceivable nature were being promptly executed, from matching a ribbon, furnishing a house, buying a trousseau or layette, to guiding and escorting to medical appointments. One Aunt met a monkey at Paddington at 3.15 and saw it safely off on the train to its new home in Kent!

People wanted surprising things. Those from the country, without a London home of their own, wanted to hold a party, ball or reception in a private setting. Gertie found one or two friends and relations who were willing to rent their houses or flats for an evening, so long as the next day's Court and Social duly described the venue as 'lent'.

Americans began to request chaperoning of their daughters – making use of this band of English women whose prestige and *savoir faire* was most valuable on the Continent.

Interior decorating was becoming fashionable: ladies were falling for the mistaken belief that only an outsider could know how their homes ought to look. The service being called for, Gertie recruited two new Aunts to supply the need. Both got themselves into print:

Lady Nelson, who did such useful work as the wife of Sir Frank Nelson, the ex MP, has now been engaged to run the home decorating department of that fast-growing organization 'Universal Aunts'. No fetish of an idle moment, it is a serious ambition backed by sound talent.

'I have to earn some money like other people,' said Lady Nelson. Dressed in a pretty blue overall, she expounded the theories of the interior decorator of the day. 'The era for modern furniture is dying out, as soon as it is bought it begins to lose its value. The same with modern materials, they do not fade and age and mellow with the artistic charm of the old materials.

'The day of pictures hanging on the walls has died out. Only good pictures are ever hung now, as a sense of space appeals to most women. Photographs, of course, are as dead as the dodo; to be kept in albums and drawers, never displayed. Wallpapers are practically dead; the modern idea is to have painted walls.

'The bare necessities for comfort are the only things we have in our rooms, we do not indulge in rocking tables and odd ornaments.' Lady Nelson smiled for the accompanying photograph.

The other, Miss Elizabeth Tarver, made her own pronouncement to the press.

'Anyone wishing to make a success as a decorative artist, working for other people, must have sympathy to see into the mind and interpret the ideas of her client. You may think their ideas are in bad taste, but you must interpret them with good taste.'

She was commissioned by Dame Clara Butt to decorate three rooms in her house. Dame Clara formed a good opinion of the work of the Aunts and extended her patronage to the hiring of a dressmaker and a silver cleaner.

Gertie recalled the words in Joshua Steed's letter to her and placed another *Times* advertisement:

UNIVERSAL AUNTS
The Hon. X is willing to caretake a town house
unoccupied by owner for winter or longer.

Behind such announcements often lay the story of misfortunes. Many women in society were well-known to be in straitened circumstances and, under assumed names, to be applying for posts of all kinds. To fulfil the office of steward in the master's absence was an assignment for which they were particularly well-qualified and later undertook with such success that a regular clientele was built up.

Business was now becoming too booming to be conducted by the penny postcards. It was a big moment when Gertie arrived in the office and announced, 'A special surprise. Installation of a telephone, and the number to be Victoria 4366.'

It was a daring decision! She was certain that the telephone was going to be the heart of the business.

Gertie waited a while before she sprang her other surprise – a portable Underwood typewriter, to be paid for by hire-purchase. The Underwood man had explained to her how such an arrangement worked. It seemed sensible when there was no money to spare.

Gertie had made one important decision from the outset. It was still very new for women like her to engage in business and she felt in need of a shield. She gave herself a *nom de plume*, Safara Fort. It was, in fact, the name of a place in India where sister Min had been stationed as a nurse.

This caused some confusion and mystery (which Gertie did nothing to dispel) as it was generally assumed that there were two Founders. Journalists and businessmen and women interviewed and wrote to Miss Fort, who was clearly the figurehead of the company; thus the elusive Miss Maclean was not their target. When they could not trace her in Debrett, for Miss Fort was obviously 'a lady' with connections, the newshounds were on the scent.

'Whose was the hand behind this rather daring idea?'

'Was it in fact a ruse?'

'Was this organization really competent to give the service it advertised?'

Gertie was skilful at evading their probings and turned their attention to the work of the Aunts rather than personalities. The journalists came up with jolly, evocative headlines in medium print on inside pages:

'AUNTS FOR ALL.'

'ARMY OF AUNTS AS GOOD FAIRIES.'

'TAKE WILLIE TO PICTURES OR CHAPERONE GIRLS.'

'WOMEN'S NEW IDEA IN BUSINESS.'

'A NOVEL PROFESSION.'

'A NEW OCCUPATION FOR WOMEN.'

'A PRETTY TRIFLE.'

'GUIDES FOR SCHOOLBOYS AND AMERICANS.'

The texts made even wider claims. So far, however, it was not only harmless but a useful source of free advertisement. Overseas publications had been alert to pick up a story and there even appeared the somewhat extravagant claim:

'AN ASSOCIATION INVALUABLE TO ANGLO-AMERICAN RELATIONS.'

Gertie was delighted. With an office and a telephone, a typewriter and two files, a card-index box of workers and a basket full of requests, her expectations had been surpassed.

1921

BETSY

Harrods' Ladies' Rest-room – Help – A big splash

Gertie and Emmie and most of the Aunts had been schooled by their mamas in a well-proved course of survival: 'If you need anything not immediately to hand, pop along to Harrods.'

By the restrictive tenancy regulations, their friend and landlord Mr Smith the Bootmaker could only permit the use of the office until mid-day. Unlike ladies' clubs, Harrods had not foreseen the necessity of banning business negotiations within their Ladies' Rest-room. A well-known venue of all the ladies, it sprang readily to Gertie's fertile mind when she needed further office hours in the afternoons. She and Emmie padded along there after lunch, just a short cut down Hans Crescent, with their papers in a large embroidery bag that had belonged to Emmie's mother.

To Hilda, the spruce afternoon attendant, in her black dress and small frilled white apron, the whole proud purpose of her life was to cater and care for her ladies and their every need. Her own private cubby-hole held everything from small gold safety pins and ribbons and thread to stamps for their letters. Their little ways were an unquestioned mystery to her. If Madam Miss Maclean, whom she had known for many years, wished for the permanent reservation of a corner table and sofa, she, Hilda, would reserve it for her. Miss Maclean seemed to hold court to quite a lot of friends there, she noticed. It became famous as the afternoon office of Universal Aunts. The incoming and outgoing Aunts saw nothing at all strange in being briefed and dispatched from Harrods.

Gertie's enthusiasm for the typewriting machine had waned; instalments became due and it sat there unused. Neither she nor Emmie knew anything about typing and, in those days, it was hardly a skill for a lady to acquire. 'Someone is needed to master it, Miss Faulder,' Gertie announced; 'in fact, we now need an office girl for it and the telephone.'

Emmie agreed. 'We could send her to an evening typewriting course and she could soon be doing our letters.'

No sooner said than done. At Gertie's command, into the office walked Elizabeth Rowe. No explanation was offered to Emmie, then or in the future, as to her origins. It was a long time before Betsy, as she became known, succumbed to a heart-to-heart with Emmie, and that only in Gertie's absence abroad.

Elizabeth Rowe's mother, Annie, had been born in Paradise Walk, Chelsea, then a respectable but poor place, now a millionaires' row. At seventeen, already pregnant, she married Barney Rowe, flower-seller and wreath-maker of Kings Road and Kensington, whose clientele were ladies and gentlemen of some standing, among them Miss Gertrude Maclean. By 1913, four children had been born to Barney and his wife; Elizabeth in January 1907, followed by William, Frederick and Arthur.

The war raged and by 1916 the losses were devastating. The small Standing Army had been dispatched to the Western Front as Old Contemptibles. Patriotic fervour was uppermost and middle- and upper-class ladies were convinced that though the slogans calling every man to fight might be Kitchener's words, they were God-inspired. They sent their own men to war and became agitators to persuade all others to go and replace the brave dead.

One day Gertie stood in Kings Road beside Barney's barrow, with her arms full of blooms, and her eyes rested on the display of wreaths. As she handed her money to him, she said, 'I ought not to have the luxury of flowers for my rooms, Barney, and you should be where they need you, on the Somme.'

'It's my family, Mum, Annie with the four little kids too young for her to go out to work. The allowances being 11s 1d a week for her and 1s 9d for each of them,' said Barney.

'I shall visit and help them while you are away,' answered Gertie, expecting him to do her bidding.

He did, and within six months his penniless wife was a twenty-six-year-old widow with her family to bring up. Gertie kept her promise and did her duty, with visits, small presents, and help to claim any extra allowances due to them. Annie was a brave, undefeated young woman. She struggled to get any small 'outwork' she could do at home, and kept the house and children spotless.

It seemed to Emmie that this humble family bore no ill will towards Gertie for having sent their father to war. Indeed, she had only done her duty as she saw it, and he had done his. Only once, Betsy recalled, had Miss Maclean 'acted funny' and upset them.

One afternoon Gertie sent a note to say that she would come to visit them. 'Ma decided to do something special to please Miss Maclean,' said Betsy. 'We couldn't buy her a present, so we spent our food money and got some butter and sugar and a bar of chocolate. Ma baked a cake, we hadn't ever had much cake.' Betsy was remembering every detail. 'We all got a lick of the bowl, and when it came out of the oven we got the crusty bits off the tin. It came out perfect. We kept a special table-cloth in paper in a drawer and Ma laid it on the table. It was white with coloured embroidered flowers in the corners.'

'I'm sure it looked very pretty,' Emmie said, 'and all of you would be in your best clothes.'

'Yes, and scrubbed too,' said Betsy without a smile. 'Well, Miss Maclean had been in the country. She brought us a basket of vegetables and some eggs, and a woolly cardigan for Ma and jerseys for us. She told us a story and then it was time for tea.' Betsy frowned. 'We were all excited because we knew the secret and Miss Maclean didn't. Ma came in from the kitchen with the lovely cake and held it for Miss Maclean to see. We were ever so quiet, waiting for her to smile and hoping she would cut it up for us.'

Emmie was transfixed by the bewildered, small, pale face, the sad, dark eyes.

'When Miss Maclean saw it she scolded Ma.' Betsy imitated Gertie's voice: '"Annie, I do feel that in your position you should know better than to waste precious rations making that kind of food in the middle of war."' Her voice wavered. 'I tell you, Miss Faulder, I saw our Ma's face go red and I felt ever so hot and like crying, but I didn't want to set the boys off. Ma said she knew it was wicked but to let's have a treat. She laughed, but only a bit, and gave us all a piece. We didn't like the taste as much as the crumbs off the tin.'

While Emmie was at a loss for the right words, Betsy commented, 'Ma said you never could know what the gentry would do, and best not to try and fathom. It was nobody's business but theirs.'

By the time Betsy told this story, happier times had come for the little family. For the widow of Barney Rowe had accepted a proposal of marriage from the one friend her husband had made in his short army career, Jo Wilby. He had come out of the war safe and sound, bearing the tidings and meagre possessions of his fallen comrade: his round steel watch on a chain, which he had received from his father when he was twenty-one, his penknife and tobacco tin with a picture of the King and Queen on the lid; a little oilskin pouch with brown photographs of Annie and the children; and his cap badge. Barney's only other treasure was a packet of letters from his wife, written during the short six months of his war.

Another son was born, Frank, who like the other children continued to have gifts from Gertie throughout his childhood. Best and most exciting was a pair of all-aluminium roller skates, a newly discovered metal as much prized as gold. Ordinary roller skates in the stores could be bought for half-a-crown, but everyone knew that these must have cost a fiver or more. They were the first ever seen, and the last word. Frank became the best roller-skater and star around Battersea. Another proud possession was her gift of a football goalkeeper's jersey in pure wool, vivid red and green. 'Did she imagine I would turn out to be a Communist or an Irish Nationalist?' he was heard to comment in later years!

Elizabeth Rowe was sixteen when Gertie offered her the position of office girl to Universal Aunts. This was quite a step up for a girl from her social background, when all she could have hoped for was a job in a factory or as a maid in a large establishment. For Gertie, it was a golden opportunity to make amends for any sense of guilt.

Gertie greeted her with a charming smile and said, 'Your wages will be ten shillings each week, Betsy.' Betsy's eyes glowed.

So she became the third occupant of the little blue office. Tucked into a corner by the door, she sat at a small, square table which just held the typewriter, the telephone and a basket of papers. The perfect office girl, she was slight and thin with thick, black hair, the waves pulled back and tied neatly into a big, stiff, ribbon bow. She had a calm, white, oval face and watchful brown eyes. Her ears were alert to the voices around her; she had every intention of changing hers. She always wore, in the office, a straight black dress with an immaculate white collar which she washed every night. To come and go, she put on a round, black, felt hat with a narrow brim and black cotton gloves.

Emmie's desk, in the centre of the room, dominated the small space and all callers were seated facing her. Gertie was more privately situated in the farthest corner. One almost had to breathe in while the other squeezed out, but Gertie was quite often out and about.

The workforce was unabated and determined, although the women arrived with obvious signs of nervousness and anxiety. Emmie directed them to the chair, smiled and asked, 'Now, what can I do for you?'

The fairly typical response was, 'Well, I'm untrained and so feel rather inadequate, but I am looking for work.'

Emmie was a good listener and was becoming increasingly apt at assessing the potential in each raw recruit. The 'impossibles' got four minutes and were kindly but firmly directed back to their social or charitable activities. The 'possibles' got an initial twelve minutes, during which time they filled in a personal questionnaire and gave the names of their two referees. They left the office with springy steps.

General interest in both the work and the workers had become quite a talking point among their friends and acquaintances. Emmie would be asked the question, 'Who needs these services and who is willing to perform them?' She considered the answers with care.

In different degrees, the Universal Aunts themselves were stepping into roles far removed from their accustomed lives. Most, before the war, had hardly passed through the green baize door in their own homes except to dispense their orders. Now they were on the receiving end of instructions, aiming to enlarge their horizons, giving their services to the best of their ability. They were earning their place in society. Errands in the morning and tiaras in the evening. How easily the majority took to it all.

'Within the British character is the curious belief that if you have social standing you cannot ever lose it.' This theory, which could only have been arrived at by someone non-British, looking in from the outside, was said, in fact, by an American who visited the Aunts, as much to look them over as to become a client. But it seemed to Emmie to be a good answer. There was no confusion of purpose: to receive service and to give it were instilled ideas. Also, of course, the strongest of all urges was in play; survival of the species. They were keeping form and changing colour like chameleons.

'Who needs us?' To this, Emmie would reply, 'Some of our clients pay us to ease their social or domestic problems. Others are suffering disease, death, loneliness, despair, or fear in old age. The ills of life are no less real for those in the fortunate position of being able to com-mission help. Ours is a business, but I'm glad to say that often we feel we have managed something quite worthwhile.'

The increasingly familiar words, '*I wonder if you can help me?*' were the challenge and Emmie proceeded, with determination, to do so.

Encouragingly, Emmie persuaded.

Firmly, Emmie admonished.

Sighing, Emmie forgave.

Glinting, Emmie dismissed.

Always, Emmie was fair.

The office was the predecessor of the job centre. At 9 a.m. ladies arrived for briefing, one by one. Emmie extracted their card from her box of workers and judged their suitability for the job on hand.

Mrs Barnes, who lived on Putney Hill, was giving a dinner party for six. She did not have a resident cook, the guests were important to her husband's business, and she wanted to make it a smooth and elegant evening. The cook chosen by Emmie knew all the finer points, the selection of the menu, how it should be presented, the table laid and the serving done. All she needed was Emmie to persuade her to go and do it all for someone else.

Lady Sutton was preparing for a grand ball in her house in Park Street and wanted someone to address several hundred envelopes, preceded by the checking of names, titles and addresses.

A very old lady living alone in Cheyne Gardens needed someone to restore order to a slovenly lot of servants, a state recently discovered on a once-a-year visit by her family.

A war profiteer, having made his million and so become eligible to be placed on certain guest lists, sought help for his wife. For an invitation to the home of one of London's new, rich American hostesses, how should she dress? Discretion and kindness were needed.

A newly widowed lady in Hampstead wanted someone by her side and seemed to have no family to help her through the immediate days, and to list callers and mourners.

One Universal Aunt, herself a widow and in very reduced circumstances, had little with which to pass her days other than stitching at her exquisite needlepoint. She was sent to work on the fine household linen of Lady X.

A gentleman called in to order and pay for a huge bunch of roses for his wife, of the same yellow as those in her wedding bouquet many years before, to be delivered to her at precisely 4 p.m. on their anniversary.

One morning Emmie's eyes rested coldly on the swaggering entry of a smoothly dressed, youngish, blonde girl.

'Your self-description and your references obviously overjudged your capabilities – or perhaps your ability to apply them in the type of situation you asked us to find for you.' She motioned the girl to sit on the upright chair. 'Your ambition to earn enough money to travel abroad cannot be realized by indifferent performance of the work you undertake.' Emmie gave the abashed girl no chance of interruption. 'We sent you as a cook-general. You have been useless as a cook and were generally catastrophic to the household and its contents.' Again the pause was only an intake of breath. 'Surely the number of burnt offerings and amount of broken china were enough. But any fool should know that black shoe polish is used only on the upper side and not on the undersoles and heels, that wax polishing is not continued under the hall rugs, doing which will precipitate the returning master of the house into a prone position on entering his own home.' Emmie unleashed her final blow: 'But worst of all, the use of the silver-cleaning bottle of methylated spirits to light the drawing-room fire and the ensuing burning chimney, has done your, and more importantly, our reputation no good at all!'

By then the girl was incapable of speech; Emmie finished off the interview. 'I fear that, should you be relying on your domestic skills and common sense to subsidize your world travel, you are unlikely to get beyond Dover. Good morning to you.'

Emmie saw that Betsy, with raised eyebrows, was signalling her to take a telephone call. She listened politely and replied immediately, 'No, Colonel, I'm afraid we do not have a gel who could come in each morning and bring you breakfast in bed.'

Violet glided into the office, limpid, wide-eyed and beautiful as her name. The interview took only another two minutes of Emmie's day. 'No, Violet, I'm sorry, we do not have a young, titled gentleman on the books who would like "help of any kind".'

Emmie took another call. 'We are glad', she encouraged, 'that being a Universal Aunt has made you into "a someone". Indeed, it has so made all of us.'

Victoria came in, with a pert face thickly painted and a lingering scent of cigarettes. Victoria, with excellent background and references, had been assigned to the wife of a visiting ranch-rich American, to guide the lady to shopping in the best places. Victoria did so – to the top shops and stores where she herself held accounts, having previously arranged her commission. A chance remark by the American had alerted Emmie, who then had to unscramble the sordid little business and save the British reputation. 'Think yourself very fortunate, Victoria, that we shall pursue this no further. We shall, of course, give you neither work nor recommendations in the future, so please never ask us for them again.' Victoria did not linger.

It was the end of a typical morning in the office, as Betsy produced a cup of tea for the three of them from Mr Smith's little kitchen.

Solicitor Joshua Steed had always regarded Gertie's venture most seriously, having respect for the formidable purpose of the emerging new women with the 'bit between their teeth'. He was closely involved in those early times and initial problems. Gertie made full use of his professional advice. Joshua's brother, Wickham Steed, was the eminent and brilliant editor of *The Times*, a newspaper which did not seem to have caught up with the growing interest in the Universal Aunt. Joshua thought this should now be remedied and put his brother on to the scent.

Wickham Steed asked for more details, liked what he was given, and spread the word in a warm and generous leader in his newspaper (right).

With a copy of *The Times* spread on each desk that morning, Emmie congratulated Gertie, and Gertie said it was equally Emmie's triumph for all her loyal hard work. Betsy told them both that she was 'ever so pleased' and that she had 'never thought to be in the newspapers'. Gertie had bought her a copy of *The Times* to keep.

The outside Aunts themselves were modestly elated. They called in at the office to smile at one another and be praised. A happy sisterhood of women had been created, who felt that they belonged together and really were doing a capable and rather splendid job.

Reprinted from

The ✦✦✦✦✦ Times.

Saturday, October 15, 1921.

OUR AUNTS.

PRACTICAL WOMEN'S WORK.

(FROM A CORRESPONDENT.)

Some people never consult a dictionary ; others who do are generally rewarded. For instance, if we look up the word " Aunt " we find it used (especially in America) " of any benevolent practical woman who exercises these qualities to the benefit of her circle of acquaintances," and the reference to America may remind us also that in Cornwall, at any rate, " Aunt " is, or used to be, a common title of esteem. A quotation from Mrs. Stowe, writing in 1861, carries us a step farther :—

These universally useful persons receive among us the title of " Aunt " by a sort of general consent. . . . They are nobody's aunts in particular, but are aunts to human nature generally.

And in honour to human nature, too, we would add in parenthesis, borrowing the phrase from Fielding, who, by the by, drew one notable aunt, Sophia Western's. Then the dictionary tells us to see " Aunthood " ; and there we begin to get really warm, for under that word Miss Muloch, " Dom. Stories," 373, is quoted :—

This sort of universal aunthood to the whole neighbourhood was by no means disagreeable to Miss Milly.

" Universal aunthood " ! The word is almost out ; Miss Muloch wrote, it appears, in 1862 : but it has been left to our own day to adopt her idea in the more direct and concrete form of " Universal Aunt." If everybody recognizes the term, this article will be superfluous ; if there are still readers to whom it conveys no meaning, we shall not have written in vain.

4

1920S

BUSINESS

*Shares for sale – Paris and Florence – Advertising –
The franchise – Jane*

With all this activity, the blue office was becoming too small. Also, while the iron was hot from the newspaper coverage, Gertie felt she should strike with some advertising. A larger office and advertisements were going to cost money.

Gertie now realized that finance was something she had been taught and trained not to talk about. She knew only two sources of security: inherited and invested money. Business was something else; incomings and outgoings had to balance, otherwise one's business would come to an end. Discussions with Joshua Steed had produced a simple fee structure and a salary scale for staff.

The fees to clients were all charged on an hourly basis, 7s 6d for the first hour and 5s per hour thereafter, payable direct to the office beforehand. The Aunts received 3s per hour and were charged a booking fee to the agency of 2s 6d per annum. Gertie was to draw a salary of £3 a week, plus 2s a week for any necessary travel on behalf of the Company. Emmie's salary was £2 10s per week, plus 2s per week for travel. The current outgoings were rent, telephone, the hire purchase on the typewriter, and the growing bill for stationery and postage. There was the 10s salary to Betsy, and there would soon be a bill from Joshua Steed for legal services.

Gertie's approach to the financial situation was quite stylish: shares! She drew up a plan, and Joshua Steed could not fault it. He admired her ingenuity and took a modest holding himself, although he never made a profit on it.

Shares were offered to family and close friends. They were taken in blocks of £10, £20, £50, £100 – and £500 by the more daring. The list of applicants read: the Maclean family *en masse*, Leith, Bower, Blackett,

Steed, Roche, Rolls, Eyre, Archer, Barron, Cunningham ... etc.
Several thousand pounds were raised.

With money in the bank, Gertie and Emmie took stock and felt
inclined to be bold. Expansion was tempting.

LIST OF APPLICATIONS

SPARES. No 364.—The Solicitors' Law Stationery Society, Ltd., 22 Chancery Lane, W.C.2, 29,Walbrook. E.C.4, 49 Bedford Row, W.C.1, 6 Victoria Street, S.W.1.   127.27-5-19

No. of Application.	NAME.	ADDRESS.	DESCRIPTION.
1	Maclean Mr JE	23, Cornwall Terrace S.W.7	Manager Director
2	Bower Mrs Marion	6 Ennismore Gdns SW	Spinster
3	Bower Joshua	Cornwall Manor, Knigham Oxon.	
4	Steed Joshua Owen	Melford, Suffolk. C/o National Bank J.d. N. Charing Cross	Solicitor
5	Glasspool Mr Reuben	13	Married
6	Blackett Mrs Frances		Spinster
7	Archer Mrs Ethel Maud	3	
8	Abbott Lewis P	Long Melford Suffolk	Solicitor
9	Charles C. Esqr.		
10	Blackett Mrs Lucy		Spinster Married.
11	Barron Mr Gertrude R	201	
12	Roy G Mr. F.	19 Stonewood Avenue	Married
13	Mr. G.B. Aaron		Married
14	Furehac, Miss Irene Louise		Spinster
15	Blackett Mr Francis		"
16	Cunningham, Mrs Valerie		"
17	Faulder, Mrs Emil		"
18	Wake-Wal.		"
19	Leith		
20	Harris		Married
21	Barron		"
22	Faulder		
23	Bower		Spinster
24	Maclean Ym		Spinster
25	Paton Norham G		Gentleman

Memo: Joshua Steed to Gertrude Maclean. 24 February, 1922. Floating 2500 shares. Keep ½ capital in your own hands. Once you have started the Company your only interest will be your shares and your salary, so make as good a bargain as you can.

Abroad, socializing as well as working was in fashion, and links between countries were becoming wider and easier. Women were no longer just accompanying their husbands on overseas tours, they were doing things abroad themselves. Even Mrs Margot Asquith set off for America on a series of readings of her autobiography, ex-Prime Ministers not being high on the pension list. Gertie and Emmie had the urge to become really 'Universal'. It was February, 1922. They had been in business for one year.

Gertie's brother Major Adrian Maclean, Consul in Florence, wrote that he felt 'the time was fine for abroad'. 'Billie Eyre is willing to take the word around. He's swanning a bit at the moment whilst awaiting his next posting and would take commissions from his flat to get things off the ground – Billie would be willing to do this free of charge.' At almost the same time, two American women wrote from Paris, offering to drum up clientele for a small salary plus a share of profits.

Gertie decided to accept Billie Eyre's offer. 'We will put aside £2 15s 6d for the printing of prospectuses,' she said. She felt more cautious about the American women.

'Better to consult with Mr Steed, don't you think?' suggested Emmie. Gertie agreed. Upon the advice of Joshua Steed, Gertie went to Paris to meet Mrs Hitchcock and Mrs Ashmoore. She returned with their proposals and they were invited to London and to join Gertie and Mr Steed for tea at the Law Society's hall at 4 p.m. on Mr Steed's next Thursday in London.

Following the meeting, while not advocating complete abandonment of the scheme, Mr Steed advised caution and care in drawing up the details of this proposed branch of the business – particularly when it came to finances. Gertie was irritated by his 'lawyer's rigmarole'.

Mrs Hitchcock and Mrs Ashmoore had no such reservations. Closely following their return trip to Paris, they wired that they had found exactly the right site for business premises.

'Really,' said Gertie, 'how can they imagine we could possibly make a decision on the basis of a telegram only?'

She was not pleased, but she pursued the project. She flew back and forth from London to Paris and depleted the Aunts' fragile bank balance with her expenses. She remained convinced that Europe would operate just like London.

Emmie, on the other hand, had very cold feet. She kept to her opinion that Universal Aunts should operate from one, and only one, headquarters. How right she was! Gertie bombarded Joshua Steed with daily reports and requests for confirmation. From Paris she wrote:

> You asked me before I left to make out a scale of salaries ... At present, I would suggest that Mrs H. and Mrs A. should receive salaries of £3 10s per week for the next six months. The messenger to receive a salary of 15s per week and her uniform, which is now complete and paid for and will last for some months. The only other office expenses except rent for the premises in *Rue Gaumartin* are firing, telephone calls, stationery and stamps and the hiring of a typewriter for Miss Armstrong whom Mrs H. and Mrs A. propose as the new secretary. The charges to clients and pay to workers to be the same as our scale in London. I wish so much that you could join me here. I think you would be convinced of the value of the proposal and could judge on the spot the suitability of the two representatives.

To and fro, Gertie related the numerous, various, and increasingly demanding, proposals of Mrs H. and Mrs A. to Joshua Steed. The business to be conducted from Mrs H.'s flat ... the secretary ... expenses ... larger commission ... a petty cash flow and shares in UA ... a considerable advertising budget for French *Vogue* ... and suchlike. These ladies were very American in their approach to business: serious, businesslike and determined. Their ideas were practical and farsighted. Their willingness to work and succeed was quite evident. For all this they expected to be given proper financial backing and to reap just rewards.

Mrs Hitchcock and Mrs Ashmoore were unused to the more leisurely British approach, the slowness, the lack of real financial discussion. Gertie seemed to them to have the wish to expand her business but not the will to be decisive. They were also bewildered that an Englishwoman of her class could appear to be on such a financial shoestring. Finally the exasperated Americans pressed that their demands should be met or they would not operate. It was apparent that they were going to run this so-called Branch to their own considerable advantage though, to be fair, it would be to the advantage of the organization too.

They had, however, made a fatal misjudgement about Gertie's type of Englishwoman. She was not accustomed to being annoyed in this way, and reacted sharply. Any deal was off! This was backed by a letter from Joshua Steed, who wrote his findings on the subject. Emmie thought he had shown sterling patience and co-operation throughout two months of negotiations which had seemed like years. On 17 March 1922 he wrote to Gertie, and summed up his basic reservations:

> My view of policy is that, unless an office is retained in Paris, the scope of the business must necessarily be curtailed very considerably, and for that reason, I think it highly desirable that the present office, however unsuitable it may be, should be retained. If the Paris branch is converted into an agency, run from Mrs Hitchcock's flat, it not only curtails the nature of the business, but it means that Mrs Hitchcock is in complete command, and control, and if that is her object, it means that she desires to be in command, and that London, which finds the money, will be subject to her. I do not think it unreasonable that Mrs Hitchcock should be asked to co-operate on the lines on which it is possible for us to work with her, and that she should not endeavour to dictate.
>
> If Mrs Hitchcock will show us that she can make Paris a success, there would be no limit to the development, but we are entitled to ask that she should prove the success of her methods before she asks us to spend money.

Perhaps if British flair and American acumen had been able to fuse, the combination might have resulted in big business. But would it have been Universal Aunts? Instead Gertie, in typical fashion, having gone off the whole idea, took advantage of the loophole suggested by Joshna Steed and gracefully accepted their resignation from the negotiations.

She did not, however, forgo her plans for Paris. The husband of her great friend Margery Allinson had just been appointed as one of our top men in Paris. Margery, of course, was of like mind to Gertie, and they set up a comfortable arrangement. Margery spread the word, through her many contacts, that French visitors to London could avail themselves of a whole range of useful services, and that a reciprocal service could now be offered to Universal Aunts' clients visiting Paris. Margery also liaised with one or two well-known Parisian shops, with whom the London office could then place orders directly. Ladies in London, or their husbands, found themselves able to buy French lingerie and sweetmeats straight from the rue George V, without going to Paris.

Billie Eyre in Florence, with no more than the £2 15s 6d outlay, drummed up some good business. Italian ladies commissioned Aunts to shop for them in Harrods, Fortnums and the White House or Smyth-sons. A horrid backlash was that sometimes, upon receipt of goods, they said these were not as ordered and refused to pay. 'Right,' Emmie insisted, 'it's money in advance in future.'

Travelling French and Italians who needed guides round London booked them from the Aunts. An Italian nobleman at twenty-four hours' notice wanted a gun for a shoot, to be collected from Purdeys and delivered near Verona. All was accomplished by a brisk, reliable son of one of the Aunts. Enquiries were made for respectable families to house French and Italian daughters for a season. Gertie approached some of the possible hostesses and implied that such assets as she, and they, possessed could be traded acceptably, for reasons either of personal fulfilment or growing financial necessity. Soon Spanish parents heard of this chaperonage and placed their daughters in the care of the reliable Aunts as well. A friend of Emmie's, similar to the Paris representative, was commissioned in Madrid.

The whole European approach was as simple as that, and was amazingly effective. Ladies from abroad loved this personal contact with London.

Emmie answered every request and took up every challenge, even if it meant going out and doing the job herself. She had enormous energy, and loved people and gossip and her many friends. She was alert and intent to 'take the chore out of living' for both home-based and overseas clients.

The response to *The Times* leader showed Gertie the value of putting one's name before the public. The upsurge of interest in the organiz-ation had brought increased business. She caught on to the idea of advertising and, true to form, her efforts were often spontaneous and effective. She saw an opportunity, or a need, and acted upon it.

Gertie's first effort at advertising was 'as large as life'. She was sweeping down Sloane Street one morning when she saw that, right opposite number 181, workmen were erecting a scaffolding to do repairs. She stepped across the road and spoke to the man issuing directions. 'Good morning, are you the foreman here?'

The man's hand sprang up and removed his dusty cloth cap.

'That's me, M'um,' he answered.

'Then I wonder if you would be good enough to give me the name and telephone number of your company.' Gertie took a small pad from her bag and scribbled down the information he gave her, thanked him with a

charming smile, crossed the road and went into her office. Within the
hour she had telephoned the owner of the company and requested a
meeting at her office.

Mr Williams arrived and, seated facing Gertie and Emmie, he handed
over his card:

FACTORY ARCHITECTS, CONSULTING & SUPERVISING ENGINEERS

HAL WILLIAMS & COMPANY
FACTORY HOUSE
79 & 80 HIGH HOLBORN
LONDON W.C. I
Telegrams & Cables 'HALWILTIE, WEST CENT, LONDON'
Western Union
AI Telegraphic Code
Leiber's Code

Telephone No:
CHANCERY 7873 (Two Lines).

While Gertie read these details, Mr Williams noted that not only was he
dealing with women, and that was unusual in his life, but that these were
ladies. Their office might be small but it was in the 'right' area. It seemed
well-organized, and he could see that they knew their business.

Gertie left him in no doubt of this as she briskly outlined the function
of her company and her proposition, that Mr Williams should attach to
his scaffolding, across the road, a wooden board proclaiming:

HAL WILLIAMS AND COMPANY
– PRESENT –

THE UNIVERSAL AUNTS
181 SLOANE STREET
LONDON S.W. I
Telephone No:
VICTORIA 4366
AT YOUR SERVICE. ADVICE AND GUIDANCE
DECORATIONS DEPARTMENT
Estimates for Interior and Exterior Decorations on application.
Good Modern Furniture, Carpets etc. supplied at moderate prices.

These services complemented Mr Williams's type of business. Gertie offered him a commission of 10d out of every £1 of business that might come from the arrangement.

Mr Williams accepted the offer as seriously as it was made. He was not slow to realize the eye-catching advantage of so unique a gimmick. He was also enjoying the liaison with ladies, and a small seed of another idea began to niggle in his mind, to be brought up at a later date. He erected the 4' by 4' board with its bold lettering, and a row of electric light bulbs across the top for night-time illumination.

Gertie made a couple of other less spectacular but equally intelligent advertising efforts. One day, lunching at the New Carlton Club for Ladies, as usual, she went to use the telephone. She struggled, holding the receiver with one hand, to get pencil and paper out of her bag. Then she decided to offer an easier alternative to her fellow-members. She produced a telephone pad to be placed beside each instrument, on the back of which pad Universal Aunts' name and services were advertised. The Committee were delighted, since the supply of pads was guaranteed and the organization was so reputable.

The Stafford Hotel in St James' Place, another favourite of Gertie and her ilk, also agreed to place the pads in all their bedrooms.

Gertie was, of course, always in the social swim. The calendars for the Season and the little Season, later in the year, lay to hand on her desk. 'What better advertisement than that Universal Aunts should this year make their first public appearance?' she said to Emmie.

The Annual Bazaar at the Central Hall, Westminster, in aid of the YWCA, was an important social occasion each autumn. Words were murmured in the right ears, and Universal Aunts were invited to run two stalls.

Before Gertie got down to arranging this, however, there came an unexpected result from the scaffolding project. It had already brought in enough enquiries to be engaging Lady Nelson almost full time. There were not many interior decorators around, but it seemed that they were becoming a new 'necessity' for people with money. Mr Hal Williams' seed of an idea had germinated and he requested another meeting with Gertie. She listened to his project and asked him to set out his plan in a letter to Joshua Steed, which he did:

I have felt for a long time that there is a great want in England for Domestic Architecture, in which the woman's point of view would be more fully represented than it is at present, and where the hundred and one things which make a home easy to run, and reduce labour, would receive proper consideration. I also consider that there is a good opening for women in advising upon these matters, and also upon decorations, colour schemes, and the laying out of gardens. The difficulty up to the present has been to find a medium which would bring the services of this class of Architecture, and women's work in the other spheres I have mentioned, to the notice of people who would appreciate and make use of them. I have followed the development of the 'Universal Aunts' for some time, and have come to the conclusion that the organization, if developed along the lines I suggest, would provide this medium in an admirable degree. . . .

I was brought up in New Zealand where domestic help is scarce, and I have on my staff architectural assistance, with Colonial experience, which has made a special study of house planning from the labour saving point of view, and I suggested to Miss Fort that possibly some amalgamation of interests to develop this side of the business might be desirable. She informed me that she is about to turn the 'Universal Aunts' into a Private Company, and I told her that if we could arrange matters on the lines I suggest, and other points were satisfactory, I would be prepared to take a substantial interest in the New Company, and give it all the assistance in my power. I gather that you are advising her, and I should be glad to meet you when you come to town and discuss the position further.

Although Gertie now felt more confident, having learned to deal with money crises and Joshua Steed's cautionary tales of doom, Mr Hal Williams' proposals were on such a grand scale that she felt it necessary to play it the way her solicitor advised.

The lawyer was again in favour of moderation. A check on the company had proved it to be both established and sound. So what was Mr Williams' real interest? It was, of course, to acquire the ready-made band of prestigious women who had come to his notice, to carry out his own Good Idea. The Universal Aunts had already made small-scale inroads into a market that he knew to be a fast-growing one – and one he wanted to exploit to the full.

Joshua Steed realized that Mr Williams' 'substantial interest in the New Company' was a takeover bid. He pleasantly but firmly made it clear that this was not on and negotiated a good deal on different terms.

He suggested that, although no share of the new company was available to be annexed as part of his own, Mr Williams might franchise out that side of the business which specifically called for a woman's-eye-view. Hal Williams knew that he could not organize such a team himself, and agreed. He found the services of the Decoration department totally reliable, very knowledgeable about fabrics, colours and style. From him the Aunts received large commissions to work upon. They learned about new advances in the use of metal and wood decoration, and had access to the latest designs in the furniture chosen by his clients. Hal Williams paid well and the arrangement lasted until the Second World War, which was followed by the vogue for the 'expert' interior decorator, backed by an expensive course of training.

By the autumn, therefore, Gertie had an even more thriving organization to present to the public. All hands had been called in to boost their Bazaar stalls. Emmie concerned herself with composing a leaflet describing the services being undertaken by the Aunts. Gertie was worried about her dress for the occasion. Niece Jane, with her early flair for fashion design, was by now personal couturier to the ladies of the family. Gertie telephoned her. 'So, having told you about the occasion, what are you going to make me to wear?' She rushed on. 'A soft colour, I think, for the dress, banded perhaps with a deeper shade repeated in the hat?' Jane responded with some ideas which apparently delighted her aunt.

At the Bazaar, representatives of Universal Aunts presented themselves before the public to answer questions and give out leaflets. Aunts sent specimens of their handiwork for their stall, with a small label bearing their name and the words *'Orders may be placed through Universal Aunts, 181 Sloane Street'*. Lady Alice Mahon, in support of her relative, the founder, and in charge of produce, arrived with a car laden with basket after basket of produce. She unpacked these herself and worked frightfully hard at arranging freshly dead-and-gone chickens. Only yesterday these prize birds had been pecking at her country acres: now the naked, pink mounds lay neatly trussed on plates. She unwrapped and polished apples and pears from her trees and displayed them in tissue-paper nests. Cook to the Mahons had made the fudge and toffee, plain and fruit, and tied it with coloured ribbons into round, grease-proof bundles. Lady Alice had tied herbs into bunches with green garden string, and she laid these out in a trug next to jolly little Chinese boxes of tea. Lady Alice, it was said, had already worked for three days ticketing and planning the arrangement of her stall. . . .

All went off splendidly; it was good for Universal Aunts that so much interest was shown in the stall, in the ladies in attendance, and in the items for sale. Gertie wrote a letter to Jane.

181 Sloane Street
London S.W. 1
24th November 1922

Dearest little Jane,

I must find time today to tell you that the dress you created for me to wear to the bazaar was the greatest success. I felt happy and confident in that soft rose colour. It was admired by Lady Bentinck, also helping at our stall, and when I did not hesitate to tell her the name of the designer and dressmaker, she suggested that you might find a most lucrative occupation within our ranks.

The eccentric Lord Burgh was much in evidence, modelling some of the hats he makes on his clients' own heads! During the afternoon, his sisters, Bay and Eveleigh Leith, talked with me of the possibility of a place within our ranks.

More importantly, I must tell you the financial result of sales from our two stalls was the sum of £115 with which, from small individual prices, we were delighted. So are the YWCA.

Our family gathering for Christmas will soon be upon me. I will, I think, have to take my own advice and hire a U.A. to do my shopping so that I have everything ready in time.

I look forward to seeing you then and send you my best love and thanks for the rose dress that pleases me so much.

Little Aunt.

It was not long afterwards that Jane's dressmaking talents were called upon for another big event in Gertie's calendar. The big money-raising functions were only one of the ways in which charities were supported. Ladies collected private donations for a pet charity in smaller ways within their own circle; perhaps an afternoon of bridge, or a small dress show in the drawing-room.

Every so often Her Majesty Queen Mary provided an enormous incentive to do this by receiving ladies into her presence, when they would present to her their pursue. Gertie had her own charity collection-box in the office, and was now included in a presentation.

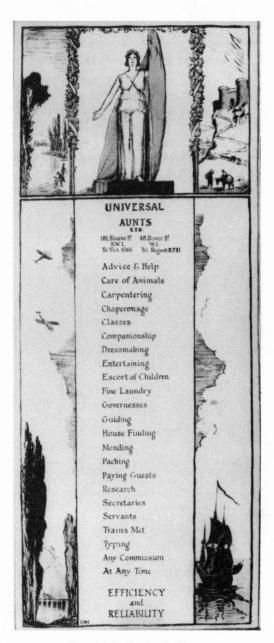

Emmie's leaflet for the Bazaar

The following morning the Court Social column included the announcement:

Universal Aunts' purse of £50 collected on behalf of Sunshine Homes for Blind Babies was presented to Her Majesty the Queen.

By the end of that second year, they had certainly got the hang of how to advertise themselves.

5

1920S

EXPANSION

A Registered Company – Women entrepreneurs –
More space – Mother Hubbards – Advisers

Quietly, behind the scenes that autumn, the organization being presented to the public had become the New Company.

Financial News, 25th October 1922
On the 20th October, 1922, Universal Aunts Limited was registered
as a private company by Jordan and Sons Limited. With a nominal
capital of £2,000 in £1 shares, the objects were: To acquire and carry
out as a going concern the business carried on at 181 Sloane Street,
SW1 and in Paris and elsewhere under the name and style of
'Universal Aunts'. To adopt an agreement with Miss Gertrude Eliza
Maclean. To act as organizers, advisers and caretakers, to provide
chaperonage, companionship, to carry on business as universal
providers, guiders, agents, furnishers, decorators, dressmakers, in-
structors, entertainers, gardeners, escorts, domestic service, arists,
secretaries, hairdressers, manicurists, masseurs, chiropodists,
laundry-workers, letter-writers, window cleaners, jewellers, libra-
rians, packers, seamstresses, miniature painters, milliners, drapers,
grocers, merchants, managers of and caterers for public entertainments, balls, Promenade and other kinds of concert.

And so on, covering most things from the business of restaurateurs,
caterers and vendors of wines, liqueurs and cigars to the acquisition of
lands and sites to build thereon.
    The first Directors were:

Miss Gertrude E. Maclean, 1 Cromwell Place,
    South Kensington, SW.
Miss Esther L. Archer, 3 Ovington Square, SW3.
J. O. Steed Esq, Solicitor, Long Melford, Suffolk.

Esther Archer was an old friend from childhood days who had become a woman with a head for figures. Gertie made her Company Secretary at £5 per week. Joshua Steed's firm became the Company solicitors. Two very progressive ladies, the Misses Barrow and Brackenbury, accountants, of 31 Westminster Palace Gardens, were appointed auditors. The London County Westminster and Parr's Bank, Albert Gate, Knightsbridge, received the role of Bankers to the Company, unchanged to this day except for the more mundane title of National Westminster Bank PLC. A Seal of the Company was produced and approved, and it was resolved that the same be adopted as the Common Seal of the Company and that one key be kept by 'Miss Fort' and one by 'Miss Archer'. 181, Sloane Street, SW1, was the registered office.

Gertie became Universal Aunts' first Managing Director, having expressed the wish that her chosen fictitious name, Safara Fort, be used in all matters connected with the Company's business. Terms of appointment were duly set out, to which the Managing Director 'hereunto set her hand and seal'.

Items number 2 and 3 laid down her remuneration and her responsibility.

2. The salary to be paid by the Company to the Managing Director shall be £312 per annum, rising by half-yearly increments of £50 to the sum of £500 per annum.

3. The Managing Director shall, while acting as Managing Director, devote her best energies and the whole of her time to the business of the Company and shall use her best endeavours to promote the interests of the company and shall not at any time divulge any secrets or dealings related to the business of the company, or be concerned in or about any other financial business than that of the Company.

As Gertie's real Aunt Augusta, Lady Whitworth, said, 'Dear Gertie's project must now be taken very seriously indeed. I shall donate some bookshelves for her office.' And she did.

Christmas came and Gertie went off to a Maclean stronghold in Scotland. Her clients, friends and associates received a booklet calendar designed by her. On the front, the services of Universal Aunts were set out while a blotter on the back hopefully ensured it a place on everyone's desk for a year. Gertie sent out 3,000 booklets and paid her printer, Thomas & Sons, £7 12s 6d.

U for the useful helps we provide
N for the nannies who can be supplied
I for interpreters ready to speak
V for a very nice aunt for a week
E for emergencies with which you provide us
R the relief that you feel when you've tried us
S is for stations where Aunts go to meet you
A for Air Terminals where we will greet you
L for the London we help you to see

A is for Aunts who will make you carefree
U is for Uncles we use to help too
N is for nothing we cannot do
T for the tours we arrange with such zest
S is for shoppers who buy you the best

L for the luggage we pack and despatch
T for the trains that we help you to catch
D for the door that we keep on the latch

Beginning work in the office in the New Year, Gertie seemed restless and Emmie short-tempered. Betsy got on with her work as usual, but 'the atmosphere gets me down', she told the family. The word 'expansion' filled the air but it meant different things to each one of them. With business going well here and in Europe, Gertie, as always, was looking for the next challenge and there were plenty about. She was not the only female post-war entrepreneur; others were also conducting businesses, wheeling and dealing. The women were kindly disposed to one another, for they felt a common cause as pioneers. Some, like Gertie, had been successful. Others were less so, and their businesses came up for sale of the goodwill.

Gertie was already involved in promoting the enterprise of her good friend, Molly Ridley. In the past they had been thrown together in their part-time war work, and Molly had confided her plans to turn her cooking skills into money. This she did in a spruce slip of a shop at 22, Beauchamp Place, where she sold boxed shortbread, biscuits and cakes. Molly's 'Hunting Chocolate' was quite famous – country gentlemen carried it in deep tweed pockets; they swore by its restorative properties for themselves, their dogs and horses. Old generals sucked it. Old ladies dunked it in their hot milk. People left it lying about in its dull brown box

because it represented quality and taste. Gertie unashamedly included a
packet in every shopping order as a kindness to Molly, putting it on the
bill. She indicated to foreign visitors that all Englishmen and women
found it indispensable!

Now Gertie was approached with a tempting proposal. The smart
little Rousslan restaurant in Knightsbridge had for several years been
completely run by a Miss Green, who served morning coffee and
afternoon tea, and had built up the business to average takings of £10 per
day. Miss Green was giving up and a new owner was being sought:
goodwill, furniture and fittings would cost £550, rent and rates £175 per
annum. Perhaps it could become part of a larger enterprise? Miss Green
wrote a polite enquiry on these lines to Gertie.

Joshua Steed was adamant. 'Either a Universal Aunt or a restaura-
teuse – not both!'

Gertie gave in, but not gracefully. She secretly congratulated herself
on her involvement with Molly's enterprise – Joshua Steed didn't have
the last word on *everything*!

As time went on, Emmie's increasing anxiety over expansion was
much more serious and down-to-earth. She was concerned that the
growth of business could no longer be contained within the blue office.
There was not enough space for the papers and files and boxes, let alone
the number of callers. It was a squash when the workers came in, and
impossible now to receive clients with any degree of elegance or privacy.
Harrods' Ladies' Room was not designed for this amount of infiltration
either. The image of the company was in peril.

Emmie now embarked upon a survey of the services being undertaken
by the Aunts. These were so many and diverse that she suggested they
could be handled better by separate departments. Gertie was anxious
about the boldness of a scheme that involved more staff and larger
premises, the exorbitant cost of a move, and the re-siting of telephone
equipment. It was a worrying decision for her but, as she remarked to
Grandfather the General, 'I don't know who, but someone said, "You
cannot stand still, you have to speculate to accumulate," and I expect
they were right.'

The General asked, 'What does Joshua Steed have to say?'

'Oh, as usual he advises caution.'

The General knew the meaning of those autocratic tones. Gertie
was, in this case, going to decide for herself. He didn't envy Joshua
Steed!

'Well, consider most carefully, make your decision, and don't look back.'

Gertie did not need to consider for long. She had no sooner put out feelers than the estate agents told her of a room near at hand in number 192, Sloane Street. Surely, it was meant to be. It was a large, former reception room on the ground floor, with two big windows fronting on to the street. The terms of £200 per annum were easily negotiated.

Since the new premises were so close, the move was accomplished at the minimum cost of 'tips'. Mr Smith led his team of bootmakers the few hundred yards in a dignified crocodile, carrying the small furniture, typewriter and lamp. Betsy, enjoying every moment, brought up the rear with arms full of files and papers and scuttled back for more. Emmie carried a Gladstone bag, brought in for the purpose, full of her personal effects, from which she would not be parted, together with the precious card-index boxes, day book, ledger, glass pen-tray, date stamp, billing file and reference file. Gertie was at the other end to receive and direct them all. The colour scheme this time was a buttery cream and she was dressed in a complementary deep shade of apricot. Desks, chairs and bookshelves had been bought as a job lot in a country sale by the General and sent as a moving-in present. At last Betsy had her heart's desire, a large desk with drawers down each side.

Gertie had arranged a select little gathering in the office later in the day. Everyone stood around and politely listened to one of the share-holders, the Revd Gilbert Weigall, conducting a short opening cere-mony. His blessing included a prayer for those who laboured therein, 'that they might be blessed in their lawful undertakings and continue to help their fellow creatures'.

Gertie included her private prayer, which was for enough fellow creatures to come along to pay for the glasses of champagne they held – not to mention other outstanding matters she didn't want to dwell on – and thus keep the company lawfully solvent.

Gertie enjoyed, as always, playing the role of gracious hostess. Emmie swayed and beamed at everyone. Betsy was attending her first party and, to put her at her ease, Gertie had given her the task of handing round the plates of tiny sandwiches and vol-au-vents. She felt very important; everyone spoke to her and she memorized exactly what they did. Throughout the gathering, Joshua Steed, a typical lawyer, looked rigidly non-committal yet benevolent. It was too late to be anything else, he thought, and he felt an affinity with the London County Westminster and Parr's bank manager, who surrounded by confident predictions on all sides, appeared bewildered after his first glass of champagne. Like many others who had to deal with Gertie's affairs, he sometimes wondered if he had missed a vital point somewhere – or perhaps she had?

A presentation was made to a proud Mr William Smith, Bootmaker, of a silver card tray with the inscription:

MR WILLIAM SMITH
IN RECOGNITION OF HIS PLEASANT ASSOCIATION WITH
UNIVERSAL AUNTS LIMITED
AS THEIR LANDLORD
Gertrude Eliza Maclean

The new office had to continue functioning while being reorganized. Three acquaintances of Gertie and Emmie were enrolled as staff to run the departments at salaries of £3 10s per week each, without consultation with the bank manager. Gertie and Emmie both kept a watchful eye and fierce control over the newcomers' every move. A second telephone line was added and Betsy worked hard to master the controls. The lease permitted a discreet sign on the windows. Gertie instructed a signmaker to charge 'no more than £5 in cost' and a square of glass was duly inserted, bearing the words in dull gilt:

UNIVERSAL AUNTS LIMITED
PERSONAL SERVICE BUREAU

Within the office, on the wall facing the door, there was placed a vast, white notice printed in bold black letters, glassed in and framed in black. Each department was listed, and every service provided therein.

On Betsy's desk sat a wicker tray with a neat pile of brochures set out as an A–Z. She systematically handed them out to all callers.

A smart commissionaire guarded the front door but he only paid lip service to the ladies. He did not hold with all this coming and going of the female sex on his premises. In his opinion, all this liberty could easily spread, even to his kitchen at home, and stir up radical notions in his own missus.

An Australian journalist made an early search for the new set-up. He saw the sign but courteously asked the commissionaire, 'Have I got the right place?'

The

AUNTS' ACTIVITIES ALPHABETICALLY ARRANGED

Advice and help in all emergencies
Animals and pets cared for and lodged
Balls and parties catered for
Children met and cared for
Companionship for short and long periods
Cars provided, bought and sold ; chauffeurs and chauffeuses provided
Cooking undertaken by the hour, day or week
Dances organized and bands provided
Dressmaking of every description ; ladies' own materials made up
Emergency workers of every kind
Entertainers provided for all occasions
Excursions organized and couriered
Fairy stories told at children's parties
Furniture and Furnishings, modern or antique
Girls and boys met, put up for the night and taken to their destination
Guides provided for London, Country and Continent
Hotel accommodation, Rooms and Service Suites found
Houses and flats found, let and sold
Indexing, filing, book-keeping, and all secretarial work
Insurance
Journeys planned and couriered
Kennel Maids provided
Libraries catalogued
Loose Covers and Curtains to measure
Manicurists, Masseuses, chiropodists visit clients' own houses
Miniature painting
Needlework and mending of every description
Orders taken of every description
Packing undertaken
Readers provided
Research work
Servants, chauffeurs, gardeners, etc., found
Schools found and inspected
Shopping. Everything supplied from a hair-pin to a Moth aeroplane
Tickets for journeys, concerts, theatres, lectures, etc.
Trousseaux made or chosen
Universal Aunts undertake any commission at any time
Upholstering of every description
Visitors from overseas specially catered for
Winter Sports Parties
Xmas, birthday and wedding gifts suggested and chosen
Yuletide entertainments
Zoo parties arranged

The man's tone and expression were deadly cynical. 'Mother Hubbards, I call them,' he said, then added offhandedly, 'Not one of them could boil shaving water!'

The Mother Hubbards, however, were getting on with the things they could do.

The workers registering on the books, in addition to coping with the work, were also a source of indirect revenue. Those were the days when, in England, they paid a booking fee to have their names on the register of an agency. It seemed to Gertie the right time to raise this fee and up it went to 2s 6d per quarter instead of per year. The workers found this quite acceptable. They got good, varied, and often enjoyable jobs.

Perhaps the children were the favourites – the little prep school boys who asked to be taken to the 'eating department at Harrods' for ices and bath buns, and the slightly older boys with outrageous pronouncements. An Aunt escorting a very young Etonian across London, train to train, for his Christmas at home in Scotland, heard him take leave of a equally suave schoolfriend. 'I'm being taken by a Universal Aunt,' he announced.

'Oh yes, I know the institution. A chap I know says that he knows a chap at Harrow who said that when one's father has travelled down from the North for the Eton and Harrow match, one could take him to them and leave him behind for repairs and get him generally tuned up for exhibition purposes.'

Gertie said she thought he was perhaps confusing them with Trumpers, but never mind, he had remembered their name.

The mother of an older young man, a first-year university student, telephoned for help. Her son was afraid to face his Bloomsbury landlady, even though he had paid his rent up to date. They had quarrelled and he wanted to leave, but he did not have the courage to go back and see her again. An Aunt was dispatched to pack his things, appease the landlady and take his boxes away in a cab.

The Advisory Interviews were extremely popular. They took place between 11.30 a.m. and 12.30 p.m., and 2.30 p.m. and 3.30 p.m.; fee £2. Gertie and Emmie were the only ones to conduct these, in a screened-off corner of the office. The advice they gave was strictly practical and they directed their clients to the best source of help, of which both had gained a wide general knowledge. If they did not know the answer, they took the details and found it out.

A mother came in to enquire about the living conditions and edu-

Gertie

The Blue Office: Emmie, Gertie and Betsy on the telephone

Aunts at work in 1921: '. . . wrapped in fine tweed and fur'

A familiar sight at the railway station in the '20s

The YWCA Annual Bazaar, 1922: Gertie with
Betsy – dress by Jane

Early advertising

Bonzo with his Aunt in Sloane Street

Safely in charge – the '50s

Emmie's retirement

Delivery by Aunt – the '50s

cational prospects of the new girls' public schools; they had Roedean in mind for their daughter. She was sent round to the educational consultants, Gabbitas and Thring.

A twenty-year-old girl wanted to go and live and work in America; could her parents prevent her? Yes, her mother was advised, until she was twenty-one. In the meantime, why not try the compromise of finding a family there, by advertising, exchange references and let her go for a trial period of a year?

A wealthy Cumberland farmer asked how to go about applying for membership of a London gentlemen's club. Few of his northern friends belonged and he could not ask them for fear of being thought 'pushy'. He had been in the army and so was given the name and address of the In and Out, and advised to consult with the secretary.

Another man wanted to know where to seek information about the Freemasons. It was only available to Masons; he should seek out a Mason and ask him if any general information was available.

One lady wished to sue her solicitor. She was sent to the Law Society with her complaint.

There were numerous parents wanting to discuss the problem of their children leaving home and living in flats. Get them a place in a flat or a bedsitter, through a good agency like UAs, where there would be a check on reasonable behaviour and on the other occupants, they were told. Then hope for the best!

There were lots of girls asking how to get into training for the professions, the law and medicine being much sought after. Each was directed to the appropriate professional body.

A lady who had got deeply into debt gambling at cards needed to know where to sell a diamond brooch. It was suggested that she talk to her husband; if not, she should go to a very top jeweller, preferably her own. They understood these things and would still bow you out when you left.

A successful lady hat-shop manageress from Manchester wanted a good opening to start up her business in London. With an envious look at the elegant little item perched on her head, Gertie telephoned and introduced her to Lord Burgh.

How to get someone an honour? a gentleman asked. Apply directly to the Prime Minister's PPS, was the answer.

These were not world-shaking problems but just needed simple advice. A willing ear was always available, and so another 'good idea' was born – the first 'Agony Aunts' department?

6

1920S

FRANCES

*Society – The arts – Politics – Meals on wheels – A nasty
hiccup – Britain on show – The death of a Queen*

The agonies brought to the Aunts were, at that time, those of a former or
current privileged class. They were dealt with by Aunts best suited for
the job: independent counsellors from within the worriers' own ranks.
The nature of the agonies was a reflection of the outside world and the
Aunts themselves were very much part of those problems. Social
intercourse had become more free and easy. Social problems remained
very class-related.

To become a Universal Aunt's client was one thing, to try and become
a Universal Aunt in order to solve one's own problems, quite another.
Both Gertie and Emmie had approaches from ladies of their acquaintance who wanted to do just that.

Certain dukes' daughters and ladies of the manor had dabbled in the
vogue for husbands and lovers of a different class. If and when the idyll
collapsed, they often came to offer themselves for work as a sort of
penance. The Bishop of Woolwich had unsettled quite a lot of wives by
denouncing the use of birth control and declaring procreation to be a
sacrament, and so they sought an outside interest. A spate of foot-and-
mouth disease in the country kept ladies from returning there for their
weekly hunting for a whole season, so they were at a temporary loose end
in London. All these had the wrong reasons for joining and they were
quite unacceptable in the ranks of the Aunts. It was, of course, a time of
exuberant people and extravagant gestures, and still wide social and
political divisions.

Several of Gertie's circle had turned to politics as their public duty,
and had mostly turned left, which appeared to be so much more in tune
with the times. There were some important names amongst the group of
society women working hard for the socialist party: the Marchioness of
Tavistock, the Countess of Warwick, and the beautiful Lady Cynthia

Mosley, daughter of the late Lord Curzon. Later, she proceeded to assist her pro-Fascist husband Oswald to campaign and be elected as socialist MP for Smethwick. They kept his Rolls Royce and her diamonds out of the sight of the electorate!

In October 1924, a general election put Ramsey MacDonald and his Labour Party out of office and Stanley Baldwin and the Conservatives into power. Gertie was delighted to be asked to join the same house-party as the new Prime Minister at the house of her friends Mr and Mrs Geoffrey Fry. She saw little of him as he spent most of his days alone, composing his new Cabinet.

Another formidable group also influencing society was the intelligentsia, who were mostly pacifists. The illustrious names of Cecil, Caernarvon, Nicolson, Strachey, Fry and Huxley, Duncan Grant, Leonard Woolf, Clive Bell, were amongst them. They had come upon one another at Oxford or Cambridge and kept in contact afterwards. The group was enhanced by some talented women, writers like Virginia Woolf and Katherine Mansfield, and painters like Vanessa Bell and Dora Carrington from the Slade and Academy schools. The women were at times feminine and engaging; at other times were *avant garde* users of racy language. They moved in and out of one another's houses in Brunswick, Gordon and Soho Squares, and were christened 'the Bloomsbury Group'.

They talked and travelled and explored, mostly Italy and Greece, came home, wrote, painted and spread their independent ideas. Arbiters of free thought and 'free love', for those with an ear to their gospels, they were gifted, creative, flawed and melancholy, producing brilliant contributions to the arts, which ensured them a following of rich hostesses to offer hospitality in return for inclusion, at least on the fringes, of the Bloomsbury Group.

The most notorious of these was the eccentric, egotistic Lady Ottoline Morrell, half-sister to the Duke of Portland. She kept open house for writers and artists of talent at Garsington Manor near Oxford. The best food and wines would be laid on for them and a production of some fashionable play in which Lady Ottoline would take the main part. Lavishly dressed, uninhibited by any effort to portray anyone but herself, she simply floated, spun about or stormed on the stage. Everything was excessive, as Dora Carrington described it to Lytton Strachey, at 'Shandygaff Hall'. Her husband, Philip Morrell, quietly busied himself outside, employing pacifists and conscientious objectors to work on his farm and land. His personal creation was a garden of such outstanding beauty that it would endure, like the works of his guests, to be enjoyed as long as it was preserved for posterity. Shielding hedges, twenty feet high, encased tropical trees and plants from far-away places. Miniature, symmetrical knot gardens were edged by box. Untamed English country landscapes spilled over acres. Evelyn Waugh wrote in praise of its delights.

There were others, not strictly within 'the Group', who were being applauded for their equally important contributions to the cultural life of the country. The writings of Shaw, Waugh and Lawrence; the paintings of Dame Laura Knight who was acclaimed woman painter of the day with her vast canvases of gipsy and country life; or the Johns: Augustus, whose passionate debauchery fed such commanding brilliance on canvas or paper, and Gwen, obsessive in her unrequited love for Rodin, who hid herself away and in melancholy loneliness produced paintings both exquisite and sensitive. Overshadowed by her brother, it was several generations later that people began to value her fully.

From out of this vortex came the Aunts who *had* passed Emmie's tireless selection process. She had on hand Aunts of all sorts: kind ones, mousy ones, knitters and bridge-players, tiresome, long-nosed, meddlesome types, pert and pretty young ladies, titled matrons, brisk women, cosy women and elderly women smelling of camphor or violets. Their common ground was that they were the ones who were not self-orientated. There was a choice for all needs – and the needs grew daily.

By contrast to the dazzling trend-setters and those in the news were other sections of the public. The vast working-class, living in poverty and overcrowded, unsanitary conditions, unemployed and in need, would shortly erupt. But they were not people who would ever hear of or come direct to such an organization. The Aunts gave them indirect, dutiful assistance. Each year they gave their free time and effort to large fund-raising events, hoping their contributions would alleviate some of the suffering. Many of those who did come to them, though not working-class were also very needy, living in the not-uncommon 'reduced circumstances': old people, the ill or incapacitated, those in tiny flats or cramped bed-sitters, many for whom shopping was a nightmare and cooking an impossibility.

Emmie coped daily with their cries for help. One day she had an inspiration. 'Why not take food to them, all ready to eat?' Thus Meals on Wheels came into being.

Gertie recalled Grandfather's shooting luncheons, and platter-like metal dishes with lids, enclosed in a hollow outer case with a little cork. Boiling water was poured into this and the food stayed hot for ages. Grandfather's pantry cupboard yielded several dozen of these treasures, and soon a team of delivering Aunts were cooking in their own kitchens and buzzing around in their motor-cars making deliveries. Standard luncheon or dinner consisted of meat, two vegetables and a pudding or savoury, costing 2s 6d delivered to your door. Special dishes at increased prices could be ordered – more expensive meat or grander pud. Later, containers were used that retained heat longer, and hot charcoal replaced the boiled water.

However, not everything was going so smoothly. There was a nasty hiccup when Joshua Steed tended his resignation as a Director. His explanation was 'inability to give sufficient time to the work of the company'. He also resigned as solicitor to Universal Aunts and 'hoped for repayment of his loan'. All this was quite gentlemanly, but Gertie had been heading for such a jolt. It had become a habit for her to write to Joshua almost daily to consult him on all legal matters, trivial and otherwise, to rely on his backing and sound advice, and to push aside any thought of needing to repay his £50 loan. He had always been a source of information and help at a moment's notice. Yet one feels Gertie would have been surprised to have been billed accordingly for this. She had exploited him in the nicest possible way and she released him as graciously. The parting was smoothly accomplished. The Macleans and Steeds were to retain a lasting and firm family friendship.

Mr Reginald S. Cockburn of Messrs Baileys, Shaw and Gillett took over where Joshua left off. They have provided a series of Mr Cockburns up to the present day.

Gertie now felt the need to appoint another director in place of Joshua and out of her circle she chose the studious, intelligent, thirty-two-year-old Miss Frances Blackett. Frances was a social-science product of the London School of Economics and an academic in manner and outlook. Endowed with a modest allowance from her eminent and scholarly family, she frequently set forth to study the social consequences of the war upon England and Europe. Frances spoke softly and with unsmiling deliberation, only when she had weighed up the matter in hand and had something to say. Similarly, she became known and respected for the precise and factual papers she wrote from the material she had gathered.

With watery pale skin, eyes and hair, thin and wand-like as a bamboo, she embarked on her travels with her rimless spectacles hooked on to her bony nose. Luggage was no problem to her: she adorned herself in numerous layers of weatherproof articles, in walking boots, and a poe hat over her hairnet to control the straggles. She carried a vast carpet-bag stuffed with her papers, writing materials, books and undergarments; threw in a few small gilt safety pins to hold together anything that might come adrift.

By then, no surprise was shown towards these lone women roaming about in the world; they were everywhere. They had been forced by the casualties of the war to adapt to living without men. They had chopped off their hair or scraped it out of sight. Their clothes were unfrilled, and their skirts were creeping higher and higher up their legs. (Not Frances Blackett's skirts; they remained always a few inches above the ankle.) Their manner was often aggressive, or at the very least confident.

Oxford had granted full degrees to women in 1920, though it was to take Cambridge until 1933 to award a titular degree. Liberated women had entered the Civil Service and the BBC, the teaching profession, medicine, the law and accountancy. They had good salaries and often a pension to come, could afford houses, domestic help, books, cars and travel. A woman could now respectably live alone, adopt a child, and hold a social position of her own.

These influences percolated through to the women of the future. The comparatively recent girls' public schools began to shape their curriculum to fit university requirements. The best of the boys' establishments were taken as models of behaviour, and girls consequently aimed for the élite classical sixth and inclusion in the First Lacrosse twelve. They were encouraged to drop their girlish wiles; tears were discouraged; to be brave and hardworking was their goal.

Universal Aunts was Frances' unexpected venture outside academic life. She liked and respected Gertie's enterprise, its aims and achievements. She had already taken shares in the Company and accepted the directorship with enormous pleasure. She was technically a non-working Director, and continued her outside travels and interests simultaneously, spreading the work of the Aunts in relevant quarters as she went. She brought back to the Board meetings some valid comments on national and world conditions, and on requirements in the social and domestic fields. She gave it her care, attention and financial backing until about sixty years later when she died in her nineties.

Frances was recognized as the 'professional' of the group. As such, she was elected to act on Gertie's behalf in her absence. To soften any kind of a slight to Emmie, the Board voted her a bonus of £40 'in appreciation of all her hard work and effort'.

Out of the office, Emmie was frequently to be seen at her favourite place, the theatre, or at a concert, often in the company of old friends whose children were destined to have their names in bright lights, like the parents of Jacqueline du Pré and those of James Mason. Emmie had catholic tastes and the theatres were then alive with sparkling productions. In the spring of 1925, *No, No, Nanette* was playing at the Palace Theatre. Her Majesty Queen Mary, in grey-sequinned toque trimmed with ostrich feathers, attended a charity performance. During one scene, the chorus appeared in bathing costumes and the Queen turned her head away from the stage. *The Student Prince, Lady be Good*, and *Desert Song* held audiences in delight, and never-to-be-forgotten songs were born. In the same season, Noel Coward was starring in his play *The Vortex* at the Royalty. His portrayal of male sexual encounters and drug addiction raised few eyebrows among the young middle-aged, but the older generation and the establishment staged a public outcry against 'such filth'.

Emmie met many friends in theatre intervals. They knew the work she was doing and it excited a good deal of interest. She was asked, 'What exactly do the Aunts *do*?'

The answer was by now too comprehensive to encompass in a few simple words: 'We can undertake this and, yes, we do that.' Emmie replied ambiguously with what the Aunts definitely did *not* do. 'No advice is given on legal or medical or financial matters, and we do not undertake detective work.' She paused, then added, 'And we are *not*, except involuntarily, a matrimonial agency!'

The theatres were not the only showplace of the best of British. Our great capital city thrived on ostentatious shows and exhibitions. June 1925 brought a grand excitement such as had not been seen since Prince Albert's Great Exhibition at the Crystal Palace in 1851: the British Empire Exhibition at Wembley opened as a market-place for our far-flung colonies.

Gertie had moved smartly as soon as it was rumoured that the Exhibition was to take place. She applied to the organizers for Universal

Aunts to be accredited agents, and as such they sold tickets and arranged parties on a commission basis. Quite apart from the considerable financial success for the Company, this proved to be excellent and widespread publicity. Americans, colonials and organized Women's Institute parties from around the United Kingdom did business for the first time with Universal Aunts.

Representatives from each country brought and showed their best arts and crafts, technological and scientific products. Visitors came in droves from all over the world to see and buy. The majority of women visitors were interested in the excellence of our fabrics; from the four corners of the British Isles were displayed cottons, linens, wools and tweeds. The couture houses and factories had also designed and made them into clothes of quality.

Gertie sent her workers from the Interior Decorating department to the Exhibition to study design. Sophisticated window displays went in for novelties to catch the public eye. Figures in plaster, wax and carved wood displayed the slinky couture dresses and wrap-around coats, ermine wraps, long multi-coloured gauze scarves and jewelled toques for evenings. The figures were bedecked in the right accessories, shoes, bags, gloves and even real jewellery. Painted backdrops, against which goods were shown to advantage, were also in vogue. To cater for the needs of Mr Hal Williams, Gertie had sought recruits to the department from art schools. This was not difficult; the Bloomsbury set had ensured that art was not only acceptable but worshipped. Their disciples, swelling the art schools, were often from the society in which they and Gertie moved, and were pleased to gain practical experience outside their studies. Their influence rubbed off on the competent amateurs already running the department, but Gertie never missed an extra chance for them to learn more.

As November of that year enveloped Britain in thick, grey fog, Queen Alexandra, aged eighty and stone deaf, surrounded by her loving family, died at Sandringham. Gertie had on several occasions been received by the Queen and felt the loss as quite a personal one. She remembered a regal and beautiful lady with a gentle manner. Walled in by her deafness and having been out of public life for two years, she was still in the hearts of her people and greatly mourned by them.

There were few republicans amongst the British people. Kings and queens were the father and mother of the family, expected to know about and suffer for their people. The cure for the ills of the nation was firmly regarded as being the business of the elected politicians.

7

1920S

CRISES

The General Strike – Irresponsible reporting

No one with a social conscience could completely divert his or her mind from the appalling realities of the vast unemployment in the country. Britain was never to regain her pre-war position in the world economy.

On the home front, the evaluation of a man's work and a woman's work was a firmly established working-class fact of life. Women in war-work had not complained about returning to their 'proper' roles when the men came home to return to theirs. Very often, though, the man could get no work and lost his position of authority in the family, even his dole money being withheld if his wife and children were earning. The wife bravely kept up appearances, darning the clothes, keeping the house, and making meals from scraps to feed her children.

Some of the worst hit areas were the great northern industries of coal and cotton. There were 300,000 miners out of work and pits were closing on all sides. The miners, having experienced the immediate post-war boom of a huge rise in coal prices, falsely expected this to be an indication of the future and were not prepared to return to wage-slavery. Too many of the mine-owners were ignorant of the true nature of the industry, which they used as a means of personal prestige and of gaining huge profits. They were not prepared to run their mines at a loss and the remedy they proposed was to lower wages or return to an eight-hour day. Discussions between owners and miners got nowhere.

A conference of 1,000 trade union delegates had, on 31 July 1925, pledged its support to the miners. Subsequent months passed in endless discussion between both sides and Baldwin and Birkenhead on behalf of the Cabinet. During this delicate state of negotiation, the scales were tipped by the printers who suppressed a publication of the *Daily Mail* because they disliked the leading articles. At mid-night on 3 May 1926 the General Strike began.

Its impact was aptly described by a young Oxford undergraduate, Hugh Gaitskell: 'A little like war, in that everybody's lives were suddenly affected by a new, unprecedented situation, which forced us to abandon plans for pleasure, to change our values and adjust our priorities. Above all we had to make a choice. And how we chose was a clear test of our political outlook.'

Gaitskell joined the University Strike Committee, set up by the Oxford Labour Party and the Left generally, to work on the side of the miners and the unions – as did many others of his time. With an opposing point of view, which was to uphold national order, but with no particular resentment towards the strikers, nor particular political leaning, others in vast numbers rallied to the call of the Government.

Recent technology lessened the impact of the General Strike. Trains and buses came to a halt, but many people now had cars. No newspapers were printed, but people now had the wireless. Soon *The Times* brought out a mini-version and women worked through the night hand-folding copies. Men rushed to drive the trams and amateur railway enthusiasts tried their hand at driving the trains; some got through and some went off the rails, but there were no reports of disasters. Some men acted as emergency police and others went to the East India Docks to collect the fish; there they found Guardsmen on sentry-go and the Guards band playing a popular selection to keep up everyone's spirits. Depots were opened in Hyde Park and other city centres; the fish was taken to these and vegetables were brought up in cars from the country. Young women became stall-holders, selling the produce, and older ones helped to run food centres for the volunteers. As described by Waugh, 'Young gentlemen from the Universities and public schools seemed to favour driving the lorries of milk churns; their baggy breeches and knee-socks gained them the name of "plus-fours boys".'

Union delegates negotiated back and forth, trying to coerce the Government and persuading themselves that they were right to organize a 'sympathetic strike'. Baldwin maintained his readiness to resume negotiations as soon as the strike was called off. Conditions for the strikers were demoralizing: hand-out clothing, soup-kitchens, and the nagging fear of even worse unemployment if they continued to stay out while other people took on their jobs. It was a dreadful and shaming sight to see them reduced to scrabbling for fragments of coal off the waste tips. Within a week there was a trickle back to work and skeleton services began again. On 12 May the Trade Union leaders went to Downing Street and the General Strike was called off.

On one side, internal wrangling and inflexibility, greed and ignorance had been shown up: on the other had been revealed, for the first time, genuine working-class solidarity. At the end of seven months, the miners dejectedly drifted back to work on the owners' terms, imbued with a staunch hatred against 'capitalism' which would raise its head again.

Business at the office was suspended during the week of the strike so that each Aunt might take part wherever she felt best suited – in the soup-kitchens for the strikers or the canteens for the volunteers. For a while afterwards, to all of them, any other work seemed trivial in comparison.

There was plenty of lighter work awaiting the Aunts and Emmie lost no time in getting them back on the road. A young green parrot in a covered travelling cage was taken to Euston and put in charge of the guard with a 2s 6d tip; he was a precious traveller and would be met by his new owner on arrival at Penrith. The mother of a young medical student asked for an Aunt to tidy up her son's rented rooms and inspect his laundry for repairs. Two eleven-year-olds on a school *exeat* were taken to the Science Museum to see the display of presents collected by the Prince of Wales on his recent tour: the Prince had visited forty-five countries and brought back gifts ranging from fabulous jewels to carved statues. A young married Aunt was needed to help another to choose her layette. An older and more sophisticated Aunt was booked to fill in as an extra dinner guest at a private house in Eaton Terrace; she had to be of good social standing and have a plentiful supply of dinner-table conversation.

One Aunt was persuaded to 'put up' a mongoose for a week while his owner was abroad. She collected him in his cage from the office and found the little animal had a ticket on his collar warning that he had a habit of running up chimneys. An Aunt was requested to make up a fourth at bridge, and another was needed to sit with a small girl who had measles and read her stories.

A high-powered, academic Aunt was engaged to decipher Aztec hieroglyphics for a young man writing a book on the subject. She questioned whether his request was serious or just a wager.

'Why?' Emmie asked.

'Because', she answered, 'at the period he speaks of, the Quipu system was in use and not hieroglyphics.'

'Tell me,' asked Emmie, 'what is the difference?'

'Knots,' replied the expert. 'The ancient Peruvian substitute for writing was variously knotted threads of different colours.'

The young man's telephone number was also false.

A shopping Aunt was dispatched to purchase a pair of corsets for a lady in Florence who had sent details of size. A sleuthing Aunt had to find a piece of waste land in London upon which a new patent fire-extinguisher could be demonstrated. So, daily, the genial, *au fait* ladies went on their way, performing tasks one might expect of one's own Aunts.

In spite of all this activity, overheads always seemed to run at more than was expected. The profit margin on the Aunts' so-called luxury services was not large enough – but one could price oneself too high. Frances Blackett was elected to make a survey and seek the best solution. She presented her proposals with the words: 'For the good of the Company and its continuation in business.' Only the clients were spared.

The permanent engagement fees to resident women employees were raised.

6d in the £ on the first year's salary up to £52 p.a.

9d in the £ on the first year's salary from £52 to £60 p.a.

1/- in the £5 on the first year's salary over £60 p.a.

The London County Council was to be notified of the proposed alteration according to the law.

It is to be resolved that £85 p.a. be set aside for general advertising, no more.

The financial position necessitated staff salaries being cut by 5s with the exception of the office girl. [That was Betsy.]

The Managing Director instructed that her salary too must be cut by the same amount.

Miss Frances Blackett herself, being unsalaried, would forgo the 5% interest on her shares.

At a quite amicable interview with the Bank Manager, a temporary loan facility of £400 has been secured, with an agreement for monthly reduction.

An accounts department was now needed to cope with the weight and variety of business, and a book-keeper was required. As so often with the Aunts, 'the network' came up with the answer in the small, round and rosy-cheeked shape of Miss Dorothy Tull, a charming lady of uncertain age, a recently retired book-keeper with the highest references. In she came and there she remained, a *tower of strength*, indomitable and happy amongst her figures for years. All Frances' proposals were accepted without question by those concerned and put into immediate effect. Seven months later the Company was again running profitably.

On 30 August there was a curious letter-card in Gertie's morning mail. Gertie did not react favourably to the contents. She left the one penny and halfpenny stamps stuck to it and just added her note pinned to it, 'not answered' (see page 79).

Betsy was sent out for the *Westminster Gazette*. The article shown on page 78 went on: 'It is so much more romantic to be met by a strange young "Uncle" . . . than it is by an "Aunt".' Gertie, Emmie and everyone in the office read it once, twice, in stunned silence. The care, discretion and complete integrity which had been the by-word of the Company from its beginning were being threatened by some smart reporter who thought he had an amusing 'modern' story. Gertie immediately contracted her solicitor.

Gertie and Emmie and all the Aunts were deeply shocked. They were quite accustomed by now to being written up in the press, but only by responsible and factual reporters, not by scandalmongers. During the following week, as the story and its repercussions filtered through the network, the Aunts gossiped and argued among themselves. Being an Aunt had been enough of a status symbol to stave off comments from friends about 'going out to work'. Husbands protesting about working wives had been silenced by the philanthropic nature of the job. The Aunts felt that their credibility was threatened and that some husbands might easily withdraw their consent.

The clients, never having encountered such 'goings-on' in their dealings with the Company, tended to treat it as a bit of nonsense and throw in a sheepish, 'Don't want one of those debonair chaps, you know!' when next they called. They received reassurances.

Gertie continued to pursue the matter. Perhaps only Emmie realized

UNIVERSAL
AUNTS
AND UNCLES.

THE SCHOOL GIRLS'
PREFERENCE.

DEBONAIR MEN
WITH BUNS.

Queer requests come to the "Universal Aunts," of Sloane-square, S.W., Miss Ford, the managing director "Aunt" revealed to the Westminster Gazette yesterday.

Universal Aunts, Ltd., are a sort of National Utility Society, who will do anything that may reasonably be requested of them, from finding lodgings to providing a companion.

A hard-working farmer in New Zealand recently asked the "Aunts" to select for him and despatch post haste "a nice girl, fond of the country, and with homely tastes," to be his wife.

The "Aunts," however, do not enter the matrimonial lists.

"We supply Uncles, of course," said Miss Ford, "and the demand for them is definitely on the increase. You see, an uncle can be so useful—especially when it comes to days on the river, motor-car jaunts where a chauffeur is required, dances, and the schoolboy's half-holiday.

BOYS SHY OF "AUNTS".

"Schoolboys are usually rather shy of 'Aunts,'" said Miss Ford, "and with the true schoolboy masculine instinct, much prefer to 'do' the pictures, followed by tea in the company of 'my Uncle,' especially if 'Uncle' is jolly and nice-looking.

"We are very careful in selecting our 'Uncles,' naturally, and never permit a single introduction to the family without the personal guarantee of one of our 'Aunts,' who are all well known to us, and old friends."

Schoolgirl "flappers" requiring to be met and escorted from one station to another also have a preference for nice-looking uncles.

the depths of her fury and the drain of her strength. Such unprecedented attacks were outside any code of behaviour she could comprehend; she was not accustomed to being a subject for public farce. She confided to Emmie, 'How I wish I could talk it over with Joshua Steed.'

But, of course, that was no longer possible. She went through the proper channels of her own competent Company solicitors. She also

69 Dartmouth Pk Hill
N.W.5
Gothard.
24. 8. 26.

Dear Auntie,

It just tickled me to read about you in the Westminster Gazette; & I should like a few particulars how to go on as I am a widow, & it probably would require an uncle to chaperone me to a Theatre or the Zoo. Anyway should love to hear from you.

wrote an indignant letter to *The Times*, asking if they would insert a paragraph of rebuttal:

> Will you most kindly spare a few moments of your valuable time to read the enclosed, and, if you think my organization is right in doing so, allow us in your personal column to deny the statement marked in the accompanying copy of the Westminster Gazette of August 27th. The whole interview as reported is garbled and incorrect, but the statement that we allow young men to meet young girls entrusted (often by parents abroad) to our charge is, of course, entirely untrue, as is the statement that the Aunts intervene in divorce proceedings. . . . The impression created by the report in the Westminster Gazette would, I think, make any right-thinking parent or guardian decide that my organization was unfit for the care of young people. We are constantly asked to take *entire charge* of girls varying in age from 12 to 20 and have the reputation of absolute reliability.

The Times's Classified Advertisement Manager, after considering the matter and reading a draft of their proposed wording, duly inserted the following advertisement in the Personal Column on 16 September 1926: 'THE UNIVERSAL AUNTS Ltd, 192 Sloane Street, SW, wish to announce that the only members of the organization who meet young people at stations are registered and accredited Aunts well known to the managing director.'

Gertie also tackled the *Westminster Gazette* directly, and their news editor wrote back:

> Dear Miss Fort,
> While I very naturally regret that a false impression should have been created in regard to the article which appeared in the Westminster Gazette of August 27th, I should like to make it perfectly clear to you that the Westminster Gazette has always appreciated the very excellent work which your organization performs and would not, for one moment, do anything that would be likely to put the Universal Aunts Ltd in a false light before the public.
> You will notice in the issue of tomorrow's Westminster Gazette I have inserted a paragraph which will make it perfectly clear that it is an Aunts' and not an Uncles' organization as the paragraph seemed to convey. I trust that you will appreciate the fact that the Westminster

Gazette is always open to do the universal Aunts Ltd good and not harm, both now and in the future.

The paragraph in question read:

The Universal Aunts Limited, Sloane Street, SW1, whose activities were described in the Westminster Gazette on 27 August, wish to make it clear that, as their title conveys, they are an aunts' and not an uncles' organization.
Miss Fort, the managing director, states that 'the only men that act professionally for us are certified tutors, chauffeurs and all domestic staff'.

The point had been reached when Gertie knew it was time to give a ladylike dismissal to the whole matter. It had ceased to be a nine days' wonder; reasonable retribution had been exacted; business was going on as usual; and the Aunts' ruffled feathers had settled. Gertie, as always, did not linger over a now stale affair. There were far more interesting prospects ahead.

8

1920S

THE AMERICAN CONNECTION

Overseas assignments – Hostesses Incorporated of New York –
The misfit – More shares – Wilton Place

Gertie, Emmie and Frances were well travelled and had many good contacts abroad. Gertie's overseas services were for the luxury market, for women with the wherewithal to engage in overseas shopping, travel or culture. A shopping Aunt in London, Paris and Rome, who would personally choose and dispatch the luxuries, brought in brisk and often regular commissions. To be met and taken care of in a foreign city enabled young, old or nervous travellers to undertake an otherwise impossible journey. A resident Aunt could be booked for the purpose: Madame Chantal at 23 rue de la Paix, Miss Wallace in Rome; far distantly, Mrs Dixon in Cape Town and Mrs Campbell in India. The business operated smoothly and easily, with the simplicity of personal attention to every detail.

Daughters came next on the list. The vogue for sending teenage girls to be 'finished', to acquire a veneer of culture in a capital city other than their own, was growing fast. In England hostesses were continuing to have several young guests per season, usually corresponding in age to their own children and including them as members of the family. These girls were selected from France, Italy and Spain. In Europe, as in Britain, many of the landed families seeking ways to maintain their impoverished estates caught on to the idea and set themselves out to receive a number of British girls for a year's duration. The ambience was perfect, the châteaux and country houses were treasure-troves of paintings, books and music, and marvellous centres of rich family life. Gertie matched up families and conducted negotiations on both sides of the Channel.

The name and work of the Company had filtered back from those 'best kind of Americans in England', as one newspaper described them, and reached the ears of an august body of ladies in New

York. Their President, Mrs Courtland D. Barnes, wrote to Gertie.

Hostesses Incorporated of New York, with offices at 26 East End Street, had been established for three years. As described by Mrs Barnes, they were basically undertaking services similar to those of the Aunts and 'gracefully and competently fulfilling their roles of accomplishing whatever jobs befell them'. She asked whether they might 'act on behalf of Universal Aunts on that side of the world'. Gertie thought the invitation a bit flowery but agreed that the idea should be thoroughly discussed, if possible in person. The Americans were serious enough to send over their representative, Miss Lucille J. Platt, who first handed over their list of patronesses, a formidable bevy:

Mrs Courtland D. Barnes, President
Mrs Barry A. Curtis, Vice President
Miss Virginia J. H. Furman, Treasurer
Mrs Woodward Babcock
Mrs August Belmont
Mrs Fulton Cutting
Miss Lydia Dadmun
Mrs Joseph E. Davis
Mrs Hamilton Hadden
Miss Camilla Miller
Miss Virginia Potter
Mrs John T. Pratt
Mrs William K. Vanderbilt
Mrs Richard Whitney
Mrs Macculloch Miller

Friendly discussions and a little British hospitality for Miss Platt went on for a few days and then she went home. Gertie returned the courtesy and sent her own list of patronesses, which stood up quite well:

The Duchess of Norfolk
The Dowager Duchess of Abercorn
Albertha, Marchioness of Blandford
Lady Blankenberg
Lady Selby-Bigge, OBE
Lady Burgh
Miss Gilbert

Mrs J. K. Jackson
Major A. Maclean of Ardgour
The Hon Mrs Maclean
Mr and Mrs Maclean of Lazenby
Major C. Maclean, DSO and Mrs Maclean
Miss Frances Maclean
Lady Alice Mahon
Mrs Alexandra Part
Lady Roche
The Hon Lady Shelly Rolls
Major and Mrs Charles Tristram
The Revd Gilbert Weigall
Mrs Hugh Reig Griffin

Universal Aunts advertised their new American link:

Miss Platt also took back to New York the authority for Hostesses Incorporated of that city to act as sole agents for Universal Aunts in America. She also made the apt observation that: 'Money is not mentioned until one leaves. In England, as we know, money is regarded as the axle-grease that runs the machinery and is not to be seen, but felt.'

This amicable relationship lasted for some ten years until Hostesses Incorporated passed into other hands, when the Directors reported that 'relations with Hostesses Incorporated have been severed'. American awareness of Universal Aunts was by then established and lasting. From the outset, however, there was one recurring American request which was declined: to supply English wives.

On the home front Gertie coped with a stupid little niggle. The care with which she and Emmie chose the women to run each department was such that the office was a compatible and happy place to work. The rare misfit was instantly a source of irritation and best released to find employment elsewhere, which Gertie arranged without hesitation. So several ladies had come and gone pretty speedily, ones who had generally accepted that it just hadn't worked. One, though, had become a nuisance and a disturbing influence within the office, and following her dismissal she indulged in some imaginative gossip. It soon travelled on the grapevine to Gertie's ears, and she dealt with it.

December 1st 1927

Dear Mrs X,

I have been told on reliable authority that there are rumours that the Universal Aunts Ltd are not doing well and that the organization cannot possibly last. May I assure you that I personally have never felt happier about the Aunts' position and prospects.

I should be glad to hear that in future you will contradict any false rumours as to our instability. I should also like to make it quite clear:

1) That we do not make it a *sine qua non* that workers engaged by us must invest in the Company.
2) That we do not run a matrimonial bureau.
3) That I never allow any member of the Company to use the office or telephone *for betting*, and that I have never allowed friends or workers to do so.

You will be, I know, pleased to hear how well Betsy is doing. Her position and pay have both improved considerably. Some time ago I suggested we should get her another post, but she wished to remain with the Aunts. She is a straight and loyal little worker.

> Yours truly,
> Safara Fort
> Managing Director.

Gertie certainly did not make it an 'indispensable condition' that her workers invest in the Company. On the contrary, invitations to do so were kept for her own friends and people of her circle. She offered shares to them and, sometimes, favours in return for their investment. Perhaps one of the things Mrs X had resented was that she was not one of the chosen few.

One who was given the opportunity, in October 1927, was the writer Marion Bower. She and Gertie had struck up a friendship when Gertie wrote to express her pleasure in her book, *The Quince Bush*. Miss Bower reciprocated with her admiration of Universal Aunts. A regular correspondence developed between St Margaret's House, Bury St Edmunds, where Miss Bower lived with her ninety-year-old father, and 192 Sloane Street.

Gertie made known that up to 300 7½ Participating Preference Shares were at that moment available and Miss Bower expressed herself very happy to take these up. Miss Bower had a niece coming to London who wished to hire a room, and this was found for her by the House department. Miss Bower herself was leaving on a tour of America (having arranged with her sister to care for their father) where *The Quince Bush* was to be published by Messrs Bobbs, Merrill and Co, who gave her a 'handsome contract'. Gerties introduced Miss Bower to Hostesses Incorporated of New York, who helped to make the tour even more comfortable and successful, and she undertook to enclose a leaflet advertising Miss Bower's book list in all Universal Aunts correspondence. 'A notice to fit the envelope in which my letter of today comes to you would be best,' she wrote on 10 October.

As far as Gertie was concerned, business was everywhere and it was her duty to capture a share. Commission had become the popular incentive in these dealings, for companies were willing to pay a percentage for the introduction of new business. Clients were introduced to the novel idea of holidays in small guided groups, packages, for winter sports or summer travel; the tour operators paid Universal Aunts. Ladies' clubs in provincial cities circularized their members with

Gertie's latest brochures; Universal Aunts paid them on any subsequent transactions. She even engaged in trade! One of the ladies' clubs with which the Aunts had a liaison was in Sheffield. 'The home of the Master Cutler,' said Gertie. 'We could enquire about tableware to offer to "home leave" clients.' Both she and Emmie had lived in India with serving families, and knew that, during home leave, the wives liked to replenish the household with simple, good quality British goods to take back. The secretary of the Sheffield Ladies' Club wrote that she could purchase, for example, knives, forks and spoons in good Sheffield plate, with 7 per cent discount off the quoted price. She suggested to Gertie that a subtle form of advertising would be to have Universal Aunts' name etched on to the blade of the knives, at a cost of 2d per letter. Gertie initially ordered half a gross of each; the line sold well and orders continued for some time.

Gertie turned down as many offers as she accepted, the standing of the company or the commodity not meeting her requirements. Accommodation to let was then too plentiful to take any more on to the books, even with some very tempting prices indeed. A quite typical offer came from R. Perrin & Co of Cockburn Street:

> To let in a well furnished and nice large house in South Kensington, each accommodation comprises a bedroom and sitting-room next to each other and meals would be served in the sitting-room by the butler and footman. The inclusive charge, with the exception of fires, 7 guineas per week.

The House Department attached a note to this correspondence for 'Miss Fort's' attention. 'They are not of value to the House Dept who already have so many rooms on the books. The profit margin is not large enough to be shared.'

Gertie had never been one to make long-term plans. When she was involved she was fully engrossed while the occupation of the moment ran its course. She entered the office one autumn morning, finding everything as usual – a hub of people, telephone, letters, smiling faces raised to wish her good morning then returned to their business. Betsy had placed everything ready on her desk: reports from each of them, letters to read, decisions to be made. As she sat down she suddenly felt a momentary panic, caught up in a situation that had somehow got beyond her control. Everything had gone very nicely but, for the first time ever, she did not seem to have written the last act of this charming production.

Gertie looked up. No one was looking at her. She sat very still and surveyed the room. Women sitting at desks, women coming in at the door, women going out of the door, men and women on the telephone, correspondence from all over the world. A delightful feeling crept over her. She said to herself, 'This time, I just don't want to go on to something else. There is everything here.' She smiled to herself. 'Of course, I'm in control as never before.'

How true! She had set the course for a long run, with or without her. Gertie's introspection usually heralded something important and this time she initiated a big step. She suggested moving to premises suitable for business on a bigger scale, with more than a hundred workers.

Once again the search was brief and the new premises were close at hand, at 37 Wilton Place. Three small floors were taken, linked by a narrow staircase which, it was noted in the lease, must be kept well lighted at all times. Radiators heated the rooms and certain furnishings were retained. The top floor was let as a self-contained flat, at 2 guineas per week, to a professional man, and the basement could be rented out in future. Universal Aunts would occupy the middle floor themselves. This had three useful-sized rooms, a landing and bathroom, and large windows which overlooked the elegant sweep of Wilton Place and Knightsbridge. The one discordant note was the rumble of old water pipes in the section earmarked for the Boardroom corner, which was to become a strange interruption during future Board meetings.

Now there was no dignified crocodile of bootmakers to undertake the removal and, in any case, there was a whole vanload to transport. Gertie and Emmie felt it only right to call in Harrods. Gertie was satisfied with the venue and the joy of more space, although she referred to the offices as 'a sardine tin tucked on a Fortnums shelf'.

Before Christmas 1927, everyone settled in easily and happily. 'Might as well be hung for a sheep as a lamb,' said Gertie to Emmie.

She promptly raised salaries by 10s a week to £3 and recruited two more young office girls to work under the now experienced Betsy at £1 10s a week. The considerable cost of the move was also very evident in the Company's affairs, and Frances stood security at the Bank.

There was a sudden set-back when Gertie slipped on some icy steps and suffered concussion. On doctor's orders, she stayed away from her duties for two months. Emmie took over complete control, and everyone else rallied and felt awfully proud of themselves to be holding things together! Gertie fretted but she stayed fairly quietly in her flat and fed on the daily reports from the office. One irritating item was that the Sloane telephone exchange had installed automatic equipment, which caused the office and everyone else for miles around fantastic confusion, as subscribers had only just got used to everyday use of the telephone.

Gertie was thankful that her particular business was sought-after and scanned the information from the office for the progress of the work. The country was still in the doldrums of unemployment and a sluggish economy; the Conservatives and Baldwin had been ejected from Number 10 and Labour and MacDonald were in power. By September 1929 attention was focused on foreign news: the American Great Depression, with its repetition of earlier British spectacular suicide-leaps out of the mess and into the hereafter.

Ramsay MacDonald crossed the Atlantic by ship to sympathize and advise. He returned quite soon and went to stay with his friend Lady Londonderry, it being rumoured that his association with this distinguished Lady tempered his views and saved Britain from the more extreme forms of socialism, then and throughout his term of office.

During her recuperation, Gertie had had time to do a little scheming. Now she made a decision which would bring in a revolutionary branch of business and also another much-needed investment of capital.

9

1920S

BAY

Air-woman – Cornwall Gardens – The silver box –
The Winchester mistake – Emmie's lectures

The Leiths had been as family to Gertie all her life; their place, Northcourt in the Isle of Wight, and property in Aberdeenshire, had been as second homes. Two sisters – Mildred known as Bay (her nursery version of Baby) who was Gertie's age, and Eveleigh who was younger – both already held shares in the Company. Now and again their brother Lord Burgh had said what an asset the girls would be to the Company. Gertie, feeling that one at a time would be the best way, invited Bay to join the Board.

Bay's mother had died when she was born on 22 March 1894, and Bay had become the pet and focus of a band of delightful, cultured women, her aunts, and the Queen Bee, her grandmother. They had cherished her in their own pursuits and she had grown up with the widest possible interests. They loved music and she was taken to Dresden and Berlin, to Covent Garden and the Queen's Hall. She saw Elgar conduct his own violin concerto with Fritz Kreisler as soloist, and regularly saw Thomas Beecham conduct.

Their house had an abundance of animals; it was only natural to love dogs and she was expected to become an accomplished horsewoman. Bay's grandmother, Mrs Disney Leith, was a regular visitor to Iceland, who spoke the language perfectly, wrote books, and published translations from Icelandic into English. Bay often accompanied her grandmother on these expeditions and watched her select Icelandic ponies to be transported and established on their own estate at Northcourt in the Isle of Wight.

Grandmother had an admirer, her first cousin the poet Algernon Swinburne. Throughout his lifetime, he kept for her an undying, unreciprocated and chaste love. Thus Swinburne also influenced Bay's early years, and in December 1894 he published a poem dedicated to her.

To a Baby Kinswoman

Love, whose light thrills heaven and earth,
Smiles and weeps upon thy birth,
Child, whose mother's love-lit eyes
Watch thee, but from Paradise.
Sweetest night that earth can give,
Sweetest light of eyes that live,
Ours must needs, for hope withdrawn,
Hail with tears thy soft spring dawn.

At each stage in her life, he chose books for her and inscribed messages in them. Time passed, and Bay's real passion in life became apparent; it was not in the arts but in things mechanical. It ran in the family, for Grandmama's passion (other than Icelandic ponies) was railways and engines; she wrote books about them with charming sketches. Bay's brother also had the bug: while still the Hon Jock Leith, he had taken a wager and beaten the Flying Scotsman express from London to Edinburgh by car, averaging fifty-four miles an hour. Bay served her apprenticeship in mechanics by working in a garage. Then she decided that she must fly.

In the air, indomitable men and women were blazing a trail and linking the world. A few years earlier, in November 1925, the hero was Alan Cobham who had made the brilliant flight from Croydon to Cape Town. In January 1928, when the Thames burst its banks in winter storms, the Duchess of Bedford had reported on the damage from overhead in her Gipsy Moth biplane. In June that year the Duchess, aiming to fly to India and back in eight days, ran into difficulties and arrived some weeks later. Undeterred, she continued to transport herself between London and Woburn Abbey, which, she said, 'helped to relieve a buzzing sound in my ears'.

Bay's friend and teacher was the woman pilot, Miss Sicele O'Brien, unique holder of an 'A' and 'B' licence, daughter of the great Irishman and cricketer, Sir Timothy O'Brien. On 20 October 1928 the two were cruising 300 feet above Mill Hill golf course in Middlesex on a training flight while an exhibition match was in progress below. The engine of the Moth aeroplane cut out and the plane nose-dived on to the fairway.

Sicele and Bay were dragged out of the wreckage and rushed to hospital. Sicele's badly crushed leg was amputated; Bay only suffered concussion. Within the year, Sicele had been fitted with an artificial leg and was back in the air. Bay, after the requisite hours, achieved her ambition, and received her 'A' licence as a member of the London Aeroplane Club.

Bay embarked upon her role within Universal Aunts with enthusiasm. She hoped to extend, through the organization, the opportunity for a greater number of women to take part in the exciting new age of the car and the aeroplane. Bay set up the Car and Air Department which she ran by herself at the salary of £3 per week.

CAR AND AIR DEPARTMENTS.

Sales. – All makes of cars supplied new and second-hand. Part Exchange Deals. Deferred Payments. Sales with guarantee of re-purchase, etc., arranged.

The finding of sound second-hand cars a speciality.

Hire. – Special Service of medium-sized, owner-driven cars from 9d. per mile. Daimler and Rolls Royce Landaulettes, tariff on application. Drivers supplied. Driving Lessons. Insurance, etc.

Flying. – Advice re Tuition. D.H. Moths and all makes of Light Aeroplane supplied.

Motor Boats. – All makes supplied.

Universal Aunts were appointed agents for the Automobile Association and for the Car and General Insurance Company, receiving commission on all recruits. Bay arranged to obtain all makes of car at a trade discount, and undertook the sale of new and second-hand cars, with all car accessories and after-sales service. Car-hire, bookings for air travel, driving lessons and flying lessons were all provided.

Clothes, to Bay, had to relate to the job in hand, so that in winter this meant her long leather coat, in summer her short leather jacket. In the office she did refrain from wearing her flying helmet with a woollen lining and flappy earpieces, in which she resembled a cocker spaniel. Yet she was always correctly dressed to step into any machine, ground or air, that happened along. She smoked continually and elegantly, using a slim holder and a thin, gold, monogrammed cigarette case.

There was a sustained public interest in this still revolutionary group of air-women. They were great characters and the newspapers offered up every detail of the exploits of 'our lady flyers':

Miss Sicele O'Brien
Her Grace the Duchess of Bedford
Lady Drummond-Hay
The Hon Mrs Montague
The Hon Mildred Leith.

They were quick to discover and report that one of their number, the Hon Mildred Leith, had joined the board of directors of the well-known social bureau, Universal Aunts. There, in an advisory capacity, the celebrated Miss Leith could be found and engaged, for a fee, to give advice and practical instruction on flying.

Scores of ambitious girls and women appeared at the office to ask, 'I want to fly, but can I make a living as an air-woman?'

'Yes,' Bay replied, 'if you can afford to hang on and wait your chance. Some women are already earning a living in the air as teachers and stunters, and every year there will be opportunities for more.'

She gave them details of the cost of her training: 'Clubs charge £2 per hour for dual flying, £1 per hour for solo pilots. Most pupils go solo after 17 hours or less.' She always added, 'These training costs are remarkably low compared with those of other careers. For your "A" licence, you have to fly at least eight hours dual and three solo, and pass an examination on air traffic regulations followed by two practical tests. A medical examination must also be passed.'

She warned them. 'Then you are qualified to fly for sheer joy. For a career, you should go on to get your "B" licence. You will need a further ninety-five flying hours, plus more medical and technical examinations.' Her listeners were always surprised when she advised: 'If possible, buy your own machine.' She said it as though it needed as little courage as buying a new hat. 'An aeroplane is a sound investment and generally re-saleable at a comparatively small loss.' She warmed to her subject. 'A new Moth two-seater costs no more than £600, a good second-hand plane £300–400. Garaging comes to £1 a week. On average, one can do 15 miles per gallon of petrol at moderate 75 miles per hour cruising speed.' She encouraged them with her enthusiasm. 'With your plane you can stunt at shows and garden parties, take passengers on short sightseeing trips, chauffeur private individuals and, after you are well-established and confident yourself, give lessons. Prospects for those without a plane are more limited.

'First and foremost are excellent health and eyesight, needed to pass the very stringent medical tests,' she continued. 'Endurance and being able to stand long hours in the air is more important than downright physical strength. You need a happy, medium temperament, neither highly strung nor very phlegmatic, good nerves, good judgement and a bent for mechanics.'

As the prospective flyers took their leave, Bay added, 'Now that you know the technicalities, I suggest you consider very carefully the essentials for a good air-woman and relate these to yourselves.'

On New Year's Day 1931, Amy Johnson, former solicitor's typist, set off on a solo flight to Peking, lost her way and ended up in Cologne. It was not long before she was successful, for the following year she made the epic flight in her Puss Moth to Cape Town and back.

Bay wrote to Sicele O'Brien on a matter crucial to all the air-women. It was sadly to be the last contact she had with her friend.

37 Wilton Place
S.W. 1
June 12th 1931

To Miss Sicele O'Brien
George Street
Dublin

My dear Sicele,
I was so pleased to receive your letter. It is such very exciting news to hear that you are about to take possession of your new Blackburn Bluebird.

I greatly look forward to my coming visit and to being with you and Sir Timothy. Apart from which, as you know, Dublin is a city dear to my heart. As you say, we have much to discuss.

The fact that there are, so far, no woman pilots in any of the various air services here and throughout the world is regrettable.

It is very understandable that the men with long air service records, obtained during the war, naturally have preference.

However, I am convinced that very soon, women will be employed as air chauffeuses for little trips to the Continent, the saloon model light aeroplanes that are so popular with women owners, lend themselves to such a service.

In my role here at Universal Aunts, I am often able to encourage these aims in the increasing number of women who seek my guidance through our motor and aviation department.

I look forward to our meeting next month.
Your sincere friend,
Bay Leith.

Six days later, Sicele and a passenger took off from Hatfield in her new aeroplane. The machine came down in a spin-dive and was engulfed in flames. Both women were killed.

Flying was life itself to the air-women, who showed a spirited disregard for anything but the job in hand. When Princess Lowenstein-Wertheim had recently left for America in her tiny Fokker monoplane, two hat-boxes had been espied among her luggage. Sadly, it was soon announced that the aeroplane was missing and she was presumed dead. The Duchess of Bedford, stepping into her plane, snapped down a sensation-seeking reporter who accosted her: 'A "thrilling venture", certainly not. Interesting, yes, but not thrilling. I am never thrilled.'

The loss of Sicele was a bitter blow to aviation in general and to Bay in particular. She was relieved to have her work at the Aunts to take her mind off the tragedy. She and Gertie decided that they needed to live somewhere close to the office. They found a large flat in Cornwall Gardens with spacious Victorian rooms, and invited their friend 'Blackie', as they called Frances, to share with them to cut living expenses. The three of them had only just moved in when they acquired a magnificent grey Persian cat called Katten. They sent out invitations to the house-warming, Bay insisting that they carry on as planned, as Sicele always had.

It was a modest evening in a busy season when the dinner-tables were buzzing with party gossip. An American millionairess was attending the social scene in a pearl necklace that had once belonged to Catherine the Great. And the first streaker had appeared – a twenty-two-year-old baronet, appearing at a party dressed as a woman, had later in the evening stripped and attempted to Charleston stark naked!

They all stayed fully clothed at Cornwall Gardens. The gramophone was wound up for a non-stop selection of records; silk slippers and patent-leather pumps tapped out the Jog Trott, the Missouri Walk, the Shimmy and the Black Bottom on floors and tables. Strains of 'Ain't we Got Fun' and 'Chili Bon Bon' echoed into the night. Most smart neighbourhoods expected to rock to the sound of a party from May to August, so no one complained; if neighbours weren't at this party they were, no doubt, at another one. The house-warming ended well, with

Jock Leith dangling a fellow-guest upside-down by his toes from a top
floor window; luckily, they both survived.

At that and other private parties, another new and unwelcome hazard
had begun to invade the scene: gate-crashers. As one hostess declared:
'The problem of the uninvited guest will have to be dealt with most
severely.'

Office work was a more serious concern to Gertie, Bay and Blackie.
1931 saw the celebration of the first decade of Universal Aunts and
Gertie was presented with a gift to mark the occasion. The staff and the
outside Aunts crammed into the office to await her arrival, and Bay
placed a package in her hands. Inside, Gertie found a small, flat, silver
box, enamelled in black with marcasite hinge and clasp. On the inside lid
it read:

G. MACLEAN

PRESENTED BY THE MEMBERS AND STAFF OF

UNIVERSAL AUNTS LTD.

FEB. 5TH 1931

1921–1931

Gertie was touched and delighted and, carried away by success, she
decided to celebrate the milestone by opening a branch office. She put
this into the hands of a friend in Winchester, operating in a tiny room
near the College, and even coined an office motto: '*Your Difficulties are
Our Opportunities*'. However, this new venture did not succeed. Gertie
closed the office within a few months and decided, then and for always,
that Universal Aunts could only operate in Britain from one main office.

Most of her ideas were much more successful and she never missed a
chance to spread the word. Gertie was, of course, included in every
social event of consequence by reason of her own position. While giving
her personal support, she could often extend this to taking tickets,
making a small donation in the name of her company or, when
programme-sellers were called for, offering some pretty young Universal Aunts. Gertie could rely upon being aided and abetted by her friends
and relations; all those ladies were, in the nicest possible way, masterly at
publicizing their own efforts. So it was when her Aunt, Lady Muriel
Beckworth, headed an Appeal in aid of the Sunshine Homes for Blind
Babies, Gertie played her part. She wrote to the Social Editor of the
Daily Telegraph, enclosing a paragraph about the Appeal, transmitting

Lady Muriel Beckwith's request that a report of the Concert might be inserted, and offering to send tickets.

The concert on 14 May at the American Women's Club (in aid of the Sunshine Homes for Blind Babies) will be attended by the Princess Helen Victoria. The artists are: Adila Fachiri, Kathleen Long and Reinhold Von Warlich. Amongst those who have already taken tickets are the Lady Allington, the Lady Muriel Beckwith, Lady MacGowan, Lady Glentaner, Mrs Frederick L. Hammond, Mrs George Crawley, Mrs Arthur Penn and Lady Piggott, who has organized the Concert in response to Lady Muriel Beckwith's Appeal.

Bay was taking a more active part in Company affairs than either Gertie or Emmie had envisaged – quite apart from running her own department. When in the office she was all ears and eyes. She looked up from her desk one morning and turned to Emmie. 'You know, Miss Faulder, apart from our founder, whose human and social interests are two of the greatest assets to the Company, versatility is more to be found amongst the outside staff than here in the office.'

Emmie considered this statement, then said, 'I hope this is not so, but I believe you are right. When one is dealing with such a wide range of enquiries all day, one does now instinctively categorize them. This can certainly lead to a tendency to refuse things which do not fit in.' She continued, 'Whereas the daily work of the outside Aunts is always to answer the conundrum. If they don't know the answer, they find it out.'

'In fact,' said Bay, 'they act for people who have no time, those who are helpless, and others who don't like to think for themselves.'

'They are paid to think,' said Emmie.

Bay gave an unexpected reply. 'Personally, I am afraid I do not really have the right temperament to be an outside Aunt. My mind runs in a business-like groove and, if I don't know something, I would a thousand times rather pay somebody to tell me than try to find it out for myself.'

Emmie laughed. 'Luckily, there are a lot of people like you, Miss Leith.'

With the '30s came an even greater number of women seeking work, women not educated to earn their living but desperately in need of some kind of job. Adding to the numbers were refugees coming from unsettled Europe. There were few more qualified to view this problem than Emmie who said, 'Our advice to young women today is to take a

course and make yourselves efficient before you look for a job. Odd jobs
for the amateur may turn up, but they are few and badly paid. Only a
background of training, efficiency and experience can ensure a living
wage in these competitive times.' She added, 'We are here to serve the
public and supply their needs. We cannot make the jobs and, like other
agencies, the number of these unskilled people we can use is quite
limited.'

But the interest in becoming an Aunt remained widespread, and
Emmie was sometimes asked to talk to a group of ladies. She always
wore a trim skirt, a jacket and a neat turban hat edged by a short wave of
her hair. Being a tall lady, Emmie liked to sit at a small table facing a
gathering of up to twenty. She was a good and logical speaker, her large,
smooth and ringless hands resting loosely on a small pad of notes, to
which she seldom referred.

'The type of person who says when asked that she can do everything,
but when further questioned is unable to type, do shorthand, drive a car,
has had no nursing or business experience, and ends by lamely suggest-
ing that she could write letters or do the flowers, is a type which is not
only very often maddening to deal with but, in many cases, very tragic,
where the need to earn is real and the chance of earning is so desperately
remote.

'I feel that perhaps the very versatility of the Aunts raises in vain the
hopes of many women of this kind. We do exercise dogs, meet children
and even sometimes write letters in longhand, but few people realize the
physical strength required to do three or four walks in the park of
perhaps an hour each, or the dependability needed for an escort who has
to meet a crowded train and pick off it some small individual who might
well like to give the Aunt the slip, or may just as likely turn up by quite a
different train from the one she was instructed to meet. Neither do they
realize that this is a comparatively small demand and is carried out by a
few regular workers, while the number of applicants for jobs such as
these runs into perhaps a dozen a day.' When Emmie had finished
speaking, questions with tea were popular.

To begin the second decade properly, Gertie applied for Universal
Aunts to become members of the Employment Agents' Federation.
They were duly elected and received the certificate.

10

1930s

SOCIAL CHANGE

Employment – Package tours – Social change – Arrest in
Munich – The King – The Court – Women off the ground

Going into the '30s, the Aunts embraced the ever-growing serious
national employment problem on one hand and, within the wide scope
of its own work, catered for the needs of a changing social era on the
other.

Emmie's regular workers, who had made the grade as Aunts, were
some of the forerunners of change. These women were learning the art
of becoming completely versatile. Emmie considered their individual
characters to fit the job in hand, weighed up the size and responsibility of
each job, and gave them a variety, so that each had a share of the plums
as well as the small, everyday commissions. They responded to this fair
sharing by giving their best efforts to each. No one who thought anything
too small for her got anything big; they soon learned the ropes.

Mrs Strickland, who lived in Bridgewater in Somerset, wrote to say:

Although I am now eighty, I like to keep up appearances and my dear
husband expects me to. My haberdasher here died some months ago
and her little shop has become modernised. Apparently they no
longer wish to cater for old ladies, whose hair has gone white, and they
stock only brown and black hairpins. I wonder could you obtain and
post to me a packet of blond pins? I feel sure you ladies will
understand the importance of this request!

Of course they did, and Aunt Mrs Madge Cookson, whose own hair now
needed the same carefully tinted pins, was down to Harrods' haber-
dashery counter and had them in the post that same day.

She would not, however, have been quite the right person to send off
on the next assignment of the day. A certain French count with a passion
for sport spent each hunting season between his French châteaux and

his Leicestershire hunting box. No hound he had in his own pack at home could equal what he found in England. He therefore made arrangements to export an entire pack of 42½ couple and two Jack Russells from England to France. A tough, knowledgeable English lady of his hunting-field acquaintance, Tabby Colebridge, was also a Universal Aunt. It intrigued him, through her, to commission the Aunts to get suitable transport, arrange the export licence, and deal with the shipping formalities. Then, with a kennelman to control and care for the hounds, Tabby Colebridge and one other hardy Aunt drove the van, negotiated in French on the other side and delivered man and animals safely in Bordeaux. At the conclusion of all this the *galant* French count expressed the opinion that 'not only did we breed the best hounds but ladies *par excellence*'.

Meanwhile, Bay Leith was busy on a shopping expedition bigger than for hairpins, in the vast, bleak buildings of the aircraft manufacturers. She bought, as requested, a Moth aeroplane, strapped on her flying gear and flew off to Europe to deliver his purchase to an overseas client. Another Aunt was already on a different route to Italy, in the company of a distraught wife whose husband, on business there, had sauntered into Switzerland without a passport and had been locked up. With no other language than English and no knowledge of the country, the wife had cried for help. The accompanying Aunt was experienced in both and, with suave diplomatic assistance, soon had the couple reunited. Though as she told the office on her return, she didn't envy *him* when *her* relief and joy turned to fury!

Life for Bay, Frances and Gertie had always included visits to Europe where, like that national hero Pooh, they had many 'friends and relations' to receive them, so that it was always home from home. They realized that there was a new trend for a wider public to cross the Channel, and their first-hand knowledge of hotels, restaurants, cultural pursuits and exhibits could be put to good use. In a joint effort they became ideal organizers of the first 'package tours'. They produced itineraries, made reservations, and selected the groups. Neither Bay, Frances nor Gertie personally accompanied these tours; they used reliable friends or experienced acquaintances as couriers, often choosing Miss Constance Douglas and Miss Adelaide Gretton, who advertised themselves as 'Travel Made Easy'. When not making travel easy, those two kept themselves in a little room at the back of Madame Fifinella, couturier, of 43 Buckingham Palace Road, and made necklaces to adorn her creations out of beads and stones collected on their travels.

One of their itineraries at that time was as follows:

THE RHINE AND SWITZERLAND
Three weeks on the Rhine and in Switzerland
40 guineas

This tour is personally conducted, and includes second-class travel, with first on the boat, meals en route, tips, hotel expenses, taxes and service charges, also all excursions as scheduled, and on these occasions, the services of excellent local guides are provided.

Extras   These consist of baths, wine, afternoon tea, laundry and registered luggage.
Also any excursions or sight-seeing beyond what is mentioned in the itinerary.

An extension of the tour can be arranged in Paris at a moderate cost, as the tickets are valid for 45 days.

ITINERARY

1st day   Leave London for Cologne at 10 a.m. via Dover and Ostend, arriving about midnight.

2nd day In Cologne, visit Opera.

3rd day In Cologne, visit Drachenfels, etc.

4th day By Rhine steamer to Koblenz.

5th & 6th days in Koblenz. Excursions arranged.

7th day By afternoon train to Basle, arriving about 9 p.m.

8th day From Basle to Interlaken.

9th day In Interlaken.

10th day In Interlaken. Excusion to Lauterbrunnen, etc.

11th day In Interlaken. Excursion by Lake steamer to Thun.

12th day From Interlaken, excursion to Schynige Platte.

13th day To Montreaux by Bernese Oberland Railway.

14th day ⎫
15th day ⎭ In Montreaux or Glion, as may be arranged.

16th day ⎫
17th day ⎬ Excursions to Geneva, Chillon, Villars, Gruyère and Rochers de Nays, will be arranged during the
18th day ⎭ stay.

19th day Leave Montreaux for Paris.
20th day In Paris. Free for shopping etc. An optional sight-
      seeing drive can be arranged.
21st day Leave Paris for London.

On the home front, Gertie was fiercely protective of the Aunts' social
image. She worked on committees, made appearances on behalf of
Universal Aunts and gave the necessary donations to the right causes.
She was particularly keen on advertising and, since the *Westminster
Gazette* affair, watchful of every word of any reports of the Aunts'
activities. A sharp note from her would follow any inaccuracy, and the

THE   QUEEN

1861

Telegrams "Queen Newspaper, London.
Telephone Hop 4900 (7 lines)

BRANCHES—
Birmingham, Manchester,
Newcastle-on-Tyne, Bristol.

17. 8. 35

Hatfield Street.
Stamford Street.
London. S.E.1.

Education and Careers Bureau

Dear Madam
I am sorry the mistake was
made of putting *agents*
instead of *Aunts*. I don't know
how it occurred. I have
known & recommended
Universal Aunts Ltd for years.

I will give the correct name
should I refer to yr work.

Yrs truly
F. B. Low.

reputation of the organization, more often than not, ensured a swift apology. Even *Queen* slipped up, received a rebuke, and apologized (see below left).

This satisfied Gertie; she knew that they would get another flattering write-up shortly, with the name of the company correctly reported. Two advertisements for the price of one!

The minutes of the Board meeting of 3 January reported:

> It was decided that Miss Fort should keep a careful note and claim all expenses for transport, meals, donations etc. in connection with Committee works. A sum of £75 to be set aside.

Also reported was the renewal of the lease on 37, Wilton Place, at £230 per annum inclusive of rates. To celebrate this, Gertie ordered one of the newest and smartest of business status symbols – an eye-catching neon sign at the door, costing £15.

Her advertising was arranged with *The Times* and the *Telegraph*, a weekly insertion in each newspaper, not to exceed 3 lines at a cost of 3s per line. The *Tatler* took a series of ten for an overall of £18 10s. She began a campaign to attract more 'professional' workers on to the books and aimed at slightly down-market publications.

> In a rut?
> A change of occupation is good for everyone. Hospital nursing is a strenuous life. At your age you might find the strain too much. Consult a good agency such as: Universal Aunts Limited, 37 Wilton Place, SW1.

Gertie's 'Let's take the chore out of Christmas' advertisement met with bumper success when a 'top' person's rather delightful response was printed as a follow-up.

> Christmas is in reality a most appalling business. The rush of presents and the outlay of hard-earned cash, the orgies of over-eating and other items in the melancholy pursuit of peace and goodwill. Can it be true, this little advertisement I read, restoring my faith in the opportunism of my fellows? 'Are you ready for Christmas, if not, ring up the Universal Aunts; shopping done, parcels dispatched, children met, etc.' Does this mean she will be a real benefactor and choose the presents as well?!

One man and two women had been among the headline-makers of
1935. In May, Lawrence of Arabia had died, following a motorcycle
accident; a mysterious black car seen at the time and place of the
accident had not been traced. And the Prince of Wales was reported
as being besotted by Mrs Wallis Simpson and was more openly to be
seen in her company. In August, Prince Henry became engaged to Lady
Alice Montague-Douglas-Scott and rumour revealed that the future
Duchess of Gloucester smoked cigarettes!

Bay was increasingly interested in the employment and shifting role of
workers, and the recruitment of the new domestic class to Universal
Aunts' force. Town and country houses were closing, partly for financial
reasons, partly for lack of the necessary expert staff to run them
properly. Domestic situations were unpopular, not so much for the
nature of the work but the element of loneliness. The great houses that
had remained had reduced their staff to three or four, and the old
chatting, snobbery and togetherness had gone with the servants' hall.
Also, the training under a skilled expert and the prospect of rising in the
pecking order of one's craft were no longer available. The younger
mistress of the house had become more considerate to her maids: she
and her daughters had more than likely washed up in canteens during
the slump years and rubbed shoulders with the working-class. Coal had
been rationed, and they had shared it with the staff quarters. Those
daughters danced the night away in smart night-clubs and the staff now
wanted to be free in the evening for the picture palace and the new
palais-de-danse. The Lady Help, the untrained, genteel spinster, began
to extend her duties from governess or companion to house-parlour
work, now that machines had removed the drudgery.

The government stepped in and ran special training schemes for
domestic work for women overtaken in their own jobs, in office or shop,
by the trade depression. Housemen, parlourmen and male cooks also
joined the scheme, as their traditional work opportunities became fewer.

Some of the old-style establishments, of course, remained, together
with the traditional methods of staffing and running them, vacancies
being eagerly filled by word of mouth. Employers on a smaller scale
made do with perhaps two male and two female staff. Often they chose
young girls who had sunnier temperaments than the older women; more
important, the girls tended to leave and marry, where the older ones
would normally seek a rise in pay, or promotion.

Domestic service was a hot topic and produced a good deal of correspondence in *The Times*. Bay had her own view and sent a letter: the main problem lay in the status of domestic servants, she felt, which work should rank with that of shop assistants, clerks and such-like. To the general suggestion of membership of a trade union, she countered with her idea of a Guild of Domestic Workers. Such a guild would not only protect its members but accept only those of good character and properly trained. Employers and reputable employment agencies would play their part by employing only those who were accepted by the Guild. This excellent idea was not taken up by the powers that be.

Frances had made preliminary investigations into a scheme to put Austrian maids in touch with English country employers, for there were many families in Austria who wanted their daughters to get away from the unrest in Europe. A Board meeting was called, at which Gertie expressed her view that there were already too many complications in the domestic field, and the idea was dropped. Her second point was that now that they were getting some of the newly trained domestics on to the book, the need to import was becoming less. Gertie then passed round the pages of Emmie's Day Book, showing the typical examples of one day's bookings from various departments (see overleaf).

Universal Aunts was, as always, quite a weather-vane of outside events. Gertie's instincts against involvement with foreign workers was quite understandable, there being a good many political rumblings all over the place and not least in Europe. Frances was, as always, deeply involved in her fact-finding missions in Europe. Strictly speaking, these were on prevailing social conditions, but by now – in Germany, at least – such research spilled over into the political arena. One February morning, Gertie received an early telephone call at her flat: the news it announced was confirmed in a report when she opened her newspaper.

Munich. February 6th, 1938.
Miss Frances Blackett, an Englishwoman, was arrested in Munich last night while attending a public political meeting. Kept in custody in the Ettstrasse political prison all night without being allowed to communicate with the British Consul, and released at noon today without any charges having been brought against her. The German Foreign Minister yesterday apologized to Sir Eric Phipps, the British Ambassador in Berlin. The explanation was mistaken identity.
A kinswoman of the late Sir Arthur Blackett and a director of

A page from Emmie's Day Book

TUESDAY, NOVEMBER 30th.1937.

DOMESTIC.

Nov.29th.

```
Livingstone fee.............................£ 0. 2. 6.
Ziegler fee.................................£ 0. 7. 6.
                                             10. 0.
```

Nov.30th.

```
Batten wants cook
Macdonald says her post with Burgh permanent
Barrett not sufficiently trained for post offered
Ward having interview with Best
Moore Ede wants work for daughter
Gendwine wants cook-general
Prentice leaving Tabor
Whitehead fee..............................£ 0. 2. 6.
Stanley Cox fee............................£ 0. 2. 6.
Allsopp fee................................£ 1. 6. 0.
                                           £ 1.11. 0.
```

HOUSE.

Nov.30th.

```
Foster wants service flat
Tower list of expenses
Fowell has sold cottage
Lanigeon cottage to let
Grosvenor House re increased commission payable on lets
Watson flats to let
Nelson wants rooms
Apex Properties Ltd. re rooms vacant at 28 Basil St.
```

GENERAL.

Nov.29th.

```
Etchells still wants work
T.B.Jones Ltd. invoice
```

Nov.30th.

```
Armfield & Sons Ltd. receipt
Priestman cannot continue Agency
Tulloch re carpet wanted
De Lalande re taking guests at Chamonix
Potter re Brass Cleverly re Howison
Turner wants tin of Overhaul for car
Roberts for escort of daughter..................£ 6. 0. 0.
```

Universal Aunts, Miss Blackett was formerly a political speaker for the Metropolitan section of the Conservative party in England.

At the meeting Frances had been accused of taking notes and failing to give a Hitler salute. When asked why she was taking notes, she had replied by demanding whether it was a political offence now to take notes in Germany. Her notebook and all personal papers had been confiscated by the police, and were returned on her release.

Unrest of a different kind was about to beset Britain. On 20 January 1936, at five minutes to midnight, King George V died at Sandringham. People were uneasy about the succession of Edward VIII, the first bachelor King since George III; what about his friendship with Mrs Simpson? The death of the King overshadowed that, two days earlier, of a favourite Englishman, the world's most highly paid writer, Rudyard Kipling.

By the start of the Season, the Court was out of mourning and the King decreed that social events should take place as planned. The London Season provided extra special requests for the Aunts, the ritual Presentation at Court bringing forth enquiries on behalf of girls without a mama or female relation who filled the essential requirement of having herself been presented. At the then immense sum of £1,000, an eminent chaperone could be provided. These ladies of decreased fortune were known to Gertie, who was trusted to supply 'suitable gels', and were very willing to enjoy those few, bright, butterfly months of nostalgia and their due reward. Gertie creamed off her own little reward too.

The English upper classes were selling themselves extremely well. The Americans who had survived the depression were very rich and influential, and were now seeking this considerable cachet for their daughters. Gertie, prevented by being an unmarried lady from making a Presentation herself, was always on hand to see her protégées as they prepared to leave for the Palace.

Lovely, young, rose-like creatures, with clear pale skin and sparkling eyes, were adorned in a long, white evening gown, full-skirted or slender according to the dictates of current Court fashion, with a modest neckline and a single string of pearls. A narrow, jewelled headband held three white ostrich feathers, arranged upright and worn towards the back of the head, and slightly to the left. Attached to the back of the headband was a short veil of white lace or net, no longer than twenty-seven inches. From the shoulders of the dress was draped a train no more than two and a half yards in length, thereby restricted to trailing no further than eighteen inches backwards from the heel of the slippers. Long, white, skin gloves wrinkled to just above the elbow, with a row of tiny pearl buttons fastening them on the inner wrist. The girls held a closed fan of ivory or pearl, or a small, round bouquet of white flowers.

Having seen the chaperone and her debutante off, Gertie would recall the scene. Tourists and sightseers at the Palace gates as the car slowed to enter. Up the red-carpeted steps, a short walk, and into the hands of the ladies' room maids, who had seen it all so many times before. Nervous chatter and anguished squeals as clothing came adrift, pearls broke and scattered, strands of hair fell down or someone stepped on and tore a train. The calm maids had all the aids on hand; they combed back straying curls, adjusted slipping feathers, put a quick stitch in a hem, and assisted in the need – urgent now but nearly impossible to negotiate – to spend a penny without fatal damage to the train. Out of the strictly functional cloakroom with its sweet, powdery scents and into the Palace, all scarlet and gold and crystal. Handsome footmen lining the corridors, magnificent Aides and Gentlemen smoothing one's passage and soothing one's nerves. Into the anteroom where mama or chaperone waited to inspect, and tweak, and cast a last, gimlet eye.

One's name announced. A well-rehearsed glide into the Presence, pause, a flick of the left heel to the train, head upright, eyes demurely cast down. A deep curtsey to his Majesty the King, praying not to be the deb who wobbled. A slight move to the right and the curtsey repeated to her Majesty the Queen (This year, however, there was only a King, this romantic figure linked to a now-divorced woman, the subject of gossip columns and speculation at dinner tables.) Backwards and out of sight, and one was launched. Even if the delights of the waiting world were not as magical as expected, that royal moment was certainly memorable.

In the world outside, the plans for the Coronation continued and Gertie obtained a batch of seats to sell. Beneath this public façade seethed the turmoil of the King and Mrs Simpson, and on 10 December came the abdication. However, Gertie's seats were still eagerly sought for the revised plans and the Coronation of the new King, George VI, which took place on 12 May 1937. An uncontroversial, gentle King now reigned, supported by a beautiful and popular royal lady as his Queen, two little Princesses and a batch of corgis. It was the stuff beloved of the British; there was great rejoicing and a sense of relief. Divorce might have become fashionable in certain quarters, might be openly discussed and a new Act have passed through Parliament, but it was not acceptable for the King of England.

Twenty-two days later the marriage of the uncrowned King (now given the title of HRH the Duke of Windsor) to Mrs Wallis Simpson, took place in France. She was denied the style of HRH by the British Government.

The Queen was the epitome of wife and mother and home-maker, a role once more in fashion in the depressed '30s. Although thousands of women had won their entré into politics and the professions, commerce and sport, the great feats of physical endurance had gone almost unchallenged by them until they climbed into the cockpit. Land and air had been the two testing grounds of the twentieth century so far. It is a tale in my own family that several intrepid ladies begged to accompany our kinsman Shackleton to the Antarctic, though it was never disclosed to my ears, and perhaps never known, whether their principal wish was for personal achievement or to 'camp follow' their hero! Even they could not overcome resistance to the idea of women on ice and as part of a team in 1924. The wife of Scott made no secret of her longing to accompany her husband and, had it been within the realms of possibility, that lady would surely have done so.

But women could, and had, conquered the air and now it was no longer a pastime for the rich. The surge of women aiming to join came from wider quarters; with single-mindedness they saved their money to pay for lessons and join clubs. In March the superbly nonchalant Duchess of Bedford had disappeared in her de Havilland Moth off the Suffolk coast. Only bits of her plane were found, and she was presumed dead. Such reports failed to deter others; they defied hardship and death to fly. In doing so they lost the feeling of being 'grounded' by their limited roles. By flying, they soared above restrictions to self-reliant freedom in the skies. All this was not unnoticed at ministerial level and it was announced that 'The Hon Mildred Leith, sister of Lord Burgh, air-pilot, has become advisory expert to women wishing to learn the art of flying.' It was a fortuitous decision in the light of escalating events in Europe.

1930s

WAR

Aunts at war – Special Services – Buying a bomber –
Forgotten wine – Like the Windmill – Pearl Harbour

The morning of Sunday 3 September 1938 broke over a London freshly washed by rain and steaming in the rising sun of a perfect summer's day. Gertie was in London that weekend, alone in her flat in Cornwall Gardens, feeling languid and suffering the headaches that had continued on and off since her concussion twelve years before. Her windows were wide open and she leaned out; there were few people about apart from those in uniform; the sense of uneasy, suspended time was heightened by the sight of piles of sandbags. Through other windows the sound of wireless programmes floated out and Gertie switched on hers. At 11.15 a.m. came the weary voice of Neville Chamberlain announcing that the country was now at war with Germany.

Gertie felt weary too. It was exactly a year since Chamberlain had returned from Germany, waving his bit of paper and declaring 'Peace with Honour', but on all sides people had gone on preparing for the worst. Many of the services offered by the company had been increasingly sought; the energies of Emmie and Bay had grown with every demand; and the staff had responded with superb enthusiasm. Yet Gertie, at the peak of achievement at last, after eighteen years, realized that her enthusiasm for day-to-day activity in her venture was waning. Like a mother whose child is ready to go it alone, she felt a gentle desire to let it do so, having equipped it well. She now found the office role tedious and preferred to burn herself out enthusiastically on occasional promotional projects.

With this in view, as long before as the previous 17 November, Gertie had given the Board six months' notice to change her Agreement with the Company. On the following 18 May a new Agreement had been reached which released her from playing such an active role. On 28

August it had further been voted that: 'In case of outbreak of War, Miss Emily Faulder would automatically become an additional Director' – a move long overdue.

On Monday 4 September Gertie was, of course, in the office early with the rest, ready to put into action the emergency plans that had been made and agreed on months before. Three departments were instantly closed: Social, Foreign, Car and Air. Legislation of the motor trade was already in force to restrict the sale of second-hand cars.

The most serious loss to the Company was that Bay was already on her way to take a key post in the Women's Motor Transport Corps. It was decided that those called up would not be replaced. All salaries, except the two office girls' and Betsy's, were cut to £2 10s a week and the managing director's, Gertie's, to £2. The Directors had agreed to forgo interest on their loans for the duration. Sleeping bags, blankets, pillows, candles, matches, oil lamps, tins of food, books and first aid supplies had been boxed and were now unpacked in a basement room earmarked for an air-raid shelter. Black-out curtains had been made ready for each window and these were hung that morning. Office hours were changed to open one hour later in the morning and close one hour earlier in the evening, to save light and fuel. Gertie announced that cheaper white writing paper would be used instead of the expensive blue. Preparations for war had been well thought out.

All occupants of property in Wilton Place were summoned to a meeting to recruit people for training as air-raid wardens and fire-watchers; everyone fit enough volunteered, and Uni-Aunts, as the locals called them, took their turns on night patrol on the roof and in the street throughout the war.

Everyone became alert. Gas masks were tried on and people checked where to reach the nearest air-raid shelter when the sirens blew. Strangers in shops and streets and on buses smiled or spoke, linking together to share the terrifying prospects of war, of bombs falling and Germans invading our shores. Ration books and petrol coupons were organized. Black-out curtains and, in some cases, boarding-up of windows, was top priority; all outside lights were extinguished. In large houses, rooms were shrouded in dust sheets and closed up to save heating. Sandbags were stacked round historic buildings and old stained glass windows were taken out and stored with other art treasures in deep, secret vaults. Khaki, navy and blue uniforms appeared everywhere.

The Government organized an immediate exodus of children and pregnant women from London and all big cities. Voluntary workers shepherded hundreds of children to the stations; labelled and carrying their meagre possessions, they looked lost and bewildered. Most had already said good-bye to mothers and fathers, although some mothers had been persuaded to go too. The Aunts were called upon to play their part, travelling as supervisors on the train or escorting the disabled or the problem child. The country women, waiting at the other end to receive the evacuees, felt that they were helping the war effort.

Disillusion soon set in as the evacuees brought the social problems of the inner cities with them. Many children had arrived with nits in their hair; hundreds had inadequate clothing for the winter and the Government quickly voted a grant to buy more. They disliked 'wholesome' food and were afraid of the animals and the darkness at night in lanes without street lights. Lonely women were lethargic and hated the country. They missed their husbands and, even if their men had gone to war, they missed the closeness of their neighbours. Many drifted back to the cities. Pregnant women were housed in converted country mansions where they spent a month before and after the birth. They bloomed with such care, and the mortality rate of both mother and child dropped.

Back in London the sky was full of floating whale-like shapes, dull silver barrage balloons, their ropes invisible except at close range. Otherwise there was a lull. Thousands of women wanting to do war work were frustrated at being told to stick to being housewives, to care for their homes and collect paper and tin and anything else that could be recycled.

Special Services had been one of the original departments of the Aunts and now it was flooded with calls. People gave up their London flats as they left for the forces or war-work. Small possessions, such as paintings, books, silver and ornaments, were accepted for storage at a few shillings a week, and packing and removals were in great demand. Repairs to bomb-damaged flats and houses could be arranged and, by the spring of 1940, this was in big demand.

In April 1940 the German armies had taken Denmark and Norway, and then began the invasions of Holland, Luxembourg and Belgium. By May they had reached the Channel coast, and the Luftwaffe made nightly raids on London. Winston Churchill had become Prime Minister, comparatively young at sixty-five, with Ernest Bevin as Minister of Labour and National Service. Suddenly women were needed; like men they could be called up for National Service and could be directed to perform important services such as those in Civil Defence, food production and war industries. Like Lloyd George in the First World War, Bevin upheld the rights of women and this time won men's rates of pay for men's work on their behalf.

Unmarried women were directed into men's jobs, married women into other women's jobs. Nurseries were set up for children and grannies were used as mothers when the children were at school; the homes still had to be run. Within a year, all those younger than forty-five had been registered for employment and had the choice of the essential industries or the women's forces. In industry they met certain trade-union taboos and some men flatly refused to work beside women; if and when it did happen, the Government considered that such existing conventions should be upheld. The manning of the women's forces fell into the natural order of things, as expected: upper and middle-class girls, particularly those who had experienced boarding school and college, were eager volunteers of the forces and became officers, while the 'other ranks' came from the working-class. (There was, of course, always the jolly rebel from a castle who became a private and was determined to remain one!) In the ATS Bay Leith was commanding Aircraft Ferry Pilots; others chose to join the anti-aircraft gun sights, the Ack-Ack girls, the only women in the war with a licence to kill.

Upstairs in the office it became quite a familiar sight to see a baby in its basket parked in a corner, its bottle warming in the kettle. Its mother would quite probably have rushed up to London to snatch a brief meeting with its soldier father passing through on a troop train. Downstairs, in the basement, Peter Ustinov's own aunt was installed at £1. 10s a week rent; she carried on a business making hats out of every available fabric and ribbon. A surprising war effort? Not at all, an astute lady. Hats were being worn, the only bit of finery that was coupon-free, and those who couldn't find them or afford them, home-made them. Off duty or on leave, women tried to dress for the occasion. Theatres, night clubs, dance floors and restaurants were packed with those living for the moment: escorts appreciated their women out of khaki, navy blue, grey or sludge green. In April when a landmine fell outside the Savoy, diners and dancers hardly paused! On 11 May a bomb fell on the Palace of Westminster, destroyed the Deanery of Westminster Abbey and hit the Chamber of the House of Commons; they too pressed on.

As the war escalated, so did the casualties. On 3 June, 200,000 British soldiers were evacuated from Dunkirk. At home there was also devastation and death on a terrible scale. At night the bombs rained on the closely packed outskirts of the cities and the mean, terraced houses fell like domino structures. The great army of the Civil Defence Services moved in before the last bomber was gone, to fight the fires and dig for victims. Those who were not dead were housed in bleak reception centres where control of the children and care of the old was difficult, and weariness and frustration flared into rows. They spent daylight hours listlessly looking amongst the mounds of rubble, to find which had been their place and any remaining scrap of their possessions. They had never had much and now they had nothing. The women were demoralized; now they couldn't even 'keep the home fires burning'. But British resilience returned and they gradually made the best of what was offered.

The railings in front of Buckingham Palace and Brooks Club were taken off for tanks; by the autumn the Palace was hit, wrecking the Chapel and dozens of windows. St Paul's had a vast hole above the High Altar; the Guildhall and eight Wren churches were destroyed. The King and Queen were widely pictured climbing over their own ruins and their people felt close to them in the shared experience, as they made very clear during royal visits to bombed-out areas.

Gertie decided to buy a bomber. She wrote to the Minister concerned, Lord Beaverbrook, to see whether the launch could get official backing. From the Ministry of Aircraft Production came the reply that the Ministry was not permitted to take any part in the formation of funds. All gifts must be entirely spontaneous. Appreciation was expressed for all the trouble that Universal Aunts were taking to accomplish their goal, and the sensible suggestion was made that an approach to the Press Association in Fleet St might result in publicity for an appeal.

Gertie took the advice and approached the Press Association who were glad to help the Aunts in their latest and greatest effort. Publicity was duly given, and envelopes came from Aunts, Uncles, Nephews and Nieces all over the world, and also from individuals and associations. The amounts added up. A woman going into hospital for an operation sent her wedding ring to help keep up her efforts until she could resume her collecting. In country areas produce and fruit were sold and the money donated. Colonial women, far away from the action with their men fighting over here, sent precious items and not only money. The

following letter, for instance, came from Vancouver, Canada on 16
September 1940:

> The Treasurer of the campaign for 400,000 shillings.
>
>   Dear Madam
>
>   Having read in Vancouver "Daily
> Province" of Sep 13th of the campaign launched
> by "Universal Aunts Ltd to raise the sum of
> 400,000 shillings for purchase of a bomber plane,
> I am writing to ask your acceptance of two
> Shillings which are some of those minted to
> commemorate the coronations of King Edward VII
> & our beloved King George V
>   I have not had the rings removed by which
> they were attached to a silver bangle, as possibly
> they could be sold for a larger sum than
> their face value, & again worn as trinkets.
>   If this small contribution reaches you
> after your objective is reached, would you
> please pass it on to some other fund.
>   I enclose cutting from "Daily Province."
> With good wishes for your success
>   Very sincerely yours

In the office stood a large box which had long overstayed its rented
space. All endeavours to contact its owner had failed; maybe he was a
war casualty. Gertie had an idea to swell the funds, which was headlined
in the Late Night Final *Star* of 16 October 1940.

Forgotten Wine May Aid Bomber Fund

In these days when good wine is hard to find and even more difficult to
buy, it is almost incredible that a case of white wine left with Universal
Aunts, Wilton Place, two years ago, should be forgotten by its owner.
The case has been broken, but there are ten bottles of Chablis 1921 –
experts refer to the vintage of that famous year as bottled sunshine –
which must be claimed by 30th October. Universal Aunts announce
that if the owner does not claim his wine by this date, it will be sold in
aid of the Aunts' Bomber Fund.

The owner did not appear. Offers poured in and the wine fetched a bomb itself. The determination that the Aunts' bomber would be ready for the spring offensive was fulfilled; it flew, a tribute to thousands, and Gertie felt pleased.

The Aunts often carried on their good work in harsh discomfort, even danger. For instance, Alison Greig, fifty-year-old exschoolmistress Aunt, was detailed to be the lone chaperone of a train compartment of forty schoolgirls, London to Scotland overnight. The train was halted by the ferocity of enemy aeroplanes. 'Girls in groups of ten, holding hands, step out of each door as I open it!' Miss Greig's voice rang out. 'You then follow me instantly into the undergrowth, carrying nothing with you except your bag. See that you are wearing your hats, coats and gloves.'

Having shepherded her girls to safety she then made heroic rescue journeys back and forth for cases, hockey-sticks, teddies. The now-empty train had several hits but her girls and their belongings were safe.

Numerous Aunts braved blitzes, bombings and lack of porters at all the railway stations, waiting for hours to collect children off the trains when they did eventually arrive. Other Aunts were sent to clamber through bombed houses to find personal belongings.

Second Lt Bertie Barton wrote from a military hospital overseas:

> I am recovering from a bit of a shoot-up and will be sent home on the 29th on 8 weeks' leave before rejoining my Regiment out here. I have no relatives left in England, so can you plan my leave for me? I would like to be a paying guest in a family and have some yoga lessons. London please, I still want to be in the action. I have saved up quite a bit of pay while in hospital and shall come to settle with you as soon as I land.

The Aunts checked; it wasn't a hoax, the boy was quite genuine. It was not hard to find a family willing to welcome a soldier, but it was more difficult to find a yoga expert. On his last day in England, Bertie Barton arrived in the office smiling and fit, with flowers and chocolates and kisses for everyone. As far as they could gather his hosts had become his new family, his yoga had taught him to relax under fire, and the Windmill Theatre, who, like the Aunts, '*never closed*', had taught him a whole lot more; he seemed to have spent a good deal of his leave inside their doors! That night he was taking his 'family' to the opening of Noel Coward's *Blithe Spirit* at the Piccadilly Theatre.

Each day the news bulletins, the casualty lists and war news were of paramount importance. A sad headline in March, 1941, caught public attention: Virginia Woolf, on the 28th, had taken her own life, drowning in the River Ouse in Sussex, leaving her walking stick on the bank and weighing herself down with a huge stone in the pocket of her coat so as not to fail in the attempt. So very many others were not being given the choice of life or death. In August, Churchill crossed the Atlantic and met Roosevelt in Placentia Bay, Newfoundland. On 7 December 1941, the Japanese bombed Pearl Harbour and the Americans entered the war.

12

1940S

END OF AN ERA

Cameos of war

On the 26 January 1942 the first American troops landed in England. As soon as their feet touched the ground, most were whisked off to Norfolk where over a hundred American air bases had been prepared for them. The boys had arrived from diverse, pulsating young landscapes across America. They were faced with the watchful silence of Norfolk, its aged brown ribs of earth embedded with frosty sparkles, braced for the invasion of human hordes once more at war.

The first subdued overall encounter with the 'old country' momentarily stopped them in their tracks. A few days of briefing on how to get along with their new allies, and they burst into view and stunned the locals into surly communication. They were not welcomed with open arms. The Brits were proud of their own Tommy, well turned-out in rough khaki cloth tucked into blancoed puttees above gleaming black boots which were obviously designed to stand up to the conquering march across Europe. They were glad to buy him a pint. The 'foreigners' all looked like 'orfficers': smooth, slick-cut jacket and trousers, shoes on their feet, with money in their pockets to order and offer drinks that had long gone under the counter in the British pubs.

Worse things quickly became apparent. They had no restraint. Like wolves on the fold, their attack on the female population was thorough and successful. Girls loved to be offered goodies that most had never seen before; nylons, candies, lipsticks and tinned foods. To appear on the arm of the kind of chap they had seen on the films, so travelled, experienced and rich, and to dance the night away to racy new tunes and steps, was very good news. Fathers forbade meetings but daughters found devious ways of disobeying; and the strains of 'Oh Johnny' and 'Deep in the Heart of Texas' hit the night air.

The GIs were frankly bewildered by the curious, rigid distinctions but relaxed social conventions of British life. There were no restrictions on coloured soldiers, the general British public having until then rarely encountered anyone dark-skinned. The fraternization so frowned upon by American commanding officers knew no colour bar. Even more to be discouraged was intermarriage between any of their troops and British girls; but it happened.

The day-by-day running of the organization was now firmly in Emmie's competent hands. Gertie's enthusiasm and efforts had gradually waned until she concerned herself only with Company matters, such as her application for a reduction of rent; she got £30 per annum off that for the duration of the war. She was seldom seen in the office except for Board meetings; her manner seemed vague. By February of 1942, she was in a London nursing-home suffering from a minor breakdown.

Betsy seemed to lose momentum and within two weeks she presented herself at Emmie's desk. 'I want to join up, Miss Faulder,' she said nervously.

Emmie was taken by surprise. 'I think we're doing quite good work here, Betsy,' she answered gently.

Betsy was not forthcoming and looked at the floor.

'I've already filled in the papers to be a typist for the Ministry,' she said.

Emmie sadly knew that was that. It was a blow, and another severed link with Gertie.

In June Emmie alerted Bay, who got a few hours' leave and went with Frances to the office for a hastily called Board meeting. The summons came as no surprise by then. A formal letter from Gertie was the subject of the meeting and, having read it, Bay expressed their thoughts. 'It is the end of an era, but not the end of Universal Aunts which by now is a cast of hundreds.' Part of Gertie's letter is reproduced overleaf.

The Directors wrote to Gertie in reply:

The Directors thank you for your letter of June 3rd, giving notice to terminate your agreement with the Company. They deeply regret the necessity for doing so and very much appreciate the gesture you have made.

They very much hope that when the time comes to consider a fresh agreement you will be in much better health and able to help them again on some modified basis.

23 Cornwall Gdns.

London S. W. 7

June 3/42.

The Directors
Universal Agents Ltd.

Dear Mesdames,

I wish to give
notice to terminate my
Agreement with the Company,
as Managing Director, in its
present form.

I feel that at the
present time a full-time
Managing Director is not
required

As from 3 June 1943, 'Miss Fort' was appointed Chairwoman, to be paid £100 a year and with six months' notice on either side.

Gertie might not have admitted approval of their foresight in having lined up a tenant for her room in anticipation of the event, but it was exactly what she would have done! The minutes of the meeting concluded:

> It was reported that the room recently used by Miss Fort had been let to a milliner, Mrs Edwards, at a rental of 27s 6d a week on a monthly basis.

It was not only Betsy who went into war work. The office staff thinned out and were not replaced. The ever-staunch Dorothy Tull remained, beavering away at her accounts books. Emmie kept one other and the three of them doubled up in the office by day and took their turns in tin hats on the streets by night – all at a saving of £65 a year on the overall salary cheque.

Emmie missed the bustle and chat of a room full of workers. Her war became a series of small cameos. Her young and middle-aged Aunts, in a rush of patriotism, had also gone – or been swept – into the services. When on leave, they popped into the office with the snippets of gossip she loved.

'Sarah, have you been shot?' she cried as a figure limped in.

'Nothing so super, Miss Faulder,' groaned Sarah as she bumped down into a chair and a thickly bandaged knee became visible. 'I stood on the parade ground at the head of my Company, stamped to attention for the march-off, and sank to the ground with a dislocated knee!'

'Were you carried off?' asked Emmie.

'Not likely,' boasted Sarah. 'I cracked it into place and marched off, after which I was put into an ambulance and into hospital, and here I am on a week's sick leave.'

'I'm sorry to laugh; it must have been awfully painful,' said Emmie.

'Oh well, the General sent his ADC with compliments upon a good show, except for the sight of the Company Commander kneeling down on the parade ground,' Sarah grimaced. 'A black mark there. However,' she cheered up, 'the ADC was super and he's taking me to dinner tonight.'

Emmie later attended their war-time wedding.

Poppy Bolt, until recently a young Aunt who was 'good news' to any needy client, was now enlivening her WAAF Mess and the social lives of a lot of officers. She burst upon Emmie one morning, curls escaping her cap.

'Dear Miss F., a ghastly accident last night at the Mirabelle.' Emmie braced herself for a bomb story as Poppy sped on. 'Tommy Slimbridge took me there to dance and I'd got all smartened up in my silks. As I *manoeuvred* out of his toy car, crouched half in and half out, horrors, I was *hooked* into the soft roof by a wire that had *crept* up out of the side of my bra like an aerial. Poor Tommy had to *plunge* away in all sorts of places to get me free, too shaming!' She paused for breath.

'I imagine he was only too glad to come to your rescue,' remarked Emmie dryly. She smiled to herself; she knew that Poppy's war effort would be as enthusiastic as her socializing.

Edith was of *quite* another cast, an energetically bossy Aunt to whom Emmie had always allotted the children and clients who needed a firm hand. In her element in khaki, she was a female version of the photographs she had once shown Emmie of her Brigadier father, just minus most of the whiskers. She marched into the office and sat with piano-legs planted somewhat too far apart while Emmie politely offered her ear to a brisk series of war stories.

'On kit inspection one morning, half-way down the Nissen hut was a bed with a hump in it, no sign of the occupant who should have been standing to attention at the foot of it,' boomed Edith.

Emmie's eyes widened behind her spectacles and her brows lifted upwards, indicating her breathless interest. Not that Edith, in full spate, needed encouragement. She shot on. 'I motioned to my sergeant, who threw back the bedclothes and *what* do you suppose met my eyes?'

Emmie's eyebrows crept higher. Indignantly, Edith continued, 'There, in that bed, was not only my missing private but a new-born baby too!' She drew one second's breath. '"This", I said to her, "is an army barracks, not a maternity ward!" And I had her and it removed.'

'How quite amazing,' was all Emmie could muster. She privately felt sure that the poor little baby would have been ordered to be wrapped, for decency, in a rough, correctly creased and folded army blanket.

Dodi had always been a favourite of Emmie's – good-natured, inclined to bumble, but with specific, written instructions in her hand she would care for her charges to the last, loving breath. When she arrived to visit Emmie there was a noticeable pale patch on the sleeve of her uniform where her corporal's stripes used to be.

'Oh dear,' said Emmie. 'What happened?'

'Well,' said Dodi wryly, 'on Tuesday we were lined up on pay parade and suddenly a V2 came down. We heard the cut-off and awful silence and dived under any furniture to hand.'

'Wouldn't we all?' said Emmie.

'Well,' Dodi went on, wonderingly, 'apparently not, because when everything had stopped crashing about and shaking and we crept out, there, still sitting at the pay desk with her arms shielding the boxes and papers, was the Lieutenant.' Dodi paused and gritted her teeth together as though in pain before going on. 'She was furious with me and said that I had shirked my duty under fire, which was to keep to my post and set an example.'

'I fear, then, that I wouldn't have made any headway in the services,' sighed Emmie.

'The Pay Officer said that theft of army money could have occurred and that was enough for me to be demoted, and here I am with a bare patch for all to see,' finished Dodi in a sorrowful rush.

'Another cup of tea?' said Emmie, patting the disgraced shoulder.

More often than not, the news shared with Emmie was far from light-hearted. Husbands, fathers, brothers, lovers and friends were reported killed or missing. Over each day hung the pall of war. Close at hand was the blazing nightly destruction of bombs on the East End. Distanced by space, so less acutely felt, was the scale of Allied losses in the field, the atrocities of rape, murder and pillage across Europe.

The Aunts ploughed on in the same general discomfort and danger as everyone else as they went about their work. Emmie felt they were due for a morale booster and gave them a rise in their rates of pay, plus a regular small war bonus when profits allowed.

When 'Salute the Soldiers' week came along in March of 1944, Universal Aunts took out the £500 they had on deposit at the bank and bought the 3 per cent Savings Bonds, stating that they were 'proud to lend this to the Country'.

One incident was to rebound some forty years later. On a black February night, Emmie lingered on at the office after closing time, she and Dorothy having arranged to eat a snack there and go on to see the film of Noel Coward's *In Which We Serve*. The scream of sirens sounded the alert and a close rain of bombs began. The best place for the two of them was up with the fire-watchers on the roof and they spent the next

few hours there. By the time things were quiet they were in no great
hurry, which was just as well. As they stepped out, on the office doorstep
they stumbled over a couple who seemed somewhat stunned. Emmie
and Dorothy helped them inside and up the stairs by the light of a torch.
Once upstairs with the lights switched on, they discovered a neat, pretty
girl and a slight young man in the uniform of an American GI, who
introduced themselves as Elmer Pope of Staten Island, New York, and
Nona Holly of Crouch End. Having been blown over by blast they were
covered in dust and obviously shaken.

Dorothy made tea and Emmie set about being helpful.

'Mr Holly is sure going to be mad if I don't get his daughter home
tonight,' explained the agitated Elmer.

'There will be no transport to get you out to N8 tonight,' said Emmie.
'Has Nona's father got a telephone?'

Having discovered that he had not, but that his neighbour obligingly
took messages, Emmie got through and waited for Mr Holly to be
fetched.

'Mr Holly,' she called loudly down the crackling line, 'my name is
Emily Faulder, Miss Faulder. I am telephoning on behalf of your
daughter Nona and her friend Elmer Pope.'

She caught the worry in his pleasant Cockney voice, 'Are they all
right, Miss Faulder?'

'Quite safe, Mr Holly. They were caught in a raid but suffered
nothing more than bruises. I have them here in my office in Knightsbridge and they will stay here overnight and be with you in the morning.'

'Me and the wife are very grateful, Miss Faulder,' answered Mr
Holly. 'We can sleep easy, I take it, with our girl in your hands?'

'I assure you that you can,' said Emmie.

She and Dorothy stayed dozing overnight in the office with the young
couple and saw them on their way at dawn. A few days later a delivery
was made to the office of a large box, inside which were American
goodies, tinned meat and fruit, Hershey bars, maple syrup, fresh
Norfolk duck eggs from a farm near his B17 bomber base, and, most
exciting of all, two lipsticks and four pairs of nylon stockings. A note lay
on top.

Thank you ladies for giving us your hospitality. Most of all for saving
Nona's reputation and my own. Keeping her out all night would not
have gone down with her Dad. I hope the eatables are to your liking

and that the personal items will be acceptable. Maybe I will be in your direction again some time.

Yours very sincerely,
ladies,
Elmer Pope

He was indeed to be so.

War rolled on, like some grim stage production with a world audience awaiting the next scene.

Churchill, the greatest producer, battling with intermittent bouts of grave ill-health and gigantic set-backs of battle, never wavered. His cast of famous warriors directed events at the head of their troops of staunch, unyielding followers, each one fighting and sweating and often hideously dying for Britain's freedom. The vast majority of fighting men were from the ranks of the 'have-nots', their world so much less than perfect; but they were determined that no bloody foreign upstart was going to walk their lands and dictate their lives in steel-shod boots.

On 3 May 1945 at 3 p.m. the leader's voice resounded across the land: 'The German war is at an end. The evildoers now lie prostrate before us. Victory in Europe has come.'

The killing was not yet over. On 15 August, atom bombs descended on Hiroshima and Nagasaki, with wholesale massacre; but judgement and mourning were set aside as the world rejoiced in Japan's surrender. War was over, but in the aftermath hard austerity would continue for several years to come.

Five months later, in January, thousands of British war brides were gathered together at Tidworth en route for Southampton and the great liners, Queen Elizabeth, Queen Mary, and fifteen others which sailed them away to their new American husbands and homes. Nona Holly was not amongst them.

The Company had soared to dizzy heights, was flooded with work and showing a record profit of £2195. A newspaper wrote that 'Universal Aunts has filled a real need in the daily life of the public in the war years'. The general public expressed their appreciation in letters.

As Emmie said, 'That justifies the directors having kept the flag flying through many difficult years!'

PART II

13

1940s

CECIL

*Post war – Avalanche of work – Welcome back, Bay –
Cecil – Mrs Stokes*

The small, fatigued war staff stood up to the first post-war calls for help.
Food, clothes, goods were still going to remain in short supply; jobs had
to be found and ordinary life re-established. But, for the moment, there
was widespread elation and optimism.

People opened up their houses again and needed cleaners, decorators
and staff. They used the family clothing-coupons to get what material
they could for curtains and covers, and sewing women were called for.
When paint was not available, walls were washed down; and with no
wood for shelving and repairs, attics were searched for old doors and
furniture and carpenters set to work to be inventive.

Everything in the shops was reject stuff, anything first-class went for
export. Ladies of the house needed Aunts to take over the burden of
trailing round to find the best they could. It was not permitted to look
through a pile of china plates to find the least defective; you took the next
half-dozen from the pile and if they were badly chipped, that was just too
bad, madam. On an income of £800 a year a staff could be kept; a cook, a
parlour maid, a housemaid, possibly a butler and a couple of outside
man-servants. The staff department began to advertise for anyone with
pre-war training to come back into service. Some did, but even the
scarcity of other jobs could not persuade many to give up their freedom.
Rations were hoarded until there was enough meagre food for a party,
then calls came in for help to make it as smart as possible. One cook had
to deal with the problem caused by the family cat sneaking into the
dining-room and licking the tops off every one of the nicely prepared
dishes. Luckily for him, he was an adored creature and his stunned
mistress just remarked, 'Oh well, I suppose he's equally fed up with
war-time food.' She returned to the kitchen and handed out one tin of
spam, one of sardines, and one of pink salmon. 'That's the end of our

stores; do what you can, or re-hash what's left in the dishes, and pray no one gets any cat disease. I shall leave it to you, cook.' She swept out. Cook did a bit of all three and the hostess was noticeably kept far too busy with her guests to bother with eating! 'She just looked anxious when she saw her husband tucking in,' cook told the office later.

People returning to London needed accommodation to rent or buy. Reunited husbands and wives popped off for second honeymoons and needed Aunts to care for their children and pets. There was a rush of owners collecting the stored treasures that had been kept safe in the huge cupboard behind Emmie's desk, bringing a nice influx of cash as final instalments were paid off. Children still needed to be met and chaperoned, old people cared for, and dogs walked.

Bay was welcomed back after her war service. Her first task was to establish herself in Gertie's place as Managing Director, but also to let it be known that she was going to be a day-by-day part of the working staff. Emmie and Dorothy breathed a sigh of relief that their lone burden was over. With delight Bay faced the avalanche of work, remarking, 'The real assets of any company of this kind lie in its relations with the public, its capacity for personal service, its high reputation for fair dealing and the feeling of confidence which it inspires.'

It was clear that reinforcements were called for, and Bay proposed the name of Cecil Scott as an addition to their ranks. The Scott sisters, Cecil and the younger Phyllis, were friends of the Leith sisters, Bay and Eveleigh. By chance, Cecil had been an ambulance driver in the American Red Cross with Eveleigh, and Phyllis in the motor transport service with Bay. Both families were of staunch pioneering stock and the Scott home had been a comfortable place for the Leith sisters to spend brief respites on leave, presided over by Mrs Scott, an intelligent, delightful and sprightly elderly lady. Her husband's career, beginning in the army, had later led him into more diplomatic channels where he served all over the world. Some time had been spent in the Middle and Far East, and they had been long enough in Switzerland to make a home there, where Cecil was born and spent her early years. His greatest adventure was in the wake of his friend Cecil Rhodes in Africa, after whom he christened his elder daughter. They were a close family and after his death and the loss of her only son in the Great War, Mrs Scott moved to London and kept an elegant and lively home in Queens Gate as a base for her loving daughters and a wide social circle of guests.

Cecil was one of the thousands of women the course of whose destiny was determined by the events of that war. Not only did she lose a brother, but also a fiancé, and thereafter she engaged herself in helping other people when and where she could. This gave her a full enough life and a host of friends and acquaintances, but she was not interested in socializing.

Cecil was a very strong character, full of vitality and interested in everything and everybody. She was quite tall, slender and pale-skinned, with wide, misty eyes neither blue nor green. Her wavy hair, worn longer than was the vogue, showed to advantage its pure golden colour. She loved clothes and dressed well but not fashionably; her main vanity was tiny feet, expensively shod. She was a resilient, quick-witted woman with a great sense of humour, and, with a slightly loud, ringing voice and authoritative manner, was a natural leader of people. She was kind, generous and hospitable as well as being a good listener; a positive person, constructive, never destructive.

So this sparkling personality with a zest for life was welcomed on to the Board and into the office on Wednesday 1 January 1947, to run the House and Flat department (letting and selling) at a salary of £4 10s per week. At the same time, the brisk and commanding Bay took over the London and Country Accommodation department, (bed-sitting rooms to let and country holiday homes) at the same salary.

Both these departments were soon bringing in enough business to rival almost any of the well-known London estate agencies. Plenty of people back in their London houses had a room to let to help pay the bills. Even more people were looking for work in London and could only afford to rent a bed-sitter.

As war clouds rolled away, Britain, the British, and the English language were popular all over the world. From Europe and countries as far afield as Persia, requests arrived for children to be placed in holiday homes to learn the language. There was no shortage of host families who were willing to take the young people either on a financial basis or in exchange for a visit abroad. Bay had to deal most carefully with the transactions, for the foreign children had their own views on food and amusements, and it was no good putting two or three young, French, say, in the same family.

Cecil was equally busy and reported to Bay, 'I don't know whether it is due to belief in our integrity, rather than a hope in our succeeding, but I now have on our books a house to let in the Bahamas, several flats in New York and a plot of land to sell in Australia!'

'It may take a little longer, but you'll do it,' encouraged Bay; and gradually Cecil did.

As soon as she had engaged two or three attractive young additions to the office staff and everyone had settled in, Bay put her mind to Company matters and called a Board meeting. The directors gathered. Except for Gertie, the distant, ailing, hospital-bound Chairman, they were there in force.

Bay, who had relinquished some items of uniform dress, reckoned there was more stout wear left in others. She therefore appeared for this first peace-time meeting dressed in shirt and skirt of khaki, rather as a captain at the head of her troop, having laid aside only her jacket, cap and insignia – a somewhat unnerving figure, clearly in charge and capable of leading a brisk pace through the agenda. Emmie, greyer and wearily upright, wore elderly, well-preserved tweeds. Frances had donned a favourite, faded, calf-length tartan kilt of a kind and a somewhat darned hip-length cardigan. Cecil looked spruce and fresh in grey flannel and immaculate white shirt for her introduction to the élite number.

Bay announced the main item: an invitation to Dorothy to join the Board in recognition of her sterling years as Company Secretary since 1927. A delighted rosy-round Dorothy was called in to sit in the vacant chair placed ready for her. The Articles of Association had been altered to increase the number of directors to six.

The remaining agenda followed.

'The financial position is good,' announced Bay, 'and apart from Miss Tull's appointment I wish to propose a rise in her salary to £8 10s per week.' She paused. 'Miss Faulder has agreed also to take a rise to £7 10s per week.'

'I second that,' said Frances, gazing over the top of her spectacles. Bay sped on.

'Approaches from outside to act as Universal Aunts agents in the provinces and abroad have in the past proved unsatisfactory. We have recently received several more and I suggest that my reply should be that it is not our policy to appoint agents.'

There were murmurs of approval.

'Mrs Symon, photographer of interiors and exteriors of houses and portraits, wishes to make us her agents. She offers 15 per cent of her profits from any introductions by us.' Bay paused while there was a rustle of discussion, but only gave them a moment. 'I have checked that

Mrs Symon is a reputable person. I think we should say yes and offer to include her leaflets in our correspondence at the charge of £1 10s for 1,000 and 10s 6d for 500, agreed?'

Heads nodded. 'Agreed.'

She went on to the next item.

'As you are all aware, with the upsurge of clients wishing to employ and of people coming to us to seek employment, I put in an application for a London County Council licence to register us as an employment agency, and this has been granted.' Bay paused while they all expressed their satisfaction. 'For the benefit of Miss Scott, who has not had time to acquaint herself with the various regulations, I will explain that this type of employment is distinct from our sending our own Universal Aunts out on assignments. They are employed by us.'

'Thank you, Miss Leith,' said Cecil, making a note on her pad.

'We are already sending nannies and ladies' maids, butlers and other trained staff, to the strangest places in all parts of the world. I'm glad to say a lot of them seem to want to go for a time, so we can satisfy our clients,' finished Bay. 'Our work as insurance agents for Eagle Star and Liverpool, London and Globe is increasing daily, and with the war over I feel there is considerable scope there and a steady percentage income.'

Bay paused and looked around the table, but they were all out of practice at planning a future, being too busy with the present and glad to let Bay carry them through the meeting. The slow, sonorous voice of Frances answered for them. 'Your proposals seem sound business ideas in which our investment is hard work rather than financial commitment, and with the possibility of growth from these small beginnings. I'm sure we'll all like that recipe.'

Bay closed the meeting. 'I cannot let this moment pass without expressing the sincere thanks and appreciation of us all to Miss Faulder and Miss Tull. Without them, Universal Aunts would have been another casualty of war.'

Emmie replied, 'And on behalf of Miss Tull, I have to extend our deep admiration to all the rest of you whose war efforts were so much more hazardous, and our thankfulness that you are safely back.'

They shuffled their papers together with little coughs and slightly embarrassed sighs, politely saw Frances off, and got on with the day's work.

The success of the Aunts in coping with the normal seemed to inspire the general public that, with a telephone call to SLOane 5101, the answer to just about anything could be found. '*I wonder if you can help me*,' over the office telephones, answered by, '*We shall do our best*,' brought in some amazing requests, and the amazingly versatile workers usually managed with great success. Often Bay, Emmie and Cecil helped the departments with preliminary searches for the unusual or with the planning of detail, from their own store of experience. '*That's all right, we can manage that*,' would ring out encouragingly from Cecil's desk, and her girls loved her for it. She seemed able to get on with her own work and have antennae out all across the room at the same time, so no one felt lost. From her host of friends she recruited sons when furniture-heavers or butlers ran short. 'You've seen how it's done in your own house,' she would tell them. 'No problem.' And there never seemed to be.

Once or twice Cecil was 'taken in', but she took it in her stride. A client demanded that the Aunts find him ten peacocks for his garden fête. That was a tough order to fulfil. Cecil set herself the task of visiting all the bird shops she could locate in, and a long away outside, London to find that number of birds for sale or hire. Punctually at zero hour a van was at the client's door, complete with the correct number of birds. It transpired that he had only wanted to make a costly experiment with the Aunts. 'Worth every penny,' he announced as he paid up!

For some curious reason, the monks of Ampleforth wished to make an addition of a Dutch breed to their goat herd. 'Surely goats are goats?' said Emmie, ignorant of the finer points. An Aunt was despatched to the station and the guard handed over a small, pretty, female creature, white and brown and docile, attached to a short rope. Although not speaking the language, she munched and gazed steadily into the distance. The line of taxi-drivers were all sceptical and, with a fine disregard for anatomy, they declined the fare.

'Is 'e 'ouse-trained?'

'No fear, lady, 'e could eat the 'ole cab at a sittin'.'

'Them creatures smell to 'igh 'eaven.'

Down the queue they moved, and found an animal lover. He put the Aunt and goat in the back, spread his newspaper on the floor and stopped in the middle of Hyde Park – 'for to give the little madam a chance to obey the call of nature and get in some good English grass.' Blessedly, he meant the goat.

'Madame, my trousers are with you,' came bellowing down the phone in fractured English, totally unnerving the recipient of the call who, pink and breathless, cried, 'Help!' Cecil took the receiver and ascertained the problem in perfect French and a smattering of Spanish. On the other end was 'Mr Ambassador', no less, from South America, accredited to Paris and there called upon to present letters of credence sooner than expected. His morning-dress trousers were with his London tailor for alteration. 'Please to get and bring with, no hesitation.'

A diplomatic débâcle was avoided, a young, ravishingly blonde Aunt was sent to the alerted tailor, on to the soonest ferry, got some funny looks and remarks – which she happily did not understand – from perplexed French customs men, and delivered the Ambassador's trousers.

Bay took a call to meet a hawk en route from Scotland to a private owner in Devon, to convey it train to train with several hours' delay in between. She arranged for her sister Eveleigh to do the job and rang up London zoo to ask what they should feed it on if no instructions were attached.

'Catch a few mice,' was the response.

'I feel it an insult to my clean flat,' Eveleigh told Emmie.

There was a trunk call from Tahiti asking for an Aunt to be despatched to Switzerland to purchase a special plate-warmer that could only be found there, and if she could not safely mail it, to take it to Tahiti. There was no lack of willing Aunts for that job!

A London banker wanted to hold a three-day summer fête on a houseboat sailing down the Thames. Except for his plan, the client had nothing else available – no houseboat, no supplies, no waiters, no drinks. Curiously, everything was smoothly put in hand except for the ice. No sophisticated, nor indeed simple, freezing method could be found for the amount of ice and length of time required. A resourceful member of staff came up with the answer: fresh intakes were arranged twice a day from pubs along the route.

Angling parties in Ireland were popular and it was soon known that Universal Aunts seemed to have the right contacts, for Bay and Cecil had a number of friends with a stretch of the rivers, from whom they could arrange to rent tackle and permits to fish in some beautiful spots. Their service extended to laying on good hotel accommodation, among other necessities.

Such was the variety of the post-war scene that the war seemed in some cases to be receding fast. All these jobs were a pleasure to fix and brought in the most profitable fees.

Early in 1945, Emmie's twenty-five years with the Company had slid by in the midst of air-raids, without celebration. Now, two years later, another milestone was reached. Mrs Stokes had come into their lives through Betsy's mother, who had put in a word when 'Miss Maclean' got her first tiny office in Sloane Street. Every day since then, Mrs Stokes, short, plump and rosy-faced beneath a woolly hat, had walked along by the Thames from Battersea to Chelsea in the company of others similarly employed. In the quiet, chilly grey office, donning a flowered pinny, she emptied baskets, swept, polished and dusted to perfection, turned on fires, and left. Through twenty-seven years of personal joys and sorrows, births and deaths, war and peace, hunger, strikes and marches, two hours of every day had been unchangingly spent keeping 'everything nice' for the benefit of 'her ladies', few of whom even saw her. Now she made history. Mrs Stokes retired but she established the only dynasty in the annals of the Aunts by passing the mantle to her daughter, Mrs Hacker, at a salary of £2 per week. On 27 July a tea-party was held in the office and Emmie presented a parting gift in the absence of Gertie. It was the sum of three months' wages and the cheque was for £25. To the Aunts' great good fortune it was to continue 'like mother like daughter' for many years to come.

14

1950s

DEATH OF THE FOUNDER

Horizons widen – Advertising – Emmie eases off –
She stoops to scrub –
Jobs for the boys – Death of the founder

Bay was meticulous in sending regular reports to Gertie, who showed neither the strength nor the inclination to leave her hospital surroundings. In 1948 Bay wrote delightedly,

> The Company has soared to dizzy new heights of profit, for the first time above the hundreds to £2,195. I know that the reading of enclosed copy of the yearly accounts will be a pleasure for you.
>
> The Company is in a better position financially than ever – to face whatever the future may bring. I assure you that the directors will continue to pursue the policies as laid down by you, to remain reliable, resourceful and ready for whatever may be demanded, above all to retain the personal touch for which it is so well-known. In its own small way helping to solve some of the problems of mankind.
>
> It will come as no surprise to you to hear that Tull wishes now to retire from her position as Company Secretary. Through the necessities of war she has extended her hard working days longer than planned; you, more than any, appreciate the skill and application she has given to the affairs of the Company for so long. In recognition of this vast contribution, the directors propose, with your approval, to present her with a year's salary.
>
> Tull will of course remain on the Board as a non-working director where we can still have the benefit of her advice.

Financial success brings with it many dangers. With improved conditions, horizons widen.

The Company's lease on the office premises came up for renegotiation. This having been successfully accomplished, it was agreed that a

new look was called for, that the shabbiness of war-time restrictions
should be banished, and a list was drawn up:

> A heater for hot water during the winter months. A 3-gallon one hired
> from the electricity company –
> COST: 5s 6d per quarter.
> New linoleum on the staircase and passages –
> COST: £49 13s 6d.
> New carpeting in the main office and cleaning of old carpeting where
> good –
> COST: £65.
> New curtains and renovating old ones –
> COST: £20.
> Washing down and repainting of all rooms and staircase –
> COST: £222 17s.

The local council, by chance, added to the renovations by changing all
the street numbers, and Universal Aunts became no longer 37 but 61
Wilton Place.

With £2,000 safely invested and £100 on deposit and thus a warm
feeling of security, Bay decided on several more expenditures: a contract
for monthly maintenance of the typewriters at 2s 6d per machine per
month, and an overhaul of the telephone system. 'The lifeblood of the
office,' she remarked. Advertising was next on the list, and an increased
estimate of £178 for the year was decided upon. The hardy annuals were
kept on – *The Times* personal column ('1 series advert. per month') at
£51, the telephone directory at £29, and Kelly's directory at £7 10s –
which left a balance of £87 10s for more adventurous placings. Masses
of magazines and papers were bought, studied, and discussed, and the
final choice was considered to cover a good cross-section, from radio
listeners to shoppers to families, with the *Radio Times*, *Vogue*, and *Home
and Country*.

As Gertie had discovered long ago, free advertisement could be
two-edged, and while the Aunts appreciated the unabated interest in
their doings and the valuable write-ups that resulted, misquoted interviews were bad business and so they seldom now gave any. At that
moment, however, an approach was made by Mr George Kent, editor of
the *Readers' Digest*, who had the notion that an article on the Aunts would
appeal particularly to his large American readership. It was agreed that

Emmie and Cecil would talk to him on condition that the article was vetted by them before publication. He sold the Aunts well! A shoal of letters came with requests for shopping, research, holiday accommodation and promises to call when next in 'London, England'.

Best of all was the request that an Aunt should be available as part of the entourage to accompany a valuable racehorse bound for Kentucky. This was all in a day's business, but there was just a hint of anxiety in the Aunts' question as to why the horse needed a female presence? 'Highly strung and used to stable girls,' came the answer. A horse-mad Aunt was chosen, who was also considered level-headed enough to cope firmly and charmingly with the four rather dashing male members of the party, should they seek evening diversion while the animal slept. Both horse and Aunt had a very good trip and survived unscathed, so the Aunt reported back.

It was noticeable that Emmie, tired by the war years, had eased off her work load and, with Bay in firm control of Company matters, now referred the general running of the office and making of decisions to Cecil. Between them, Bay and Cecil possessed a degree of training or experience that enabled them to be receptive; they realized that the post-war work of an employment agency was going to be different, less like the old 'personal service bureau'. Although Bay decided, 'As our main business is with private posts, we are not really in a position to deal with openings for qualified women in various businesses and professions.'

Cecil agreed and added, 'The most worrying aspect of the present times is the inequality between supply and demand. A dozen or so employers are on our books demanding a cook, and perhaps one, or at the most two, of those elusive creatures is on our register. But to another desk, dealing with non-domestic employment, there come perhaps a hundred people in a day wanting work, and not one with qualifications to suit.'

The situation gradually became more balanced by outside forces, as the former 'domestic classes' relinquished even more their rights of tenure by seeking greater status and declaring their newly acquired expectations. There were takers waiting on the sidelines. What had begun as something of a lark for some Universal Aunt applicants had become stark necessity; they now had to earn a living and not just supplement their luxuries. What they lacked in experience they made up for in enthusiasm, and they aimed at competence. Small, smart domestic-training schools sprang into being with short basic courses, and became more sought after than finishing schools. So Cecil's placings became easier to make, although it was for some still the days of fitting work around play. Employers from Richmond to Hampstead could be forgiven a certain curiosity as to whether the striking young thing at the moment cooking their dinner menu or spring-cleaning their drawing-room at an hourly rate of 10s, did other things too – and the answers would frequently have amazed them.

Virginia slept till noon after her or anyone else's coming-out party, and at one o'clock would be on the job as a much sought-after cook. Rose, a peer's daughter, cleaned for a nice bachelor and as his charwoman could not properly accept a date, although she knew that one day, sure as fate, they would come face to face at the same party. In old ski-pants and boots, deb Sarah scrubbed and polished and dusted for all and sundry. Camilla switched from flower-arranging to working at a petrol-station, while Emma and Angie waitressed in Belgravia coffee bars. Prue had opted for a summer job abroad, and scrubbed the St Tropez villa early so that she could finish in time to lie, in pretty bathing-costume, on the beach with the villa occupants until it was time to prepare their dinner. Prue and her like had been found to be far more reliable and consientious than the local cleaning-women, by those renting villas in the south of France.

As in all things, it was different for the boys. Their jobs were undertaken between studies and for the express purpose of subsidizing their pleasures – paying the instalments on their fast or ramshackle cars, buying tickets to far-flung places, or skis, books and paintings, May Ball tickets, dinners for girls. They butled in black tie and trousers, waitered in white shirt and linen jacket, and hoovered in old cords and sweaters with near-elbowless sleeves.

Julian cooked and served breakfast in bed for an American tourist on her birthday. 'If you have your head screwed on, you take the job that pays the most,' said this up-and-coming young accountant, owner of a voracious Sunbeam Rapier.

Nicholas hoovered up m'lady's real pearls with the fluff under the bed. 'Thank God they didn't bust the hoover,' he said. Harry researched a pedigree at Somerset House and discovered he and the client were related. Richard of the tasteful wardrobe and good looks sat in with some luscious models on a photographic session. 'And I shall need all the odd jobs you can give me to pay for taking as many as I can out to dinner,' he confided to an understanding Aunt. Behind a fork, a rake and a hedgecutter, Miles was the joy of several London garden-owners, until he made up his mind and embarked on his future career, as they all did, sooner or later.

There were just two older Uncles on the books but their uses were limited. 'Uncles are all right,' said Cecil, 'but when the chips are down it's the Aunts who really count. It's pointless to send a fiery old Colonel to the airport to greet a little girl, "Hello, my dear, I'm your Aunt." He'd probably be arrested anyway. Besides, an Aunt should be not only patient and resourceful but when necessary, ruthless, and women are much more ruthless than men.' She thought for a second. 'I can give you a good example. A Universal Aunt collected two children off a train at 2.30 to catch the 5.35 plane for Germany, only to discover they had left behind both passports and tickets. She knew her job and bustled about collecting replacement documents, then rushed them off in a hired car.'

'Did they make it?'

'They did not. The little boy was sick all the way to the airport and they missed the plane. But –' she paused triumphantly, 'the Aunt did not give up. There was an alternative flight with two vacant seats, and two Germans were just about to take them. The Aunt brushed them aside, loudly demanding priority for English children, and succeeded.' She drew breath. 'A man would never have done that. He wouldn't have thought it sporting. Nor was it, but the chips were down.'

Cecil liked the continuity of old clients, as she explained to a new recruit to the office staff. 'Every spring, regular clients ask, "Where are you going to send us for our summer holiday this year?" We work out a tour of the British Isles or on the Continent, mapping out roads, booking hotels, getting tickets, and providing timetables and advice on Customs. We shall most likely then pack for them and sometimes find a holiday home for their children so that parents can have a holiday on their own.'

She took the girl over to the Meetings department to be introduced. 'Children too remain in our safekeeping for many years. They are going to school much younger now, and such is the progress of travel that whereas in the old days their holidays would have been spent with relations here, or in a holiday home, now they can join their parents in the Sudan, Germany or Hong Kong, within a few hours. We meet and escort them en route each time.'

Cecil finished explaining the departmental work. 'On the other hand,' she went on, 'we are still dealing a lot with the personal, with small but important easing away of anxieties.' Her tone became softer. 'A recent invitation to one of our own clients was to attend a Buckingham Palace reception. "Horrors, do I eat canapés with my gloves on or off?" she asked me. "With them rolled back," I promptly advised her.'

In the stout days of Cecil Scott, her devotion to the organization, became her 'cause' – all things were possible. A young Swedish girl wanted to come to England to learn sheep-farming, shearing and weaving and all about textiles. 'At the same time, I want to brush up my English so that I can teach too when I return,' she requested.

'Nothing to it,' said Cecil. 'I simply have to find a shepherd who happens to be a weaver and a professor of English literature.'

There was a general mood of affluence in the country and a buoyant money market in the city. Backed by expense-account big spenders, restaurants and clubs renovated and reopened. Food rationing was not to end until 1954 but that did not prevent a good deal of socializing. The criss-crossing of classes had come, and the making and spending of money was an acceptable aim and topic of conversation, although the first aristocrat to open the doors of his stately home as a business, the Duke of Bedford, was frowned upon by the other Dukes until they saw the profits, and moved in on the act. For the working classes the whole of the '50s moved towards the later statement of Harold Macmillan, that they had 'never had it so good'. There was a material uplift in their standard of living to which their parents would never have aspired. Luxuries were no longer enjoyed by the few but were now regarded as normal expenditure for the young – television, cars and telephones, electric gadgets and foreign holidays.

There still remained a respect for the law and a belief that it should be observed. There was neighbourliness, and in family life the responsibility of, and to, parents was upheld. Pride in the country was strong and the government decision to hold a great Festival of Britain was grasped as an opportunity to show the best of British arts, sciences, and business methods to the rest of the world. Thousands were employed, ideas flowered and production flowed. On the Battersea South Bank site, skeleton constructions began to tower above the trees and the foundations of the permanent theatre complex were laid.

The Festival was to open in May. In January, Bay called a Board meeting to finalize the Company's plans for Festival year. Emmie was not present, through illness – the first meeting she had missed since joining the Board. It had been arranged for a Universal Aunts representative to distribute literature to visitors from the provinces and overseas at strategic places; the Chase Bank, American Women's club, English Speaking Union, the Royal Society and the Overseas League. Back and forth they discussed the type of business which might result, and the 'making ready' necessary if they were not to be caught on the hop by a hoped-for rush. Other business included agreement to the approach by Miss Shapiro of the Italian section of the BBC to broadcast about the activities of the Company, and one more item. Bay's departmental assistant was leaving to be married and it was reluctantly decided that in those days even Universal Aunts staff expected to be paid on a realistic scale. Her replacement, Miss Cave-Brown-Cave, was not to know that she therefore joined the staff at directorial level, financially speaking, at £5 per week!

Crowds thronged together on the day in May when eighty-four-year-old Queen Mary graced the opening of the Festival. For her public appearances she now sat in a wheelchair, to which she gave all the dignity of a throne. She was upright and superb, in her pale, near-ankle-length fur-collared coat, her matching toque upon close silver curls, her throat and ears regally jewelled and a long rolled umbrella lying in her gloved hand. Her slender feet in their strapped shoes resting on a little platform, she was slowly wheeled by a uniformed Crown attendant with his shining row of medals. Of course, it rained, so a dignitary held his huge black umbrella above her. The crowds loved it and thundered their applause.

Five months later the British were cheering another great and ageing figurehead, although merely seventy-six, as Sir Winston Churchill returned to 10 Downing Street after an absence of six years, bringing with him his favourite bed. Momentous national events bring great joys and sorrows, and with the British people the world was plunged into deep and stunned mourning when the news broke on 6 February 1952 that His Majesty the King had been found dead in his bed at Sandringham by an under-valet. Nine days later, in silent grief, the people watched his funeral procession from the streets or on television, to the muffled beat of the drums.

Businesses at once began their preparations for the new Queen's Coronation. Bay put out immediate feelers for seats along the route, and came face to face with the fact that only the big companies such as Keith Prowse could compete in taking up the allotments at 10 to 15 guineas each, on which there would later be a splendid profit with overseas visitors waiting to pay any price.

'Money makes money,' said Bay, 'but we cannot risk laying out such an investment.' As for the previous Coronation, the Aunts simply handled those seats that came their way through friends and acquaintances. The office was flooded with requests for accommodation, theatre bookings, sightseeing trips and general advice. Aunts were detailed to buy and dispatch items of bunting, decorations, and souvenirs that had been advertised in magazines and newspapers. Staff for parties, babysitters and Aunts to push wheel-chairs were needed for 'The Day'. Americans wrote for historical details about the royal family.

While all this was going on, the Company suffered a personal loss. In January, Emmie tendered her resignation, to take effect on the last day of June. For over thirty years she had served the Company; it seemed inconceivable that it could function without her. Gertie, withdrawn in her hospital ward, hardly understood the news gently broken to her. Dorothy, from her own retirement, realized most of all that the time had also come for Emmie. Bay, Frances and Cecil tried to persuade her to stay on with a lighter work load, but Emmie was adamant. The Board had no other alternative than to accept her decision, and voted her a gift of £750 tax free, and one month's salary. Bay solemnly tried to put their feelings into a few words.

'It is the opinion of us all, the Board, the staff and the Aunts, that the success of the Company is largely due to Miss Faulder's wholehearted service over thirty-two years, a debt that can never be adequately repaid. It is to our continuing benefit, however, that Miss Faulder will be remaining on the Board, so that her help and experience will still be at the Company's disposal should they be needed.'

As the preparations gathered force towards the crowning of the new Queen, with what myriad of memories the grandmother Queen must have driven out from Marlborough House to inspect the stands being erected in the Mall. On 24 March, her life quietly ebbed away.

By the late spring preparations were under way for the Coronation, and Bay ordered a new electric sign to be placed facing Knightsbridge, to be left on a time-switch until midnight. £15 was spent on a Union Jack and red, white and blue flowers outside the windows. Often office hours were extended to cope with the work and the staff were paid a bonus. The rain poured down as, on 2 June, the new Queen rode out to be crowned, but her smile was serene and brilliant, and her subjects were jubilant and loving. The office, like every other, was closed and all the occupants were at their own particular vantage points. It was a night of parties and grand balls and flowing champagne – 3,000 bottles at the Savoy alone. Universal Aunts toasted 'The Queen' and in their own case were able also to celebrate a nice increase of £1,046 to the Company's yearly profit.

A few weeks later the Directors gathered and Bay reported, 'Miss Fort, owing to ill health, is no longer able to act as Chairman of Directors.' The meeting proceeded and their resolutions were entered in the minutes:

> It was resolved that the Company should give Miss Fort notice to terminate her agreement as from 31 December 1953. In lieu of the salary of £100 per annum now paid to her as Chairman it was proposed that, as Founder of the Company and in token of her services to it, she be offered a pension of £240 per annum to be paid monthly. This proposal was agreed and Miss Leith was asked to write to Miss Fort on these lines and to express the Board's regret on her continuous ill health.

In fact, Gertie never relinquished her post as Chairman nor took up her pension. Gertrude Eliza Maclean died on 17 October. Bay once again put their feelings into words. 'The tradition laid down by the founder will be cherished throughout the present and into the future,' she said. The minutes of the meeting record that 'The Company owed [Miss Maclean] a debt which could never be repaid and her death is a great loss as well as a great sadness. Owing to her death, it was necessary to elect a new Chairman and it was proposed by Miss Faulder, seconded by Miss Tull and unanimously agreed that Miss Leith be elected Chairman of the Company in Miss Maclean's place.'

15

1950S

PROXY PARENTS

Emmie's retirement – Molly Sheppard – Proxy Parents

By natural progression over the past eventful months, shifts of power had taken place. Emmie was to remain Consultant Director, Bay became Chairman of the Company, and in January 1960 Cecil stepped into the role of Managing Director. Miss Vera Ockenden, a lady similarly experienced to Dorothy Tull, had slipped into that vacancy as Company Secretary and, having by now proved herself, gladly accepted a proffered place on the Board. It was also entered in the records that Miss Molly Sheppard had joined the Meetings department to deal with the large flow of work in billing and receiving money when school-children were on the move at the beginning and end of term.

With post-war enthusiasm and activity running high, with the recent profits enjoyed by the Company, and the continued stream of business, it came as no small surprise when a Director's Report from Bay to the others sounded a warning note.

'Expenditure has a way of creeping up until, before it is realized, the resources that have been so slowly and painfully piled up are suddenly swept away. The profits have certainly mounted but so have the outgoings – the inevitable rise in staff salaries and recent increase in the cost of our premises and service charges. World conditions today do not allow us to make a corresponding upmarking of our charges. Outside events have always had a great effect on the Company. However, as businesses go this Company is still young and its past history has shown it capable of weathering many storms. We must move with the times.'

What Bay did not, of course, mention were the recent gifts from the Company to the working directors who had retired to a non-working role. They were most willingly given, but they depleted the deposit account, nonetheless.

Notice of Emmie's retirement soon came to the attention of the journalist watchdogs. This was too good to miss and there was quite an influx of them padding down Knightsbridge to make a final record of a lady who had surely been one of the pioneers of businesswomen and had successfully spanned the decades. Her dealings with them had always been a model of courtesy and mutual respect.

They were met at the interview by a trim and vigilant figure.

'I have no note of your first name, Miss Faulder,' queried one hopeful lady journalist, with pencil poised above her pad.

'We don't believe in giving our Christian names,' Emmie replied, and smilingly awaited the next question. It was a simple one.

'Any failures you can recall?'

Emmie pursed her lips and after the slightest pause, truthfully recalled, 'Naturally there have been some *errors*. Clients have failed to co-operate, mails have been delayed, or children have been deliberately naughty. Sometimes boys come on earlier trains than expected, just to get off on their own. We have had some pretty bad moments, but we have so many resources that we always manage to pull out. We have friends at Scotland Yard, in the fire department, the post office and all the transportation services. Attendants in parks and public buildings, MPs, plumbers, doormen, stationmasters, aeroplane hostesses; they all know us. I suppose we've been lucky; nothing dreadful ever happened. But on the other hand you must remember that our loyal and watchful team of Aunts do all that is humanly possible to make this a certainty.'

'As it is end-of-term week, Miss Faulder, how are you coping with the great climacteric?' enquired the journalist. Emmie didn't much like the word, since as far as she knew it meant 'constituting a crisis', and she answered rather sharply, 'Unhurriedly, for in thirty-two years of existence we have built up a foundation of decorous efficiency.'

But in her usual manner, Emmie quickly thawed and laughed. 'But I will tell you two little conflicting stories. One happened last term, the other only yesterday. A small boy boasted throughout the Michaelmas term of the smashing Aunt who was to meet him at Paddington. When a more homely representative was despatched to collect him, his chagrin knew no bounds. "You," he said, "are not the Aunt I ordered."' This, thought the happy journalist, is really good. Emmie went on, 'An Aunt arriving to take charge of an American boy was greeted thus: "Gee, I'm glad it's you, I thought they'd send an old bag." Now that *was* nice,' she finished.

A final prompt from the journalist and Emmie wistfully repeated the

question, 'How far has the organization come in my time?' She felt that
was best answered by several significant pointers.

'I suppose imitators are a measure of one's success and we have had a
number, the latest being a new service agency starting up in Eastbourne
under the name of Universal Aunts. Having informed them that we have
a copyright on that name, our solicitor was able to report that they were
changing the name to Helpful Aunts.' There were plenty of instances
that Emmie could continue to quote. 'The Budapest telephone exchange has started a new information service which can answer almost
any question from a caller. They have named it the *Universal Aunt
Service*.' Emmie waited for the girl's pencil to be poised to go on. 'A
recent obituary in *The Times* read "To a much-loved sister and Universal Aunt."'' Emmie began to end the interview by slightly pushing back
her chair from the desk. 'It is my belief that by now our name is stamped
on the blotter of every consulate in the world,' she said.

The journalist was quite sincere as she shook hands to leave and
remarked, 'What a splendid heritage you are passing on.'

As Bay had reported, calls for the services of the Aunts were as
plentiful and varied as ever. Typical meetings were taking place by the
hundred.

Universal Aunts Ltd
61 Wilton Place SW1

Mrs Binnie
c/o Imperial Chemical Industries
    (India) Ltd
18 Strand Rd
Calcutta   Ref A

Dear Madam,

We thank you for your letter of 7 July and confirm that we are
sending one of our escorts to meet your children on Saturday 28 July
and we have arranged for your daughter to travel by a train from
Luton that gets to St Pancras at 3.13 p.m. She and the escort will then
meet your son at 3.55 p.m. and both children will stay the night with
the escort.

We note that they will have their passports, air tickets etc. and that
they are to be taken to be at Airways Terminal about 8 p.m. on
Sunday, 29 July (we will verify this).

Our charge for this service is 10s for the first hour and 3s 6d for each following hour plus expenses and 10 per cent which we have been obliged to add to cover our overhead costs.

All your instructions will be given to our escort who will take great care of the children.

Yours faithfully,

Universal Aunts Ltd

PS There is an additional charge of 5s for Sunday work.

Once parents had experienced the reliability of the Meetings department, they sent along their instructions with touching faith. Sometimes the most vital detail of all could slip the mind of a busy mother and be omitted. The mother of one young regular sent her letter airmail and postmarked Katchin. By the time it arrived at the office, the twelve-year-old boy had left Bombay by plane. He was to be met and housed by his escort for several days and to be outfitted with carefully listed clothing. Also taken to a performance of John Gielgud's *Much Ado About Nothing*, and to a cricket match at Lords. He should visit his uncle in Hampshire with his hair neatly combed. On the Sunday morning he was to go to church and in the afternoon be put on a train for Rugby with a box of sandwiches and two pounds sterling. There was a minute description of the child, and a photograph was enclosed with the cheque. The only thing this meticulous mother neglected to mention was the flight number and date of arrival. A couple of staff got the telephone buzzing to check passenger lists, and within an hour of the letter's arrival, the situation was in hand and an Aunt en route to the airport.

It had been announced that the formal presentation of debutants at Buckingham Palace was to cease. 'A long overdue step' said some, expecting the entire deb scene to thereby die away. 'Those poor little darlings who expected to be received by the Queen,' cried others. The Special Services department of Universal Aunts just went on supplying the right ladies to introduce the gels into what remained of so depleted a Season.

A commission of some historical interest was also placed in the hands of the department. Mr Evelyn Waugh of Piers Court in Gloucestershire was bent upon privacy for himself, his wife and children in their eighteenth-century pile with Tudor fragments. He placed a sign on the gate which read:

PRIVATE ENTRANCE
NO ADMITTANCE
ON BUSINESS

'*No admittance on business*' was repeated in finely engraved Gothic lettering on a brass plate on the front door itself. When Mr Waugh was asked where he had the engraving done, his surprising reply was, 'Universal Aunts, they get anything done for you – an invaluable body of women. Some Hungarian cousins of ours were caught there by the Socialists after the war. The British Government tried to get them out. Frank Pakenham, who was in charge of Germany, did his best. All no use. We put Universal Aunts on to it, they had 'em all in Tasmania in three weeks!'

How Universal Aunts achieved this where Ministers failed has to remain part of the story which cannot be told.

A Canadian wrote to say that his mother had willed her ashes to be returned to the United Kingdom and scattered over Beachy Head. He asked that the Aunts undertake this grave responsibility and the ashes were in due time delivered into their hands. A soberly dressed Aunt was despatched by train and then taxi to the site. On the chosen day the wind was so strong that the taxi-driver had to grip her with both arms round her waist as she leaned over to complete the task; they were as decorous as possible. The Canadian sent the Aunts a Christmas card every year for the rest of his life.

Apparently the start of the shooting season had crept up on someone unawares and the department was alerted: 'Go to 100 Crawford St, W1, collect 2 guns, mid-calf shooting boots, in cellar, breeches in spare-room cupboard and deliver quicker than possible to North British Hotel Edinburgh, please!' All went according to plan and on meeting up with the client in Scotland the Aunt learned that he was a professor with a Chair in Machine Intelligence and Perfection!

The world crisis of the late '50s was Suez; domestic events in Britain were mostly concerned with personalities in Government and the royal family.

Churchill had celebrated his eightieth birthday on 30 November 1954. In Westminster Hall both Houses of Parliament gathered to present him with a portrait of himself by Graham Sutherland. Churchill, in his speech acknowledging the gift, described it as 'a remarkable example of modern art.' His dislike of the painting was fairly obvious and was echoed by many other people. On the following 5 April the great parliamentarian was driven to the Palace and surrendered his Seals of Office to the Queen. Sir Anthony Eden, by then in frail health, took over as Premier and his appointment was reaffirmed in the general election at the end of May. He held the post for two years while he battled against illness and with escalating crises over Suez, attempting to prevent Nasser's traffic embargo. On 9 January 1957 he handed over as Prime Minister to Mr Harold Macmillan.

Princess Margaret was the social figure of the day, the reporters relentless in pursuit of gossip to feed an insatiable public – who escorted her to what, which dress she wore, even on one occasion the fact that she used four matches to light a cigarette! The target of interest was Group Captain Peter Townsend who, in spite of his divorced status, seemed to be the man in her life until, on 31 October 1955 the Princess issued a formal statement from Clarence House. 'Mindful of the Church's teaching that Christian marriage is indissoluble and conscious of my duty to the Commonwealth, I have decided to put those considerations before any other,' – thus damping speculations. By May of 1959 the Princess was socializing in the company of a name new to her circle, photographer Anthony Armstrong-Jones. On the following 26 February their engagement was announced. After hiccups over the choice of the couple's best man, their first being Mr Jeremy Fry, who was replaced for health reasons by Dr Roger Gilliatt, she became a fairy-tale bride at Westminster Abbey on 6 May 1960. They sailed blissfully from the Pool of London aboard the royal yacht *Britannia* for their honeymoon, to cruise around the Caribbean and land on the island of Mustique to view their wedding gift of a plot of land.

Within the office, Company finances were fast recouping, increased profits being shown in every department. The staff situation was less rosy, and there was a deputation to Cecil to say that no one wanted to work on Saturdays. This echoed the general trend, and as in many other business offices the decision was made to have a trial run of Saturday closing, followed by a review. Not without precedent, outside influences affected Company policy. It was found that the release of many men and women from Saturday work enabled families to engage in excursions and shopping together, and the move was popular. Universal Aunts' clients became accustomed to conducting business Monday to Friday, and so it remained.

There was a shuffle amongst the hierarchy. Bay, now that Company business was wholly on her shoulders, together with her continued involvement in the world of flying, decided to pass over her departmental work to her well-trained number two and not appear in the office daily. Molly Sheppard, having become a valuable member of the Accounts department, was offered a place on the Board and, after a month to consider the responsibility involved, she accepted. Her appointment took place from 1 January 1958, a day upon which another significant appointment was made when Miss Margaret Fry joined the staff of Universal Aunts. With the arrival of the new decade, Emmie relinquished the office administration which she had continued part-time and arranged to come in only on Fridays, on which days she would conduct any staff interviews.

It was therefore the eve of the company's fortieth birthday when Bay received an approach from Mrs Agnes Billiter, who offered her business Proxy Parents for sale. A meeting was arranged and Bay was to find out why this charming middle-aged lady, owner of a flourishing business of high reputation, wished to sell. Mrs Billiter, or Miss Turner as her workers called her, had married late in life and her husband was a partial invalid from war injuries. She had begun her company to support the family and had succeeded to the point of acquiring an invisible family of 1,000 children and some 250 workers. Now the Government had introduced the scheme whereby insurance must be paid on all workers who worked more than eight hours a week. The extra administrative burden had come at the same time as her husband's deteriorating health and Agnes Billiter felt herself unable to cope.

At Bay's request she made her company books available and the directors of Universal Aunts were not slow to see that Proxy Parents would be an enhancement to their own employment department. So the decision was made to purchase the goodwill. A figure of £500 was at first thought of; the Company auditors thought it too high and an offer of £300 was made and accepted. They had all liked and been much impressed by Agnes Billiter, and offered her the post of running the babysitting department which she happily accepted. By tragic irony Captain Billiter died one week after she became a Universal Aunt. Perhaps, however, it was best for her to be part of a group and no longer battling alone with ever-growing legislation.

Very quickly Agnes established her own distinctive place in the office. She gave the same care and efficiency to the babysitting department as she had given to building her own business; she soon had a complete rapport with the growing number of nannies, teachers and general babysitters on her books, the confidence of brisk hotel housekeepers, and quite a legion of mothers relying upon her utterly. There sat Agnes at her corner desk, pretty as a sugared almond, not too tall, pink and white, topped by shining silver hair, and immaculately dressed, often in a pale lavender, green, or blue wool dress and matching cardigan, set off by a discreet necklace of pearls or crystals, and always her engagement ring of turquoise. Soon her desk and bookshelf sported pots of flowering African violets, begonias, and geraniums, always in the pink of condition. Her top drawer held a bottle of eau-de-Cologne 'for cheering-up purposes' and she was to reign thus for seventeen years, quietly competent.

Agnes loved being an Aunt and her favourite quote from Jane Austen summed it all up for her. 'Now that you have become an aunt you are a person of some consequence. I have always maintained the importance of aunts! Help of all kinds at all times.'

It was clear that the addition of Proxy Parents had been a good one; there was no limit on the calls for those workers. In the first months one proxy mum, caring for the children of an American millionaire, did in fact marry him – a good beginning, though this was beyond the bounds of Auntish duties. More women were taking up careers and even more were sharing their husbands' lives and going on his business trips. Families were scattered, so that help was not to hand. Book a proxy parent!

'Can they be trusted with one's precious offspring and all one's worldly goods?' parents asked.

'Of course,' came the answer, 'the proxy mother has been hand-picked and vetted, and comes with impeccable references.'

She also came following a good pep-talk from Cecil. 'You must at all times display the invaluable gift of common sense. You will need it. You have to get used to a strange house; all houses are basically similar but it is the little things that take time to adjust to, such as the idiosyncrasies of a dishwasher and when to give it a thump! Remember where things go, especially with a determined crawler hell-bent on turning out cupboards. You have to cope with unknown localities, shopping, taking children to school, Brownie night in the dark, steep local hills covered in ice, and food – getting the right kind for instance, let us say for Americans, who think sausages are for dogs! Au pairs, granny or cleaner can be a hazard. So can a pet. You must plan for fun, activities and

outings; carry out an expedition rather than endure an aimless
weekend.' Cecil paused for a moment. 'Most of all you must remember
that you have no permanent place in the family, so give the children care
and comfort but remain detached and dispensable. Get to know places
and glimpse other lives; it is a lonely job having no social life of one's
own, but rewarding,' she ended.

Such was the popularity of the service that the *Daily Mail* thought it
worth a column and consulted Cecil. She described it admirably under
the heading 'Universal Aunts Proxy Parent Assignments'.

'Our organization is bent on disproving the theory that though you
can choose your friends you cannot choose your relations. Universal
Aunts provides instant kinswomen – they swoop into homes when
sickness or infidelity carries a wife away. At trifling cost, they provide the
service you would expect from a real dream of an Aunt.'

The Press commented, 'Their true value lies in their will to face the
unexpected.'

1960s

MARGARET

Forty years old – Margaret Fry – Walpole Street

1961 began for the Company as the year of adulation of Aunthood, for had not those most notable of *Universal Aunts* reached their fortieth birthday? It was an event that deserved not to go un-noticed.

'Forty Years Old –
Too old to be foolish
Young enough for action.'

'A happy band of 18 Universal Aunts in an office with a network of part-time Aunts and a grapevine of professional acquaintances.'

'Where to look for information
and whom to ask for help.'

'Common sense and mother-wit.'

So ran the headlines as *The Times* and others in the media kindly celebrated the occasion.

The Aunts themselves made brief comment and then got on with facing the next forty years. 'What attributes make a good Universal Aunt?' Cecil was asked.

'The ability to make a quick decision, a great deal of patience and tact and an unfailing sense of humour. Must have oodles of common sense and be able to cope and be – well – of a certain background,' she said.

'Why has your business continued to flourish?'

'People never seem to think of things on time; then they come to us,' was her quick answer.

Company's 40th Anniversary Miss Faulder called attention to the fact
that 1961 marked the 40th Anniversary of the Company, and she
proposed that a notice to this effect should be inserted in *The Times*
personal column. The Board were in unanimous agreement with this
proposal and the Chairman asked the Secretary to have the following
advertisement inserted on 23 February:

> 1921–1961 UNIVERSAL AUNTS LTD
> AFTER FORTY YEARS OF ACHIEVEMENT CARRY ON
> THEIR PERSONAL SERVICE IN THE TRADITION OF
> THEIR FOUNDER!

It was not *quite* to end there, for someone's niece decided to add her
point of view! In providing help of all kinds at all times, she suggested an
all-pervading omnipotence not entirely foreign to many Aunts.

A mere niece's-eye-view of Aunts – later with certain education of
being fifteen years an Aunt – I know what an Aunt's responsibilities
are and can recognize a good Aunt when I see one!
  She has:

Thought	can cope with deep silence produced by shyness.
Application	quick of intellect, nothing is deader than last year's slang and aunts must keep up to date; by 1949 super-duper was *out*, etc., etc.
Memory	remembers dates and birthdays
Punctuality	always where expected to be
Patience	up to the minute in present crazes and crushes. No silly ideas about right time for bed or early morning talking.
Reliability	has a range of handicrafts, clay and plasticine, easy reading, water pistols, and knows how to finish off knitting or leatherwork as a present for mother.
In short	she tries to produce order without authority, to get better results than mother with only half mother's weapons – and it's a tribute to her how often she succeeds.

Guide to good Aunting:
* In the war the best Aunts never used their sweet coupons.
* Anyone applying for an Aunt's post must possess encyclopaedic

knowledge of jet aircraft, no dislike of noise, a good collection of bus tickets and endless affection.
* Should be able to divine what is wrong with a pet mouse.
* An ability to juggle with and answer such diverse questions as:
'Well, if he's the Queen's husband, why isn't he King?' (constitutional law)
'But *how* is God everywhere?' (metaphysics)
'What makes bees fly, anyway?' (biology)
'Why can't boys wear bracelets?' (masculine etiquette).
* Hang on to your temper and count twenty when, having presented a cast-iron lucid exposition, you are greeted with an uncomprehending stare and some irrelevant remark – 'Oh, I wish I was a fish.'
* The height of the season for Aunts is around Christmas time when circuses, pantomimes and other excitements are rampant. Any holiday season is a busy time for Aunts and each requires its particular preparation – especially the beginnings and ends. The beginning's problems include whether to kiss your charge in front of his contemporaries and the exact present whereabouts of treasured pet or possession. At the end of the holidays, the sympathetic approach is called for – clean handkerchiefs to stem a tear, a promise to visit without fail, chocolate and potato crisps for the journey, and a parting ten-shilling note.
* Imagining that as school days pass, so do Auntly responsibilities – how wrong! Giving a roof while training is in progress in late teens for instance – comparing the troubles of childhood with the peccadilloes and pitfalls of young womanhood is like likening teething to appendicitis.
* Dispatch someone else's daughter to a dance with a young man whose intentions are no doubt honourable but are still unknown, while you watch the clock at home for their return.
* Once an Aunt, always an Aunt – when that splendid day is reached when you achieve the dignity and status of Great Aunthood (than which there is nothing more dignified) and a new, although less energetic career begins to open before you.

Cecil missed the staunch day-by-day support of Emmie and Bay; she found it a lonely task running the office single-handed and with no one off whom to bounce ideas. There was an obvious choice to remedy the situation: Margaret Fry, who had established herself in Accounts alongside the experienced Molly Sheppard. Fairly tall and sturdy, a tweed-and-twinset lady, upright and cultured, with a pastel appearance and silver hair, Molly often wore a fine, long, gold chain, at the end of which reposed a tiny gold whistle on which she occasionally blew a sharp blast as she walked around. When in the mood she would pause for a chat, ranging from travel, books and possibly a wireless programme she had enjoyed, to the merits of a Mason Pearson hairbrush which she strongly advocated (regularly rinsed in a sprinkling of Dettol and dried in the fresh air). She was an immaculate person in all ways, and although a Director, Molly did not seek a wider role than her calm and efficient attention to her book-keeping.

Margaret, on the other hand, was immensely interested in the entire business of the Company beyond her departmental duties. Into the Accounts department, being the heart of the business, came information from every department to feed her ideas for smooth running and greater efficiency. She was hardworking and far-seeing. The Directors' Report, instituted by her, catalogued the progress of the Company for posterity. Fresh on the scene, Margaret was struck by the variety of unusual assignments that came in almost daily and made it her duty to list them, a clever thought for which future Directors came to thank her. She put forward the suggestion that the newly popular Shannon filing system could benefit every department, to which the Board later gave their approval. Although not one for change for the sake of change, she was clearly a woman with vision.

Margaret was responsible for a striking change between management and staff. She politely but firmly requested Cecil, 'Miss Scott, now that we are all out of the army, I dislike and object to being called "Fry" in my working life.'

'I quite agree, Margaret,' said Cecil, and the habit ceased.

It was the 'old girls' network' that had brought Margaret Fry to Universal Aunts. Dorothy Tull had been educated at Godolphin some years before Margaret Fry, and it was in the way that headmistresses of course know everything, that Godolphins, when the time came, was able to put one 'old girl' seeking a job in touch with an even older 'old girl' with the right sort of contacts.

Margaret Fry had driven an American Red Cross ambulance during the war, which had been ended for her by the last but one V2. It caught her driving through Smithfield Market and she with many others ended up far below street-level with Smithfield on top of her. Neither

Margaret Fry nor history relates how she escaped, but she made sure to bring her co-driver out with her. When the pain, broken bones, traumas and horrors had receded enough, Margaret took up one or two less dangerous post-war pursuits. She loved clothes and went for a while into the exclusive Monica McGregor Salon in South Molton Street, where she stayed for eighteen months. There followed a year in Gloucester Square, personally assisting Lady Mayer during Sir Robert's preparation for his great Royal Concert. By 1950 Margaret was helping war-hero and explorer Captain Robert Ryder, RN, VC, the husband of a family friend, to canvass successfully for his seat in Parliament; she remained his secretary in the House for five rewarding and happy years. Then came the Aunts to fill her life.

Tall and striking in appearance, with the attractively unusual and distinctive colouring of auburn hair, brown eyes and fair complexion, she always appeared to enjoy clothes in joyful colours, wore them well, and set them off with carefully tended face, hair and nails. Popular in male and female company, she enjoyed entertaining and being entertained and had good, staunch friendships. Within the office Margaret was noted for reliability and expected the same from others. With her clear, decisive voice, she was a commanding and respected presence. No one seemed the least surprised when Cecil, going over to Paris for two days to interview the new 'shopper', Madame Adamian, left Margaret in charge of office matters.

Universal Aunts had been ensconced for so long in Wilton Place that they were part of the landscape there, as was indicated in *The Times* by the bard of property selling, Roy Brooks.

Good 14-year lease only £110 p.a. £4,995. Typical English Gentleman's Town House, slightly shabby, supremely comfortable and quiet where Group Captain sojourns between astonishing adventures; he spent 18 months in jail behind Iron Curtain for rescuing a beautiful political prisoner.
Underground maids' room with HIDDEN bath. Withered garden with trees – strategically placed twixt fashionable Church and Paradise (a striptease club). Universal Aunts are just round the corner in case of need.

Horrid rumours were, however, circulating that there were plans for Wilton Place which involved demolition and a linking of the area into

Sloane Street and Brompton Road. Although the current lease had two more years to run, as Cecil said, 'If in fact the building remains and becomes part of this new area, Knightsbridge rents are going to be far higher than the present £800 p.a.'

It was agreed to put out feelers for alternative accommodation; and after several obvious non-starters, 36 Walpole Street was found, just a few streets away and into Chelsea. It was the ground floor of a block of more recent flats at the King's Road end of the pleasant eighteenth-century street. A heavy outer door led into a lobby, from which glass-panelled swing doors gave on to a square hall with a large reception room on either side. Stretching beyond was a corridor with five rooms of various sizes strung along the left-hand side and windows lining the opposite wall. All was painted pale green and white, with nice parquet floors.

By July of 1962, Bay had negotiated a seven-year lease on the property (at £2,000 rent per annum, £200 rates and £100 service charge), and had managed to unload the remains of the lease on Wilton Place. She circulated a letter to the staff:

Arrangements for our new premises at 36 Walpole Street are now completed and we hope to be able to move into these on or about October 1st. As I expect you all realize, this move, which had become inevitable owing to future redevelopment plans for this building, will be a very heavy expense for the Company, and will entail a very large increase in rent. In order to meet these increased expenses the Board has given a great deal of thought as to possible means of increasing efficiency, obtaining new business, and raising fees where possible. This last decision has already been carried out and if we can maintain our business on even the present scale it should go some way to meeting our higher overheads.

The Board has also had to give much consideration to the basis on which we pay commission . . . Each department will bear a proportion of the rent and overheads, and the commission payable after deducting the higher expenses will be at the rate of 33½% instead of 15% as heretofore . . . While it is inevitable that for the moment commission will be less than in the past, you will realize that on the new basis it could be very high should we succeed in making a good profit.

As regards efficiency; the Board has decided that in future all

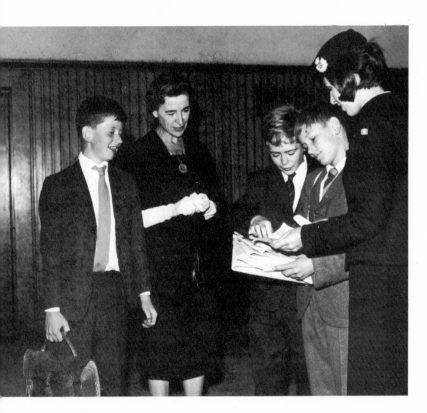

The '60s: happy travellers with their 'impeccable Aunt'

The office team in the '80s: back row from the left, Jenny, Sue, Joy, Rosemary; front row, Rhonda, Maureen (holding Galaxy) and Marion

Aunts at work: Daphne, Betty and Christine matching fabrics

Neville, the Universal Uncle,
on passport duty

Peggy at the airport

Margaret Fry   Penelope Henshaw

Angela chooses plants for a special
delivery

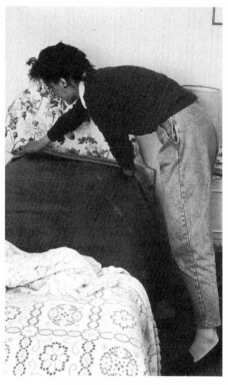

Alexandra prepares an Executive
House for its occupant

Louisa steps in when a mother is in hospital

Super cooks – Bridget and Sue

Jo and Elsie delivering children to Lulu at her Dawmouse Nursery

accounts rendered will be handled by the Accounts Department . . .
thus releasing the staff to deal with their departmental work. It must
however be stressed that it is absolutely essential that the necessary
details should be most meticulously passed to the Accounts Department so that the rendering of the bills can be dealt with quickly and
smoothly.

Another matter in which the staff can be of the greatest assistance
in increasing efficiency is in the matter of filing. It is essential to have a
well worked out method and to be sure it is carried out . . . Personally I
consider that an extra half hour keeping such matters up to date can
save hours of unnecessary work later. Miss Fry or Miss Ockenden will
be pleased to explain anything which is not clear.

We are certainly going to meet a challenge in the new premises and
I hope that everyone will meet it with enthusiasm and a determination
to make the 'Aunts' bigger and better.

Margaret wrote to Bay, enclosing the yearly report for her to read and
edit. Bay returned it promptly, without any alterations, and commented:
'I always feel very guilty that you should have to write the Directors'
Report, but I do feel that without the minute book and a more personal
memory of the various happenings which one has when on the spot, I, for
one, could never do it properly.' She added:

I am glad to hear you are all so busy but shudder to think what it will be
like moving. I wonder if I could be of any help if I came up to London
for a day or two? People will have to arrange their own rooms and I
don't feel I should be much good interviewing, but there might be odd
jobs. You can let me know when we meet next week.

In fact, everything moved faster than expected and was ready by 10
August. It was a gigantic move this time, involving the business effects
and paraphernalia of forty-one years. Even some unclaimed parcels from
the war storage were found in cupboards and were transported intact in
their old bomb-dusty wrappings and carefully re-stored. Removal vans,
and individuals with their cars stuffed with possessions, ferried back and
forth. There had been a slight reorganization of work within the
departments and each was allocated a room, reception being placed on
the left of the entrance, the Directors' and accounts room on the right.
The bustle of setting things into place took two days, and on the 13th the

office was open for business. When the dust had settled, the company was honoured by a welcoming visit from the Mayor and Mayoress of Kensington and Chelsea, who made a conducted tour of the departments.

The basic nature of the company was changing as fast as its inhabitants. What could originally have been loosely called domestic placings had gradually been enlarged. An increasing number of women were on the register wanting 'white collar jobs' in the home as chauffeuses, gardeners, and personal assistants. Training opportunities for women had brought in those looking for clerical, secretarial and receptionist or switchboard work. The number of employers was very satisfactorily keeping pace with, if not outstripping, the applicants, and the company began professional advertising, no longer for ladies in reduced circumstances to act as dogsbodies for ladies who had not been similarly reduced: 'Would *you* like to be one of London's most sought-after women? Important men begging for your company? You don't need the face and figure of a beauty queen. You just need to be a typist. One firm has provided a swimming pool. One, cream cakes free with morning tea. A 16-year-old can earn £14 a week and a top secretary £1,500 a year plus luncheon vouchers,' ran the more modern agency advertisements.

The placing of office workers was the province of the private agency, and the network between them and the employers worked well. Employers and workers felt a personal and sympathetic attention to their needs, and the conduct of the agency was safeguarded on their behalf by the expulsion of wrongdoers from the Federation and licences being revoked or refused. Non-members of the Federation were best not dealt with. Unfortunately a man in the Ministry of Labour had a bright idea and in October 1964 a Placement Service was opened in Holborn to deal exclusively with office-workers. For five years the Custom and Treasury Controls had battled against what in their view was an added burden on the Exchequer with the cost of financing such a government department when private agencies, under certain safeguards, were fulfilling this role at a charge not to the already burdened taxpayer but to the employer who could afford it. Custom and Treasury Controls churned out their watchdog statements about burdens on taxpayers, and free enterprise; as the Ministry grew bigger and bigger, presumably they didn't listen.

At the same time, in came the 'domestics' from Lavender Hill,

Battersea, Clapham and Wandsworth; the cleaning fraternity who were beginning to find that an agency did better bargaining on their behalf than they did themselves.

As well as the Ministry, other bodies were also making innovations, and someone opened the paper in the office one morning and read out: '*Ladies, You May Now Smoke.*' Following the headline, she went on, '*Women smokers, it has been decided by the General Hospital Health Committee, may take their cigarettes with them on admission to hospital, except when it would harm themselves or their fellows. Individual hospitals will have the right of final decision.*'

'We shall soon have smoking allowed in offices,' added a different voice.

'Hardly likely,' was the response from another desk.

It was a time when companies vied, with stylish little handouts, for avid newsreaders; and Cecil no less than others came up with some gems. For London:

Help with spring cleaning? More business firms are making a point of sending their executives abroad during March and April so that wives can carry out their spring-cleaning unchecked. So that he does not return to curtainless windows, coverless chairs and the all pervading smells of soap and paint – it is worth remembering that you can acquire that other pair of hands from Universal Aunts.

For New York:

To prepare our New York representative, should she be called upon to advise the well-dressed American this year, we have done our homework, with no less a person than the manager of the gentlemen's department of Saks. There is, of course, a well-known diversity of sartorial correctness in these matters between the Englishman and the American.

Taboo: Tan shoes with dark blue suits. Sports shoes with business clothes, except for smart slip-ons, which are no longer considered strictly for sportswear. Soiled white buckskin shoes.

For stout men: Loud colours and bold patterns should be avoided; rough, heavy fabrics should be passed up. Extremely short jackets accent portliness. Practically all else, in the endless range of men's fashions, is completely proper for the overweight man.

> Fashion highlight: Due to the growing popularity of fancy breast-pocket handkerchiefs, co-ordinating ties and eyeglass cases in foulard patterns are being well received in the United States. The top of the eyeglass case looks like a squared-off handkerchief when carried in the breast pocket.

By chance it was discovered that Margaret was adroit at advertising copy and Cecil was glad to pass it over to her. Margaret's fund of everyday information was also put to use when a special service had to be set up.

'There is no such thing as "we can't do it"; just hedge for time until you have worked out *how* to do it,' she often advised.

A harassed member of staff, groaned, 'We have to arrange to dispatch a Santa Claus to arrive in the South of France on Christmas morning, where one of our clients is entertaining his twelve grandchildren.'

Margaret looked up briefly from her desk. 'Presumably we do not need an export licence for him, so it shouldn't be difficult,' she said.

17

1960s

MRS DALE'S DIARY

Business survey – Mrs Dale's Diary – Days at work –
50th anniversary – Exodus

Bay was, of course, part of the old days and old ways but was determined in her aim to set the Company on its new course. To this end she commissioned Messrs Gordon Rayment, management consultants, to carry out a survey. The Board studied the report and expressed a collective opinion that Gordon Rayment was aiming at a larger and more elaborate business than the Company wished to have. However, some of their recommendations were adopted, together with the Shannon filing system that Margaret had hoped for previously. A staff letter went out:

> I feel sure that you are all wondering what the outcome has been of the detailed study of our organization carried out by Mr Evers of Gordon Rayment Ltd . . .
>
> The principal weakness which they have found in our organization may be summed up in over-departmentalization resulting in a lack of co-ordination where a client's needs may cover the services of several departments, and possibly in a lack of knowledge by one department of another's work and a lack of appreciation by the staff that in an organization such as ours the whole is far more efficient than any one part could be . . . Growing from a small staff willing to tackle any enquiry, departments were formed specializing in our various activities. These have tended again to subdivide, thus losing the co-ordination with which we started . . .
>
> The Board have, as you know, already started to centralize the accounts . . . We are also hoping to adopt gradually a card-indexing system for all departments which, while meeting their special needs, will be uniform so far as possible and make use of the same type of material such as cards etc. . . .

In order to relieve Miss Scott, who carried the burden of management in addition to her departmental work, Miss Fry will take over the
routine running of the departments so that minor queries can go to
her and Miss Scott will have fewer interruptions.

The Board have asked her to impress on all staff the importance of
punctuality which has become a little lax lately. One should realize
that 12 minutes lost each morning amounts to an hour a week. Also it
gives a very bad impression if clients ring up at 9.30 and have to be
told that the person they wish to speak to is not there. The hour before
interviewing hours is a most useful time for clearing up any back log. It
has always been a rule of the Universal Aunts that staff should not
smoke during interviewing hours in the departments and the Board
would like this rule adhered to. Also staff should not be seen having
snacks at their desks. These minor details do give a bad impression.
Telephones, which are always over-burdened, should not be used for
private calls unless there is a real necessity.

It seems that smoking in the office had become acceptable after all.

Cecil was reading the morning post. 'Margaret, I have a rather nice
invitation from BBC Radio, that Universal Aunts could be brought into
the programme *Mrs Dale's Diary*,' she said, looking across the room at
Margaret.

'Very good publicity for us in such a popular series,' answered
Margaret.

'Just what I hoped you'd say.' Cecil passed over the letter. 'I will leave
you to telephone Mr Antony and arrange a meeting – it's more your
line than mine.'

Margaret felt anxious about her ignorance of script and recording, but
the kind and professional Jonquil Antony soon eased that. Margaret
was invited down to Portland Place to sit, earphones attached, in a small
room and watch a recording session through a glass screen. By the time
it was all over she walked out of Broadcasting House feeling quite 'one
of them'. Then the script arrived with a note from Jonquil Antony,
hoping that she would not find it silly, and adding a postscript: 'Do
say if you think anything should be changed.' It was the first script
Margaret had seen, and it all seemed a bit naïve. As she said to Jonquil
Antony, 'There are discrepancies between the script and the real-life
form of our interviews. For one thing, we would not have offered Mrs
Dale any jobs until we had her references.'

'Only so much factual material can be included in a script. Specific detail doesn't always come across well, so with a true story I have the unpopular job of adjusting it for the media,' Jonquil Antony replied, quite used to overcoming the qualms of a 'new girl'. 'The reading of a script by the uninitiated is a somewhat flat experience – it comes to life enacted over the air,' he concluded.

The whole thing went happily ahead; a great experience, nice people to work with, and much enjoyed by Margaret. The result, publicity-wise, was a small rush of dithery ladies who clearly identified with Mrs Dale and thought that they too could 'Aunt' without much effort. On the other hand, some listeners had not realized the range of the Aunts' work and rang in to ask. That was good for business.

MRS DALE: (diffidently) Of course, you must think it absolutely absurd that someone like myself should come to your agency and expect to get a job – I – I haven't any real qualifications at all –

MISS FRY: I'm sure we can find you something! We get all sorts of enquiries.

MRS D.:   Yes, but at my age – I mean, I'm a sort of middle-aged housewife and I haven't any real qualifications, not like a – a degree – or having been a teacher before I was married. I don't type or do shorthand, but I always understood that this particular agency didn't specialize entirely in that sort of thing.

MISS F.:   We find all sorts of jobs for all sorts of people. Now, if you'd give me your name – and address –

MRS D.:   Mrs Mary Dale, Virginia Lodge, Parkwood Hill . . .

MISS F.:   Telephone number?

MRS D.:   Verity 2341 –

MISS F.:   Well, what sort of thing would you say you are good at? You can cook, I'm sure, and of course, we always need people for babysitting –

MRS D.:   Oh . . . I . . . well, I mean . . . that's the kind of thing I'm doing all the time. I was rather hoping for something different . . . The money doesn't matter so much, it's just the interest of it – a change, you know, from the sort of life I lead –

MISS F.:   Yes, I do understand that, Mrs Dale. Now . . . I was just

	thinking, I do have a temporary job for next week that you might do for, it's rather nice – helping someone move into a flat, she's a very interesting and busy woman, a publisher, and she needs someone to help her just next week.
MRS D.:	Oh . . . I'm . . . I'm afraid next week . . . you see, my daily help – I – well, I have to give her a couple of days off. My mother will be at home but I – I do rather wonder if next week – perhaps I ought to start the week after –
MISS F.:	Well, we can find something for the week after, I'm sure. What about a job in a flower shop – are you interested in flowers?
MRS D.:	Oh, yes, I am! And gardening is something I do know about!
MISS F.:	It's off Berkeley Square – rather a smart place. The hours are nine to six and Saturday mornings up to one –
MRS D.:	No . . . I'm afraid that's no good. I – I couldn't be away from home all the time . . . perhaps a part-time job – I'm so sorry –
MISS F.:	Well . . . now let's see then . . . There's a part-time job here which might suit you rather well. A companion to an old lady – a client of our's mother – she's not the *old* type at all, very forceful, very intelligent – and a little bit domineering, her daughter says –
MRS D.:	Looking after someone's mother? Very – forceful and – and a bit domineering . . . oh . . . I – it sounds rather like my own mother who lives with us – it – it –
MISS F.:	(laughs) It wouldn't be a change at all?
MRS D.:	No . . . not really. I'm afraid I'm quite hopeless. I ought not to have come here at all.
MISS F.:	Now look here, Mrs Dale, I think this might suit you. Here's an afternoon job in a bookshop, two to six, in the King's Road, Chelsea. Interesting, quite well paid – it's five pounds a week – and they want someone at once. Today, in fact. So if you could go and see the owner this afternoon, she's there from three onwards – I believe this would just suit you!
MRS D.:	I – I don't think I could go and see her this afternoon – would tomorrow morning do?

MISS F.:   Well, no . . . she won't be there. She wants it settled today.

MRS D.:   I have to mind my grandchildren this afternoon! I – I've said I'll go! Oh . . . how absurd of me to imagine I ever could get out of – of all my family commitments. (suddenly) And I'm not really sure that I want to now . . . I'm so sorry.

MISS F.:   Well . . . I've got an idea, Mrs Dale. Suppose we put you down on our Emergency Rota?

MRS D.:   Emergency?

MISS F.:   Yes, we have several people on it. It's for odd jobs that come in, all sorts, cooking, shopping, minding children, meeting children and dogs off trains – oh, all sorts of things!

MRS D.:   Oh, yes, I think I'd like that!

MISS F.:   It's all rather the kind of thing you've been doing for yourself, but of course, it's what you could do and it has variety. And if you can't do the job when we ring up you have only to say so and we ring somebody else.

MRS D.:   I believe that would be exactly right for me! (she sighs) I can only do the things I *can* do, after all!

MISS F.:   It's not much money, five shillings for the first hour and three shillings after that – but most people do it for the interest –

MRS D.:   The money . . . oh, I don't really mind about it, you see. I think I should like doing it very much and it doesn't take me long to get up to town.

MISS F.:   I'll put your name down now then –

MRS D.:   Yes . . . thank you . . . But – er – not on Wednesday or Friday of next week, or Saturday morning . . . Oh, Friday might be all right – er – and of course, on Wednesday I suppose my mother –

MISS F.:   (laughs) We'll ring you up when we want you, Mrs Dale – and you can decide then and there if you can do the job! And I'm sure we can find you plenty to do. Somebody like you can be very valuable to us.

MRS D.:   (surprised) Valuable! I thought I'd be no good at all to you!

MISS F.:   But of course! People like you – who've brought up

families, run homes, coped with emergencies – you've
got the most valuable thing of all for this kind of job, Mrs
Dale – you've got *experience* – and that's what's needed!
(Fade)

'Reception' at Walpole Street soon came to be reigned over by two
indomitable ladies of advancing age, one for morning duty and one for
afternoons. Phyllis (a.m.) had been an army wife, engaged in regimental
pursuits, caring for her baby daughter Jill, and in time following her
husband on retirement from the army into the racing world, where he
took an appointment. Phyllis had been a widow for a year when in 1960
she joined her daughter to live in London, bringing with her the other
apple of her eye, Charlie, an ageing dachshund. Jill had become an
actress, and when she was 'resting' from that career she was a part-time
Universal Aunt. By then, Phyllis was dreadfully crippled with arthritis
that bent her small body forward and twisted her hands into painful
knots. None of that dimmed her sweet smile and pretty face beneath
neatly waved hair.

'I've brought Mummy in to register as an Aunt,' said Jill as she
introduced her mother to Cecil. Within a week Phyllis was recruited to
stay for a month at the Ritz as companion to a lonely American who had
also recently become a widow, but a rather richer one. Even if her Ritzy
days were past, it was very much Phyllis' scene. The evening routine
required the two ladies to make a social effort, to be dressed and
jewelled and promenade along to a table in the rose-and-gilt arbour
where Michael poured them a glass or two of champagne before dinner,
under the gaze of painted cherubs. Four such weeks had a beneficial
effect on both the widows and Phyllis decided that working for the Aunts
was a very good idea! When she was offered the vacancy of part-time
receptionist in the office, she took it without a qualm. But mastering the
plugs and wires of a switchboard, and the hustle and noise of office life,
proved something of a shock. Within a week she headed for her doctor.
'Please, a short course of tranquilizers to help me survive the trial
month,' she begged.

By the end of that month, Phyllis had the calm assurance of a
seasoned receptionist. The routine ran smoothly, callers were put at
east, and Phyllis had become friend and confidante of every member of
staff. She remained so for fifteen years.

On the brink of every afternoon shift, Rosie would arrive to take over.

A handsome, robust, craggy lady, her ample form thrown into a dress that was usually black, she removed Phyllis's nest of cushions from the low switchboard chair, settled herself in, and lit her first cigarette of the afternoon. Rosie's academic husband had died young, many years before, since when much of her time had been devoted to the considerable task of editing the official newspaper of her church. A careless aura surrounded her; a spectacular diamond ring encircled one of the slender fingers that raked through her mane of hair at regular intervals during the afternoon. Ash spilled and was brushed off. Her commanding bark, 'Come in, come in, don't stand in the door!' did nothing for first impressions – but these were not always right. Having drawn one near, Rosie got down to the task of sorting one out in a most kindly fashion. Should it be a terrified foreigner, he or she might well encounter that almost unheard-of courtesy, an Englishwoman with an excellent and charming command of their language, for she had several besides her own.

To complete the line-up, there was the stand-in, 'the floater', who came in when one of the others wanted to be away. Hazel was tiny and pretty. For her to have been twice widowed was sad, because she really needed to be looked after. She seemed delightfully vague, but her telephone conversations belied the fact that she coped most efficiently. Listeners might well feel bewildered to hear her trill, 'Mrs Watson, I've got that –' a slight pause as Hazel's forehead wrinkled thoughtfully – 'Oh, no, of course, I'm Mrs Watson, who are you?'

Earphones in place, each of the trio received dozens of daily calls. 'I wonder if you can help me . . .' A flick of a switch through to the departments followed, and frequent asides to anyone (or no one) passing through reception.

'Could you arrange to have six pairs of my socks darned?' asked a pleasant male voice.

'A conventional sort of man. We used to do a lot of that but it died out with man-made fibres.'

'I would like someone to paint my bathroom,' a lady said.

'There was a time when we had a flourishing interior decorating department, but it's now all done by the professionals or do-it-yourself operators. It would be good to corner a little of that business again.'

'Could you transport a lavatory from Acton to Guildford?' asked a harassed voice.

'I wonder why the owner is loath to leave it behind when he moves?'

'May we give you an order to deliver lunch every day to a man on remand in Brixton?' was a hopeful query.

'I've never been to prison!'

'I don't know whether you deal with livestock, but there is a curly chocolate poodle to be transported to Korea,' said a veterinary voice.

'We quite often pack a pet.'

'May we have two Universal Aunts to take the names of mourners at a memorial service?'

'Vera Bremner-Myers and Peggy Furneaux are most suitable.'

'I am a collector of the miniature "match-box" series of vehicles and have several numbers missing. What cost to commission you to find them?' enquired an American.

'Time and persistence needed here.'

Within the departments it was a different story. There the problems had to be resolved and assignments fulfilled. The character of a department grew out of the nature of its work, and its competence out of the character of its head. In Accommodation, for instance, it was necessary to be compassionate but practical: the head of department who let tears trickle down her cheeks as she listened to some of the stories had to be moved to a jollier desk. The elderly widower looking for somewhere safe and cosy and someone with old-fashioned standards was pretty certain to melt the hearts of a room full of women.

The Accommodation department had its quota of woolly-hatted ladies whom life had thrown into a persistent search for a corner to call their own, where they wouldn't be put upon, or put out, at somebody's whim. This group had to be disappointed so often, for the sad and simple reason that they could pay little and they were going to be *stayers*. Landladies wanted a good rent and *movers-on*. They had frequently lived at home in the orbit of 'Daddy'; he as frequently seemed to depart this life, leaving an unwordly, untrained daughter in her late forties and enough sporting debts and bad investments to render her homeless and almost penniless. She often had a little dog with faded fur and worn yellow teeth – an added disincentive to the landlady. The mistress would be thin as a stick and faintly blue, her pet over-plump. Sometimes a happier solution could be found.

'Hello, Miss P, come along in.'

'I'm here again, I know you *do* keep me in mind, but I always think it's a good idea to keep in touch.'

'That's all right. I know you're very anxious.'

'Well, at the hostel they have warned us that they will bring in the higher spring and summer prices on the first of January, Victoria being so sought after by tourists, and that isn't long ahead.'

'Miss P, I know it isn't ideal, but I want you to consider one possibility that came in early today. A very nice, elderly, but quite fit, lady is offering accommodation in lieu. She has a flat here in Whitelands House and is offering a large, sunny bed-sitting room and no rent, in return for having her breakfast and a light supper prepared.'

'I could easily do that, it sounds too good to be true. Could I go and see her?'

Within an hour, both old ladies had agreed terms and there seemed reason to hope for a successful outcome.

A small family group from abroad arrived to ask for budget ac-commodation while 'doing' London in a week. A couple of American college boys came round the door looking for two nights' bed and breakfast.

'What have you seen on your travels?' they were asked.

'Yesterday we went to *Blenhime* where Winston Churchill came from,' was the answer.

'And what did you think of it?'

'It was *neat!*' Which seemed one up on the British for understatement.

The phone buzzed and the head of Accommodation was summoned to a client waiting in reception – a very large, very black, lady made even taller by the height of her spike-heeled sandals, wrapped in a ginger fur coat and topped by a wide, floppy-brimmed, black straw hat with a huge pink rose centre front. A little gaudy, perhaps, but otherwise she seemed normal, until she outlined the purpose of her visit. 'I am Queen B–. I need a guardian family for my two children.'

'How old are they?'

'The princes are eleven and twelve. They will come to school in England.'

Nothing out of the ordinary there. 'I see. Well, we don't arrange any kind of legal guardianship but we do have some nice hostesses on our books who are sometimes able to take over school holidays, visiting the children at school, shopping for them and so on.'

'That might do. First we got to get them away from their father, the King, who keeps them in Africa.'

First seeds of suspicion that all was not as it should be. 'Well, as the boys are so young you would have to talk again with your husband, the

King, about this and when it is all fixed up and their school here
arranged, I shall be very happy to do what I can to help you.'

A contented expression replaced the alert wariness of the Queen's
plump, shining face. 'OK. I'll go and ask him. He's at Buckingham
Palace having lunch with your Queen just now. I was asking your lady,'
pointing to the switchboard, 'which bus I get to go there. But first I need
to buy a petticoat and she says try Peter Jones.' She heaved her
mountainous self off the chairs and shook hands all round. 'Many
thanks. I'll be back with the King.' And off she went.

It can sometimes be hard to unravel fact from fiction. But one thing
was certain; that day's Court Circular announced Her Majesty to be in
residence at Windsor for Christmas, not in London, and no visiting
potentates had been entertained to luncheon.

As time crept towards the fiftieth anniversary, more changes came
about. Bay's younger sister, the Hon Eveleigh Leith, was elected on to
the Board. Her first task was to finalize the work study of the '60s into
Company policy for the next decade, a matter that was taken so seriously
that an experienced woman executive, Miss Anne Carr, was co-opted
from outside, from 'big business', to form, with Eveleigh and Margaret,
a working committee whose job it was to keep the programme on course.

There were more resignations and replacements. Emmie left the
Board and became Consultant. Molly resigned from the Accounts
department but remained as a Director. Less expected was Cecil's
shock decision to retire and live permanently in Switzerland where her
sister Phyllis had become resident a few years earlier. The natural ·
successor was Margaret, who joined the Board and became Managing
Director on 26 January 1967. She elected two replacements: Diana
Marno, who had served under Molly for almost nine years; and a new
girl, Lola Lumb, a family friend who had been widowed in the war and
whose son and daughter were now out in the world, enabling her to take
up employment. This she did, joining Universal Aunts to run the
Flat-letting department.

New Directors, new moves. The best of the European finishing
schools had been known and frequently visited by the much-travelled
former Directors, so that the Company had for years provided an
advisory service to parents on the best school for their daughters. The
new Directors were not sufficiently in touch to provide such expert
advice, so Margaret arranged to pass that business to the oldest
educational consultants, Gabbitas Thring. In return, Gabbitas placed

their student-accommodation business in the hands of the Aunts, who already ran their own and were glad to enlarge their list of landladies. It was a beneficial shuffle for both companies' expansion.

Another expansion came through an approach from Mrs Lyford-Pike, owner of the exclusive Jean Hamilton secretarial bureau in Beauchamp Place. She wished to sell, the Aunts to acquire a bigger secretarial section.

The Press took note of the Aunts' fiftieth birthday. Denis Hamilton of Times Newspapers Ltd wrote to say that *The Times* Women's Page had already made plans to notice Universal Aunts' fiftieth anniversary, and cordially wishing them well for the next fifty years. He ended, 'Long may you continue your good work.'

It fell to Margaret's lot to be interviewed; and the Press used several statments that she made.

> The world has become a bit impersonal now – all we do is give the kind of service that once could be got as a right . . . There are so many 'problem agencies' in London now, you'd hardly think there would be room for one more . . . We're a small community, it's better that we're of a kind . . . Parents manage on their own for fifty weeks of the year and get a Universal Aunt Proxy Parent for the other two while they get away from it all.

Bay, who had been taking a back seat more and more because of increasing deafness, held a Board meeting so that an important complaint could be aired. The modern travelling schoolboys hated to wear the old Universal Aunts labels with their boldly printed instructions for all to see. Bay suggested round lapel badges in the Company's coral colour, bearing a simple UA in black. The boys could pass that off as anything they wished while still being identifiable, the old labels being consigned to the luggage. That simple updating of Universal Aunts' symbol brought Bay's reign to an end. She retired to her cottage at Friston on the east coast, and being an excellent correspondent kept well in touch with her range of personal interests and friends. Eveleigh took her place as Chairman of the Company and Bay remained, for the time being, on the Board as a non-working Director.

18

1970S

NEW BROOMS

On with the job

The early 1970s saw an influx of new staff who were to be trained into the ways of the Company by Margaret and become the longest-lasting group in its history.

Jean, married and the mother of a schoolgirl daughter, came into reception when the two part-timers, Phyllis and Rosie, retired. Jenny, a widow with three teenagers, came to run Employment. Joy, a widow with two sons at Harrow, joined Accounts. Margaret, the young one, always called Mary in the office, came on from her job with Hardy Amies to run the Accommodation department. Marion came for a part-time retirement job after some years in the City. She was a war-widow with a son on his way to becoming an admiral and a daughter on her way up to a place in the world of business. Her 'retirement' became a joke; it turned out to be a hectic, full-time job as the Special Services department grew bigger.

Two others came in on the ground floor and their progress was to be rather different from their expectations.

A letter from Kate Herbert-Hunting to family.

50 Chester Square
SW 1.
21 February 1972

As you know, Elizabeth urged me along to Universal Aunts – 'Where else?' she said, saying that I was now going to need an occupation outside home and children. She knows the Managing Director, Miss Margaret Fry, and an appointment was made, which I was dreading, not having either looked for employment nor met a lady Managing Director before. Miss Fry's manner was courteous and her nice smile never wavered as she took down the answers to the fearsome questions, their customary way of assessing one's suitability to join the ranks. Recently widowed mother of three with a twenty-one-year-old Landrover, up from the country! was all that sprang to mind. With a little prompting, more of my 'qualifications' came to light. Nevertheless, upon reading it back, I began to wish I hadn't come.

'I imagine common sense has held you in good stead in your busy family life?' enquired Miss Fry. I laughed. It occurred to me that it had. 'Our work needs a good deal of that,' she smiled and went on, 'We often interview recruits at a time when they have suffered some personal change in their lifestyles. Why do you wish to work for us?'

I said the first thing that came into my head and later realized that it was the true answer. 'This work seems to be an extension of what I've always done and that is what I like doing.' I then muttered, 'Also, I think the best thing for my children now is not to become a "wearisome widow"!'

'Good. We do not take on Universal Aunts to solve *their* problems,' she said briskly. 'It is sometimes difficult, however, for a woman who had been king-pin of her own world to adjust to *taking* orders, not *giving* them. That is the test.' Food for thought in *that* remark, I began to realize after only one day! The interview ended there as I was offered the job of running Special Services (almost anything for anyone), at a salary of £1800 p.a. on a month's trial to see if I *can* manage that vital adjusting!

So today, my first, has been an enlightening and gruelling day. All I feel really is a jumble of sensations but you will be glad to know that the over-riding one is the niceness of the people themselves.

I wasn't the only new one today; there is Marion Berlyn. She is an older and more experienced woman than I, the widow of a Naval Commander, so while bringing up her children she has worked in shipping in the City. She has retired from that now and joined UAs as a part-timer, for a less hectic occupation. She is very elegant and terribly nice.

One feels among friends. A good thing too, because one also feels pretty stupid.

Even answering the telephone in an office – the noises off make it impossible to hear, and why are other typewriters quite different from one's own at home? I spoiled so many sheets of expensively headed paper that I secreted them in my bag. At my age it doesn't seem quite the thing to be feeling and behaving as though one is back at school!

Special Services, my department, turns out to be the hub of a quite amazing selection of services, of which Miss Fry spent a large part of the day telling me and instructing me as to the way in which one must handle the job. I also met some of the workers – the UAs who go out and actually fill the assignments. I think few of us would ever have a real Aunt around whose family feeling would rise to some of these tasks! They are a variety of types, resting actresses, teachers on holiday, girls like Angie, widows, ex-nurses and social workers, and wives and mothers who now have time to give. *What* a work-force; and it seems that they walk through the door.

I'm too new to know, but it certainly seems to be something one could find very worthwhile.

A letter from Penelope Henshaw to family.

> North End House
> W14.
> 8 May 1972

Today has been my first in the new venture and although one shouldn't perhaps make such an early decision – I do think it is going to turn out to be what I have been seeking.

As you know, since my return from Kenya I have been in search of the right occupation. I believe in Universal Aunts I have found it. I enjoyed my years in Charity work, but private business somehow has a more exciting feel to it – a challenge – and although this one has been here for fifty-one years – to keep going and succeed.

When the Managing Director, Miss Margaret Fry, interviewed me, I made no secret of my hopes and aims to take a place in the Company should I prove to be what they want.

I have taken over as head of a department – Meetings. This is the backbone of the organization, the money spinner. It entails the whole and somewhat complex meeting, escorting and sometimes putting-up of some six hundred or more children at the beginning and end of each term and half term!

By the end of today, I am bewildered but determined, and have two obviously first-class workers in the department, most experienced, Charlotte and Carolyn.

I like the people here, every one of a muchness and though ages seem to range quite widely it doesn't seem to come into it at all.

Miss Fry clearly keeps a very keen eye on new girls, in fact on old ones too! Although this may be a bit unnerving, it is also a great help. She also gives one a commentary on other activities in the Company, this too is good so that one does not feel isolated and can learn about and relate to the thing as a whole.

She seems very much a strict but fair-minded headmistress and one has the urge to stand up when she enters!

Charles and his friend were with us last week. He had just returned from Washington and in an idle moment on the plane he thumbed through a guide book and there, under London, he read: 'The British think of everything. A Universal Aunt escort agency specializing in middle-aged women to take care of young children travelling on their own.'

He didn't know whether to be pleased or sorry about my new job!

I have so far only glimpsed the other departments but they seem equally hectic and the reception room today seemed always crowded. A lot of *au pair* girls passing through – in great demand with domestic help a problem and apparently now that there is less money for finishing schools, our girls are keen to get a year in Europe.

It seems that Universal Aunts has just acquired the Jean Hamilton secretarial bureau, who join our secretarial dept. this coming October, bringing their entire staff with them.

With children en route back to school, I have today met a lot of the UAs themselves, who do the escorting. All part-time and I liked them exceedingly and their dedication is enormous – winners all.

One told me of an incident with her small charge when she put him on the plane for his holidays in Bahrain three weeks ago. She was well en route for Heathrow when he tugged her sleeve and said, 'I've got an awful confession. I left my pet mouse in your sofa. I couldn't get him out.' Having got that off his chest, he brightened. 'But it doesn't matter. I've got another in my pocket.'

She seemed to take it quite in her stride and when I asked her what she did, she said she enticed it out of her sofa and kept it safely until his return journey this morning and the two are reunited!

On my remarking to Miss Fry my admiration for these workers, she told me that I would find the high quality of these women, some trained, some not, who because of home commitments can only work part-time, means that they achieve more in their hours than those who flit from job to job working full-time. She said that many of these women are better than they think they are and just need bolstering as a start.

I feel I have an awful lot to learn.

In one incident, Miss Fry showed me how the job should be done – I only hope I may sometime achieve the same sang-froid!

Following an operation, a small boy arrived en route for two months' leave from school with his parents in West Africa. Slight snag! (am I getting the right feel already?) his passport, vaccination certificate and ticket had been left at school in Yorkshire. Miss Fry seized *Whitaker's Almanack*, looked up Customs and Excise – she picked the third man down from the very top and *really persuaded* him. The child got the plane.

'You must use oodles of common sense, Penelope,' she said, quite unexhausted by it all. I was a rag, just listening!

Our day ended thus:

'Well, Penelope, how does it all strike you at the end of your first day?'

'I very much like all that I've experienced today, Miss Fry. I think the atmosphere and team spirit is so good,' I told her. I really meant it.

Margaret certainly did spend part of her days amongst the 'new girls', acting as an instructor and shock-absorber until they could get the hang of things. For instance – the head of department turned pale, put a shaky hand over the mouthpiece of the telephone, and said, 'Can we feed an elephant in somebody's garden for a week?'

Margaret took over the telephone. 'Yes, certainly we can manage that. Of course it will be a *very* expensive assignment and we shall need an *advance deposit* . . . Oh, he's rung off! That is how to deal with a hoax,' she said as she replaced the receiver. 'We recently turned the tables on another hoaxer. Had a very authentic booking for Willie Snooks to be met at Victoria and taken across London. Our Aunt found herself at the barrier looking up at a six-foot young naval officer! Unperturbed, she said, "So you're Willie Snooks? Right then, come along!" and she led him briskly to his destination. He was so dumbfounded, he followed her.'

An old lady of eighty-two in the Stanhope Court wanted a Universal Aunt to help her move her things to another room. 'Old ladies want company as much as practical help. When someone goes to help one with this sort of thing, they get chatting and she enjoys it. A week later she rings in and says, "I'm in an awful muddle again, will you come round?" Soon we find our UA is taking lunch with her once a week and getting quite attached.' Margaret spoke from long experience.

A hostess telephoned, being minus a male dinner guest. 'Oh yes, we have several nice men available, carefully vetted of course, only the most presentable candidates qualifying,' Margaret assured her.

First thing on Friday morning, Margaret ran through the oddly addressed envelopes from the week's post. 'We keep a note of these,' she said.

The International Aunts Ltd London (*from India*)	Aunts, Wives, Widows & Spinsters Walpole Street London England (*from Africa*)
The Manager of the World Aunts Organization London England (*from United Arab Republic*)	Aunts of Wimpole St London England (*from Japan*)
Universal Aunts Walpoll St, London (*from Cheshire*)	Unusual Aunts London (*from Twickenham*)
Unversal Ends Waltels St Tring Road London (*from France*)	Respectable Agency 86 Walpole St London SW3 (*from Brescia*)

Last thing on Friday evening, Margaret wished her new heads of department a quiet and happy weekend – a necessity after the normal week's work at Universal Aunts!

Confidence soon grows under good guidance and it was Margaret's policy to step into the background when she felt it time to let each head of department manage her own interviewing of workers and placing of jobs. 'Remember, however, your relationship with client and worker is a *Company* matter. Any problem or doubt you refer back to me,' she warned. 'Your work here is never going to be dull, so there will be plenty of those.' She smiled knowingly and left them to it.

The phones rang constantly and job descriptions from clients were taken down. Calls were made to workers and placings were offered. In between times there were captivating titbits to pass one to another. Hopeful, modest ladies and confident, lofty ladies arrived for interviews, out of which more super Aunts were taken on to swell the ranks – young and old, all types, shapes and sizes.

'Employment department, can I help you?' answered Jenny, and listened for a moment. 'I understand, Lady Crane, now may I check the details?' She began to write on her pad. 'Your drawing-room chandelier has just crashed to the floor, most of it on top of the butler – he's in St Thomas's, not too seriously hurt I hope?' She paused. 'Oh, good. So what you need is a temporary butler for approximately six weeks and also an antique glass repairer. Yes, I think we can supply both for you. Now may I tell you our charges?'

Only a few minutes later, Jenny phoned one of her workers. 'Mrs Dent, I have a job to offer you in Gloucester, companion to a ninety-year-old lady while her daughter and son-in-law are away for two weeks next month. Very spry, simple meals, daily help comes in, old lady likes a game of Scrabble in the evenings. There is only one thing to watch, if you use the hoover; she hides her money in the hoover bag against burglars, doesn't think anyone knows – the daily is of course aware of this. You'll take it? Good.'

A fresh-faced girl in her twenties came round the door. 'Hi, Jenny,' she said in a strong New Zealand accent.

'Hello, Karen,' Jenny smiled and waved her to sit down. 'How are things going? You've another two weeks in the job before the Wellanbys' regular nanny is back, haven't you?'

'Yes, it's been a really super job! The baby's a love and the other little one too.' The girl pulled a chair up to the desk. 'An amazing house, the like of which I'll never see again when I get back to New Zealand, full of beautiful things end to end! So many rooms, I haven't seen them all – thousands being spent on marvellous renovations, carvings and plaster, pictures and drapes cleaned, and new bathrooms. All like a picture-book story of England for me. Lord and Lady Wellanby are nice to work for and very friendly.' Karen was obviously enjoying a successful placing.

'Well, Christmas with them in Scotland will be lovely for you, too,' said Jenny.

'Yes, that's another thing! Last week an entire truck was filled with all the presents and luggage and sent up ahead of us. I wouldn't have believed that life like that exists.' Her smile was quite without envy.

'Now, you'll be free again in early January – are you able to go straight on to someone else?' asked Jenny, already checking situations vacant.

'Almost straight away. I had thought to go and stay with my sister. I've been promising to ever since I arrived in England. I'd be quite glad of a few days' break.'

'Fine. I'll mark you in for the beginning of the second week – have a really good Christmas.'

Lunchtime in the office was often an exchange of newspaper gossip over the coffee and sandwiches. This much-scorned and frivolous pursuit was of value in an organization which frequently supplied services to the darlings of the columnists, if not employing some of those same darlings itself. The information this gossip garnered, on at least two occasions, brought to light the unusual situation of a Universal Aunt working in a house of horror. One of the nannies was a regular weekly relief in the home of a much-publicized nanny murder case. The other was a Proxy Parent caring for the children of a distraught and most tearful father who had called upon the Aunts following the sudden death of their mother. He was later convicted of killing his wife and watching her body burn. The Aunts fortunately survived with no sudden and violent reduction to the workforce.

'An interviewee ready for you, Jenny,' buzzed Jean from reception, with a warning note in her voice.

A very dressy lady of middle years appeared through the door and paused while the effect of lacquered ash-coloured hair, a bosom full of gold chains, and gleaming knee-high boots stunned the occupant of the room.

'Won't you take a seat, Mrs Y?'

She did, opposite Jenny's expressionless face, and was politely asked, 'Now, what can I do for you?'

'Well, I need to get away from my husband. He's an absolute bastard – so I thought I'd take a job. There's no point in filling in your form until I see if you've got something to suit me.' Jenny mentally agreed that the form-filling would indeed prove to be unnecessary. 'I can do absolutely anything,' continued the interviewee. 'I'm especially good with *people*. I

can organize them and arrange everything for them in their social lives –
dinner parties, receptions, do their flowers, advise them where to go for
whatever they need.'

'Do you have any particular qualifications, Mrs Y?'

'Goodness no!' Pause for quick delve in her Gucci bag, then, with
lighter already in flames, 'Do you mind if I smoke? I've lived a very full
life, entertained at top level – what better training? By the way I shall
need to live in – a residential job of some kind, with nice accommodation
and –' knowing pause – 'preferably with a nice man around. I shall soon
be able to use a new husband.' Confident smile. No one was looking.

'Well, as you yourself mentioned, what you are looking for is by no
means in the usual run of vacancies on our books. I suggest that you also
contact any other likely sources for such employment and just leave your
telephone number with me so that, should anything come along, I can
give you a ring.'

'Yes, I'll do that. I shall be quite choosy, of course!'

'Absolutely! Good-bye!' As the door closed, Jenny sighed. 'Thankfully there are so few Mrs Ys who seek us out.'

The phone rang again.

'Hello, Mrs Brock. Oh, I'm sorry she isn't suiting you.' Long pause.
'Well, you didn't mention any duties other than light housework. Your
personal hand laundry and general companionship when you are alone
in the evenings are an addition to your original request.' Shorter pause.
'Yes, I know she is only about four foot six inches tall – if she can't reach
the dishwasher, as there are only two of you could she not wash up in the
sink if that is at a lower level?' Brief pause. 'No, she has no aspirations as
a cook; indeed that was the one thing she said she could not undertake. I
think perhaps as she is seventy and you are needing rather more help
than you had anticipated, it might be too much for her. Could I go
through my files and see what I can come up with – a younger and taller
one this time?'

'That client is determined to get her money's worth!' said Jenny,
ringing off and turning to greet one of her workers who had just come
in for a job. 'Funnily enough, Mrs Smith, I have one in this morning
and the client has the same name as you.' She passed over the job
description.

'My God!' exploded Mrs Smith. 'She's the woman who ran off with
my husband!'

At that moment Jean put a call through from America. 'Excuse me a moment, Mrs Smith,' said Jenny as she picked up the phone. 'You are wanting a *lighthouse keeper*,' she repeated loudly. 'I'm afraid we don't have such a man on our books,' she went on. 'Oh, a *woman*? I don't think there are such things. Where is this for?' Looking bewildered, she listened again and then said, 'I'm so sorry, I misunderstood, just a different emphasis on words. You are needing a *light housekeeper* for your home in Washington.' She finished the call and turned back to the waiting Mrs Smith, hastily getting off the subject of the husband-snatcher. 'I have a temporary housekeeper job here, three weeks with an eighty-five-year-old retired admiral; but I'm afraid he specifies that he wants a Navy lady.' Jenny was thumbing through the vacancies as she talked and was about to pass on when Mrs Smith announced,

'I'm an ex-Wren!' and a good placing was made.

A call came in just before lunch. 'Jenny!' in an urgent whisper, 'this is Anne Oliver. You know last week I rang to tell you that my eighty-year-old widower was a darling and so kind? I'll have to leave before my two weeks is up, he's chasing me round the kitchen – it's not a housekeeper he wants!'

Problems were usually quite small ones, but a police officer arriving in reception requesting an interview with the Managing Director meant that Margaret was faced with a serious matter. Police Inspector Ivory was ushered in.

'Miss Fry, I believe.'

'Good morning, Inspector. How can I help you? Please sit down.'

'Thank you, madam. I have come to ask you to check on your records for a butler whose name may be on your books, one John Z?'

'I'll just ask the relevant department to bring in their cards'

A knock on the door. 'Jenny, may I have your box of butlers in here, please?'

It only took a minute for Jenny to reappear. After the policeman had risen and been introduced, he continued, 'Do you recall a man called Z, I wonder?'

'Yes, I do, Inspector. He signed on with us about a year ago; but after doing several casual jobs, dinner parties and so on, he took a full-time job – not through us, from another agency – so we haven't seen him since. I've brought the file of references, Miss Fry, in case you wish to see those. Z's must have been all right, of course, or we wouldn't have been using him.'

As the door closed, the Inspector settled back into his chair.

'I think that will be one job you are going to be pleased not to have filled, Miss Fry.'

She passed over the blue card with the man's description and the two written references. 'As you see, Inspector, all in order there – his past employers seem to have been well pleased, and he had an excellent training. It sounds as if you have something serious to tell me.'

'I have indeed. The full-time post the man got was in an embassy, where he has been most satisfactory for the past year – but the fact that he is a homosexual has, I'm afraid, led to his ruin. Recently, in the absence of his employers, he was out on the town and was driven back in a cab by a driver with similar tendencies. He invited the man in and this was followed by one or two more visits by the driver – until last Monday evening, when the man came again and brought two friends. By morning, not only had they departed, but the Ambassador's entire and valuable collection of jade as well. We have the butler in custody and we are making enquiries into his background, so I am grateful for your help.'

Margaret shook her head. 'It hasn't been much, I'm afraid; but as you said, I am thankful we did not place him. It seems to have been a bad week for butlers, Inspector – most unusually – and we have been involved in another drama recently. Luckily a slip caught this one in time. We hadn't placed him, either, but were called in after the event, for a replacement. He was engaged by a client of ours on marvellous references and proved himself over three months to be a perfect Jeeves. At the weekend our client was due to leave his home in Jeeves's care, to spend Christmas with friends in Switzerland; the day before, he had an embarrassed man with a nice voice on the telephone. The caller announced his name, which meant nothing to our client, and explained that he had recently advertised in *The Times* for a butler, had received a reply from Jeeves with a glowing reference from his present employer, all quite proper – except that the reference was signed "Lord X". Both gentlemen agreed that it was an extraordinary mistake for a butler to make!'

Inspector Ivory intervened. 'They always make one sooner or later.'

'Well,' Margaret went on, 'it transpired that he was in the habit of scanning the "Situations Vacant" column, forging references, doing a good job for a short time so that there would be no qualms about leaving the house in his care; and when the time came, off he would go with a bag full of treasures and another job already lined up. We have now sent in caretakers to guard the house while the owners are away recovering from shock.'

The Inspector stood up to leave. 'All that training thrown down the drain! But the bad'uns can't think straight, they take such careless risks that they're bound to be tracked down.' He picked up his cap. 'I'll bid you good day, madam, and thank you again.'

Aren't we lucky to have so many really good ones on our books? Margaret thought to herself. We appreciate them, and hopefully they do us.

19

1970s

DOWNSTAIRS CHANGES

All in a day's work

Some ranks of servants had changed more than others, but the butler on the books perhaps least of all, for there can be no updating of his expertise. He had, of course, found it prudent, if not necessary, to become less of a snob, for there were fewer 'gentlemen' able to afford him and more newly rich all over the world who aspired to having him. Once they had acquired the trappings of wealth, who better than the English butler to instruct them in the ways of doing things properly? That was his training; the art of gracious living, the upholding of traditions in the house he served, had passed down from butler to butler. He had been tough enough to survive the menial years on the way up and smart enough to rise thereby to his present status; he accepted his own place in the order of things, and acknowledged the master to have his. Both good and bad master and servant have always existed, but the bad butler was in a unique position to abuse and use every loophole, from access to the wine cellar and maids' bedrooms in the attics, to exploitation of the rotten master and mistress and their idiosyncrasies. Eccentricities in a butler have traditionally been met with a blind eye, where other servants would have been dismissed without references. For the majority, however, there has been persistent pride in a job well learned and honourably carried out, and loyalty to the trust of 'their' family.

By now, some butlers had left private service for the freer life of employment with a City company or 'living out' to an embassy. This left him able to moonlight, and his expertise was hired by the hour by a wider variety of employers than his predecessors would have thought possible. Quite often delighted by his inclusion as a guide, mentor and friend of the party, he never forgot his place and protocol as a hired butler.

Cook, on the other hand, had changed a great deal. The previous demands and conditions of her job had often led her to be a demon in her own domain, with a wicked tongue, a penchant for the bottle and permanently aching feet made worse by overweight. By the 1970s many well-trained girls had arrived on the scene, and cook would be slim and brisk, conveyed by car or moped or a weeny box-like van in her favourite colours with her name on the side. Hired at so much an hour, she would produce the goods in your own kitchen or deliver them from hers in hot containers. She would wait at table (unless she spied her best friend, enemy or 'ex' on the guest list), would fill the freezer ahead of school hols, cope with large numbers and endless meals for a shooting-party, weekend guests or in-laws, and leave the hostess free to glow under lavish appreciation and praise. If used judiciously, these cooks proved to be easier on the nerves than the previous model, and seldom expected more than a bottle of plonk to be supplied to the kitchen.

Cordon Bleu, like modelling, lost some of its cachet because of naughty and less able girls whose paper qualifications far exceeded their performances. As one furious American client shouted down the telephone, 'Cooks for directors' lunches, she told me! Why, she's so bad, she couldn't sling hash for a Great Dane!'

An equally harassed but gentler lady telephoned the office, 'The cook you sent is so sweet and tries so hard, she arrives each morning with an armful of cookery books – but *please* may I have her telephone number? She has left some pale pink *thing* in the fridge for our dinner this evening – I can't make out what it is and it appears to be growing!'

The British nanny had always been acclaimed and sought after throughout the civilized or aspiring world. Now, within such establishments as the Norland, she had become impeccably trained to the highest nursery standards. This was expected by the modern mother, who had absorbed, while pregnant, all the up-to-date information on child care. Nanny was often, now, a friend of the parents as well as the children; and mother could go out to work if she chose, confident that Nanny would be upholding the solid values of the nursery: bread and butter before cake, fresh air in town or country, and correctly timed potting. It had been recognized that even those basics could be well or badly taught, and she was the expert.

One might think it could only be a dowager's voice from the past that would ask for a lady's maid, but not so. The wife of a Lord Mayor or other public official with a heavy social calendar; a globe-trotting actress with a suite at the Dorchester; an eminent socialite; a hectic professional or business woman: all of these were on the books in need of such a treasure. Even the best of London's dry-cleaners was no substitute for the personal touch of a woman caring for one's clothes in one's own home. The old lady's maid, like the butler, was a slowly trained expert who usually stayed a lifetime with her mistress, and only the death of one or other parted them. The new version would be an Aunt with a passion for needlework, needlepoint or *gros point*, beavering about in search of wools, silks, gold and silver thread, poring over books of ancient designs, her favourite venue being the Royal School of Needlework. Her hobby was an expensive one, and maiding someone else's couture clothes was quite an acceptable way to fund this. There were several such ladies on the books of the Aunts. *Permanent* was a word of earlier years, *temporary* the new style of employment; and that necessitated new introductory methods. It was up to the Company not only to sell a service but also to prove to the clients that it was a satisfactory alternative.

The Aunts on the books remained much the same: a staunch brigade upon whom the Company relied, willing, co-operative and loyal, extremely hard-working and seldom thrown by the demands of the job, which were many and varied. One week in a department had to be lived through to be believed.

From Special Services, Kate dialled a number. 'Good morning, Venetia, it's Kate – I've got a lovely job that you might like to join in.'

'Tell all,' came the answer.

'I have twenty-five Japanese gentlemen, architects and designers, who are fact-finding in England and while in London want to be entertained in an English home – so yours, for one, sprang to mind.' Encouraging sounds from the other end. Kate went on, 'This is on the 23rd of next month. I plan to split them into groups of five, each with an interpreter – they speak no English.'

'How terrifying!'

'I suggest afternoon tea as the most English entertainment and of a short enough duration to allow everyone to survive, sparkling to the end.'

Venetia had caught on. 'Lovely! Cucumber sandwiches, Victoria sponge and all the best silver out, plus a reason to dust in high places! I'll be ready to hear more about Operation Orient when you've got it planned. My thoughts are bubbling!'

Kate managed to get five bubbling hostesses lined up. The office planning involved was quite considerable. As an ice-breaker, she drew up and sent off a short résumé on his hostess to be given to each guest beforehand, so that when stepping into her house he would feel less of a stranger.

> These details are intended as a starter to a relaxed and happy visit. This English lady has a husband who is a banker, and two sons, one aged twenty at university and one at public school, and one daughter aged eighteen who is training here in London at the Inchbald School of Art and Design. Her home is a very typical four-storey London house built in the eighteenth century in an area which was then, and still is today, a fashionable part, though outward appearances are likely to be less elegant. Her interests outside her family are . . . She has travelled a little, on holiday to . . . Of slight historical interest to the overseas visitor, this family is connected with . . . so that, in their home, among other things, you will be able to see some of his small personal possessions and a very fine portrait of him.

In five London houses the top dusting was done, family treasures were unearthed, faintly vanilla-smelling Victoria sponges and butter short-breads appeared in kitchens, and transparent slices of cucumber drained on plates. Drawing-rooms were made beautiful with flowers, fires and faded scents of pot-pourri. A low table spread with an old lace cloth held the polished silver and newly-washed, shallow cups covered with roses, violets and plenty of gold-leaf edging. Gracing it all, the hostesses made special efforts – Englishwomen at their best with silk frocks, pale legs and soft shoes, pretty hair, some nice pearls for lustre and a few diamonds on fingers for sparkle.

On the day, the gentlemen duly arrived and with wide smiles they stepped into the hall, bowed low, and removed their shoes. In the drawing-room each handed a gift to his hostess. Their small figures were enveloped in the size and softness of the chairs beloved by Englishmen; they smiled and nodded while conversation flowed back and forth quite easily through their interpreters; and they copied carefully from their hostess the correct way to take tea in England – somewhat different from their own. Enormous interest was shown in all they saw – the house, the furnishings and the treasures. It was an afternoon of considerable pleasure and friendship, followed by most sincere letters of thanks for such an unexpected taste of England.

'Hello, Noel, Marion here. I have a rather discreet little job that I think you could manage beautifully, if you would consider it. A letter came in the post today from America, a son writing on behalf of his mother. She is the widow of a well-known American medical man who is to be posthumously honoured in London next month. She will, of course, be over here and is expected to attend the dinner in the evening. He would like his mother to be accompanied to this by a suitable male escort, to be introduced as a family friend.'

Marion paused while Noel went over the facts. 'Yes, thank you, Noel, that's very understanding of you. I agree we can manage to make this a much less harrowing experience for her. We've got about six weeks to put it together. Don't go . . . I have another here for you, a bit more immediate.' She flipped notebook pages. 'Someone has to go over to Florence within the next day or two to bring back the fifteen-year-old son and heir of the A's – need I elaborate? – from his college there. He appears to have a supply of his mother's cheques and a considerable propensity for forging her signature. Needless to say, his little journey home is to be a surprise to him and will be best accomplished by a person he can't argue with – in your case, a very large, very commanding Guards officer! Good, we think you're marvellous.'

'Oh, hello Toby, you've come to be paid,' said Marion as another Universal Uncle, large and military, walked in. 'How did last night's dog-sitting go?'

'Not so well. There were just two huge armchairs in their sitting-room and those brutes sat one in each and I sat on the floor for four hours. You don't argue with a Great Dane,' he explained glumly.

Beautifully dressed and scented, Jess floated in to report on the assignment she'd just finished, which was to witness a wedding. 'We arrived to find this enchanting pair, both in their eighties. He is an upright, snowy-haired general; she was obviously a great beauty in the past, and still is, in that fragile way of the very old. We saw them safely through the ceremony, and back at her flat in Eaton Square we found out that all those years ago they had been each other's first love.' She paused for effect. 'They were considered too young and were separated by their parents; both eventually married perfectly happily – she lived for years out in Nairobi until her husband died and then she bought a villa in Spain. Blow me, last summer he, now a widower, went there on hols and they literally bumped into one another. This time they decided on a secret wedding before anyone else could butt in.'

'Miss Fry, will you want me for the next hour? I'm just popping into

Hamleys – someone wants us to buy and dispatch a lovely model boat they have in stock. I happen to know the one, so it's easier for me to go.'

The Managing Director raised her eyes from her papers. 'A *model* boat! How times have changed.'

Kate groaned inwardly: 'Here it comes, something they did better than we do now.'

Margaret removed her reading spectacles. 'No assignment, of course, is too small; but in 1968 we were commissioned to buy a yacht for a Greek millionaire. I myself went along to Captain Watts to get the matter properly under way; plans were drawn up; months of nego-tiations went on; we were heavily involved.'

'Lucky Universal Aunt or Uncle who accompanied *that* to the Greek Islands!' thought Kate as Margaret went on,

'The moment of completion came and designer and client fell out over – you will not believe this – £2,000. The whole deal was cancelled. So of course was our commission.' A sigh for what might have been. 'I hope you've got the money *in hand* for this, Kate.'

'I'm so sorry, Mrs B,' said Marion, 'but I'm afraid all our butlers and maids are fully booked for the next three weeks.'

'Who in God's name is having all these parties?' screamed an American voice down the telephone. 'I haven't been asked!'

'Good morning, Miss C, what can I do for you today?' asked Marion of her all-too-regular visitor.

A brief, yellowed smile flicked on and off.

'I have 200 large balls of wool and I wonder if you have someone to knit them for me?'

'*Into a tent?*' wondered Marion silently. 'That's rather a lot of wool. What sort of knitting?' she asked.

'Well, I have collected it over the years, thinking of twin-sets, but now I have arthritis in my fingers and can't do it myself.'

'We have a very nice Miss Fowler on our books for knitting, and I believe she's very good and reasonable. Now, I'll write her name and number down for you and you can contact her direct.' Marion passed over the details and rose to her feet.

'What do I owe the agency, Mrs Berlyn?'

'That's all right this time, Miss C. Perhaps you'll be using us again.'

'She certainly will!' rang out a chorus as the wool beret was seen bobbing along just above the wall outside.

'Poor old duck,' said Marion.

Polly's head popped round the door.

'Ah, Marion, just looked in to say I'm off to little Miss Johnson. We're going shopping and then we'll visit an old friend of hers in hospital.'

'As she's ninety-one and almost blind now, does she really enjoy shopping?'

'Of course she does. She likes the articles to be described and she's most particular that they should be just right for the person concerned – even with W. H. Smith tokens, she likes to know what the picture is on each card. She can feel things too, and of course, as I've now been helping her for two years, I've got to know the tastes of her family and friends, so that's an advantage. By the way, she's not quite ninety-one, you remember how we planned the ninetieth birthday party? She had a new dress, had her hair done and looked so pretty – well, we're now in the process of getting organized for the ninety-first.'

'You've been such a blessing to her, Polly.'

'My dear, she's been one for me, taught me such a lot. Even reading *The Times* to her has widened my interests; instead of just being able to pick out what I like and skip the rest, I have to cover her tastes. "No thank you, I don't want that – find me what's reported on such-and-such a page, or about this or that." Very good for me altogether is my dear Miss Johnson.'

'Before you go, Polly, I've had a request from the Poodle Parlour for a relief next Monday and Tuesday; can you do it again?'

'My dear, I wouldn't miss it for *anything*, it's such an eye-opener!' Her eyes rolled. 'There I sit in Curzon Street, almost in the window, answering the telephone and selling the odd tin of Chum, but mostly watching the risqué goings-on outside. Early afternoon and a number of female "shoppers" suddenly appear to stand and gaze at our display of dog coats and baskets, waiting for the pub opposite to close. Sometimes a sinister man in a Jaguar is parked watching. The last day I was there, what a scene! An innocent tourist started photographing them, and the flow of *language* . . . Phew!'

'Poodle-faking,' said Jenny.

'What does that mean?' she was asked.

'I don't really know, I think it was a bit before our time.'

Marion looked up. 'It was horrid old men, before prostitution was herded off the streets – the girls in Shepherd Market and Park Lane used to have a little poodle prancing on the end of a coloured lead. It gave the men the excuse to approach.'

'Well, there you are, then, it instantly conveyed what I meant, very verbal,' said Jenny.

Adela came in and flopped into a chair.

'Mrs D totally exhausts me,' she announced. 'Though I hate to give up on a job, I think her family will have to call in their solicitor to sort this one out. I'm wasting my time and their money.'

'That's the old lady whose paperwork you were to get into order?' enquired Marion.

'So her family hoped,' sighed Adela. 'But after two weeks I haven't even begun. She has a card table in the drawing-room on which she puts every letter and bill that comes in the morning post. It's piled high and covered with a long red velvet cloth.'

'What is the point of that?' asked Marion.

'Because, enormously rich as she is, she is so incredibly mean that she refuses to pay bills, and my job, it seems, is to cook up every small excuse for her not to. Nearly seven months ago, she returned two tins of tomato purée to Harrods and she insisted that I make them check back to be sure they had credited her with them before she'll even consider their very large bill.'

'What a waste of time.'

'It is. I can't see any background correspondence because it is under the cloth, and I have to wait until the moment when she totters off to the loo to whisk up a corner and try to find something.' Adela appeared unusually deflated. 'Now the telephone's been cut off and she's furious because an equally ancient buddy had been trying to get through and finally sent a runner to see if she was dead. She swears she had never heard from the telephone people but it is all there, covered by the red velvet.'

'I shall explain matters to her family,' Marion decided, 'and advise that professional help would be better in this case.'

'I hate to fail.'

'It isn't failure, it's facing facts. You will be better pleased with the next job: your lovely blind Miss Roland is arriving to take her next elocution examination, so as usual I guess you will want to meet and escort her.'

Adela smiled. 'Now that's what I call worthwhile. She's such a courageous woman.'

An Irishwoman came in to sign on for domestic work. On her form she wrote the name of her two referees, one without an address.

'May I have that address?' asked Marion.

'For why?'

'To send for your reference.'

'She'll not be sending you an answer from Paradise,' replied the Irish-woman with unanswerable logic.

Donna had received her briefing from Marion over the telephone.

'As you know, our client is a very eminent writer. Now that she is aged ninety-two she has decided that her vast collection of papers and effects must be sorted and catalogued. Before we embark upon this, I have arranged for you to visit her and check the exact extent of the job for us; here are the details.'

Donna called in to report. 'It is a huge, cobwebbed and dust-covered house with damp patches and dark corridors. Open any door and you must pass through piles of documents and papers, boxes and books, and unknown what-else, to move about. There is no order anywhere. I saw hanging on the walls Augustus Johns and the work of other such contemporaries, who were I believe her friends. Letters falling out of boxes had famous names. The lady herself is charming but now very aged and vague and will not be able to advise in any way. It will be a long and dirty task, and I would suggest that perhaps four careful and orderly people should simply do a rescue operation, getting the dust off papers and placing them in tea-chests. The house has been sold and the old lady is going into a residential home, so everything will be moved from there. From what I saw, I think the experts from Sothebys or Christies should then take over that valuable collection to sort and catalogue it. Actually, my father knew the writer and her late husband quite well. She hadn't seen me since I was a child and invited me to have a glass of sherry and reminisce, but her mind wandered off in a few minutes.'

The Aunts undertook their part of the job in the careful and orderly way that Donna had suggested.

Julia strode into the office late in the afternoon and draped her six-foot silk- and mink-swathed self across a chair.

'Not everyone comes job-hunting in head-to-toe mink,' commented Marion. '*Really*, Julia, do all Scandinavians own coats like that?'

'Not all; this is from the good old days when I was still with Darling.'

'Very nice. The Duchess would like you tomorrow at two o'clock, then to pick up Lady Allendy and drive them both to visit the rest-house in Surrey.'

'Oh yes, we went down there before to visit her old maid who, Her

Grace told me, is the same age as herself, eighty-nine and quite spry. She takes her a Fortnum's walnut cake and they talk of the old days and have a lovely time. You know, lady or maid, I find one faces the same sad facts of life: ageing friends (or in her case retainers) with failing eyesight and hearing, tucked away in homes. Last week we collected another old friend of the Duchess for the afternoon drive, and I was feeling rather smart in my Piero de Monzi trouser suit. I was a bit dashed by the conversation from the back seat. "What a nice young man you have driving for you now, Emmeline!" "Don't be silly, Victoria, it's a Universal Aunt!"'

Dolly appeared with a newspaper and plonked it on to Marion's desk. 'I thought you might not have seen this. Our well-connected client is now in the hands of the police.'

Marion read the piece. 'For using the shopping accounts of her famous same-name cousin, I see.' The others in the room were agog. 'What did you do for her?'

'Well,' said Dolly, 'she wanted an inventory making of her couture clothes, said it was for insurance purposes as she was about to pack to go around the world. I was shown up to a dingy dressing-room lined with cupboards and when I opened the doors there were racks of dusty, unprotected, grubby day and evening dresses, coats and furs. Boxes of tatty bags and belts, and what had been delicate shoes, scuffed and dated. Thousands of pounds' worth, by their embroidered or embossed labels, from the best couture houses, and Bond Street bag- and shoe-shops. A sad museum!'

'What did she look like?'

'Sallow skin and sunken eyes and a huge lot of long dyed red hair – a bony wraith who smoked thin brown cigarettes all the time. *The* most awful thing was that I never saw her in anything but a ghastly green kimono thing – or *nothing*. I tell you, I got the shock of my life, on the first day. She suddenly appeared round the bedroom door without a *stitch* on, headed for the telephone and got put through to some man in Vienna, to whom she said, "As long as you have paid for my tickets I shall come." A listening silence, then, "I'm not that kind of woman, I shall expect you to marry me." Well, I thought, if he could see her now! Quite apart from which, I was busy keeping me between her and the door, and the one thing that reassured me was that she kept ringing *men*.'

'The only trip she'll be making now is to court,' said Marion.

Few requests any longer caused surprise, but if they did, by no sign must the client be made to feel any unease at having asked. So it was when an Australian man rang from his suite at the Savoy and wanted to speak to someone on a closely personal matter. He asked Marion, 'Could you arrange for a Universal Aunt of suitable age and experience to undertake a shopping commission? I need to purchase several pairs of directoire knickers for my aged aunt, who cannot find them any longer in Australia.'

Having put down the telephone, Marion looked up 'directoire' in the dictionary, but got no further than that it seemed to mean the 'imitation of a style prevalent during the French Directory'. And that was given as 'Fr. Hist. of 1795–9'. Surely not!

Bea, an upright, charming, grey-haired Aunt blessed with tact and humour, was dispatched to the hotel to take his instructions. Amazed, but calm, she learned that the six foot two inches of handsome, tanned Australian male of middle age intended to accompany her on the search. From one top shop to another they moved, and at her request a modest display of the articles was laid out on the counter, elasticated of waist and with knee-length legs, in peach, coffee, or flesh pink. The gentleman viewed all these but none of them suited the requirements of his Aunt – they were too large, too small, the wrong shade, the wrong shape. At the fourth attempt, Bea suddenly got a panicky feeling that *something was not as it ought to be*. He was clearly enjoying this venture and they were getting nowhere. Bea suggested that London's supply had been combed and rejected. He immediately and quite merrily agreed, took her arm, escorted her to a taxi, and thanked her most charmingly. 'Whenever,' said he, 'I hear the name "Universal Aunts", I shall say "Knickers!"' And an astonished taxi-driver drove her away. He was of course a most unlikely-looking voyeur.

20

1970S

THE BOARD MEETING

Meetings – Claims

Margaret was not dissatisfied with the progress of her team and in 1973 two unexpected changes came about.

Lola chanced to meet again, after many years, her late husband's old friend from Rugby schooldays, Murray Inglis, now a retired brigadier. Both now widowed, they recalled old memories and being guests at each other's weddings, and soon they had their own marriage arranged. Lola temporarily retired from the Board; to return two years later, but was persuaded that her superb management of the House- and Flat-Letting department, together with which she also handled Public Relations, would be a considerable loss to the Company, so she continued that part-time. Margaret proposed Penelope to fill that vacancy as a Director.

Bay, in her coastal retreat, valued her continued contact with the Company but realized that the time had come when working, rather than absent, directors were needed, who could construct Company policy from everyday contact. She too resigned as a Director, and Margaret suggested Kate. So, once again, the Board consisted of a majority of working Directors.

Margaret was its backbone. Molly, by then coming in part-time, was an assistant and support to her, and ran the stationery cupboard and all the ordering of supplies. Diana, expert and competent as ever, continued to come up from the country to reinforce the Accounts department when needed, so was well in touch. Now there were the two new Directors also. Eveleigh and the redoubtable Frances were supplied by Margaret with constant, up-to-date facts and figures, so they appeared at Board meetings well informed and with strong and carefully considered opinions.

The appointment of Penelope and Kate having been confirmed, they were summoned to a Board meeting – an event conducted in the ritual passed down since the very first meeting more than fifty years before, and usually timed for 2.30 in the afternoon.

A bustle of activity began immediately after lunch. A faded cardboard box was taken down from a top shelf, the blue and white china washed and a tea-tray laid. A new packet of biscuits, chocolate coated on one side, was placed ready to open. Two people, who turned out to be the newest Directors, lifted the ancient, black, gate-legged table from the corridor into the centre of the Accounts room, opened out its wings and stuffed a wedge of paper under its one weak leg. Chairs were placed around it, a jug of water put near the Chairman's end, and all was ready.

Signatures from Attendance Books dated 1921 to 1986

With everyone gathered and greetings exchanged, the Attendance Book circulated for signature on the already dated page. All the pages were yellowed with age and on the earlier ones were the names of shadowy figures from the past. With the sight of those came the real awareness of what was expected of oneself, a sobering thought.

During a few moments of waiting for the arrival of the Company accountant, Philip Strode, Penelope and Kate could glance at the two Directors they had never seen before.

Eveleigh Leith, at the head of the table, was somewhat austere, tall and lean and elegant; one could quite see her as the lady squash champion she had been, unemotionally demolishing her opponent, and as the matter-of-fact author of the work study which was now the Bible of their business. She took out a silver compact and fluffed a little powder on to her nose. No one else seemed to notice.

Frances Blackett, an old lady now, tall and translucent, had arrived walking slow as winter treacle between two sticks. Even Eveleigh did not sit down before she appeared and took her place on the right of the Chairman and opposite Margaret. Frances welcomed the newcomers with gentle courtesy. Her snow-white hair in a bun was covered by a hairnet, and a long tartan skirt and a woollen coat covered her. She carefully arranged her papers on the table, delved into a large cloth bag and brought out a giant-sized matchbox, out of which she took a small pair of gold-rimmed spectacles and put them on. She then removed the long wool coat and two cardigans, and was still warmly clad in yet another. No one else seemed to find any of this surprising.

Philip Strode arrived and sat at the foot of the table; small pleasantries were exchanged while he snapped open the locks of his sleek black briefcase and took out his papers. With his smooth, dark-suited, and correct City appearance, his calm manner and low, reasoning voice, he had been counsellor, guide and guardian to the Board of seven women for many years. Unruffled when they resisted his advice, uncritical when it proved they should have listened, with never a hint of 'I told you so,' he just went on from there! His reference always to 'we' gave them the comfortable feeling that for his own sake he would keep them afloat.

The meeting proceeded through the agenda, stock-taking, decision-making, questions and answers. The windows became steamy and cheeks pinker. Mid-way, with a knock on the door, tea was brought in and all talk immediately ceased until the door had closed again, so there was never the smallest bit of gossip to carry back to the other rooms.

Then general discussion began. Margaret had, throughout, been noticeably the well-primed leader, with facts and figures thoroughly prepared and to hand and all suggestions previously researched. She clearly held Philip in great respect but still gave the impression that it was after all, she who had to run the Company, which he seemed to like. It was apparent that they enjoyed bouncing ideas off one another.

The more surprising participant was Frances. Appearances had been deceptive, for it became very clear during that afternoon that she still had a razor-sharp mind and keen ear. She sat very motionless, requested enlightenment now and again, spoke the minimum on salient points, and her every word was orderly and relevant. No wonder she had been revered over the years.

General discussion followed tea. Philip continued the main theme of the meeting. 'Our present financial concern is that we have never caught up with the government price freeze, because we did not up our fees and move one step ahead of it.'

'Very true,' replied Margaret, 'but we cannot do the catching up with the massive slap of 50 per cent on all our fees now.'

'It is happening everywhere and the present, but temporary, mood of the paying public is acceptance of the necessity of steeply rising prices. We should take the step now, and not in dribs and drabs,' Philip advised logically.

Frances spoke firmly. 'As you know, Mr Strode, the working Directors are in day-to-day contact with the business. This gives them a feel as to how much increase can be swallowed at one time, before our clients can't or won't pay for our services. From their advice we take our cue. It is always a gamble, but once fees are put up they cannot be put down in the event of a mistake having been made.' Frances gave a gentle smile and went on. 'So perhaps you find us over-cautious and a trial to your patience.'

Philip laughed as he gathered up his papers, and then made a surprising statement.

'You must remember that my company has advised you from your beginnings, so not only do I have your figures to hand, but the much more interesting yearly history and struggles behind each balance sheet. Your reasoning, like your ethics, are the product of your Founder and, in today's world, the one, not the other, should give you food for thought.' No one interrupted as he went on, 'In the 1920s and 1930s, your

Managing Director received £6 for a very full seven-day week, and the Aunts averaged three shillings per hard-working hour. On the outbreak of war, their pay was frozen and other Directors' discontinued. All this was made possible because of a background of private means, and that does not breed good financial sense. By March 1944 this small company, with war-weary staff reduced to the very few, had not only survived but could support "Salute the Soldier Week" by putting a precious £500 into 3 per cent Savings Bonds. The year after, Company profits reached the dizzy heights of £2,195, enabling the distribution of a dividend. You have never charged enough for the first-class personal service you give and never properly exploited the name you have built up. Indeed, you have never run your Company at the going rate, and that is now catching up with you. I know the present Directors are making great efforts to come into line on these points – appropriate fees and salaries – but you have an awful backlog of past thinking to overcome.'

Margaret, while listening most attentively, had also had an interesting thought and had been making a pencilled calculation on the balance sheet before her. 'If we could, at this time, levy only 2 per cent on the present considerable gross turnover, our Directors' Report would make good reading; but I would wager that in whatever form we tried it, the outcry from clients would be greater than a rise in our fees.'

Without hesitation, Philip took up the idea. 'A trial run of a handling fee, which could be as easily discontinued without any disturbance to fee structures and all the work involved in that.'

'To be levied on fees, not of course on expenses,' added Eveleigh. 'It would be cheaper, and therefore surely more acceptable to clients than a rise in fees.'

'I think,' said Frances, 'that whatever words you use to describe such a levy, the clients will ask, "Surely that is included in the fees we pay you?" Although I would not vote against the idea,' she finished.

On a show of hands, it was decided that fees would be frozen for a trial period and the 2% levy brought in. As soon as this was quoted on the scale of fees and added to the bills, the clients questioned it exactly as Frances had predicted – proving that to the general public, a fee is a fee, to be accepted or not, but that what they consider hidden extras are never acceptable. The experiment was discontinued.

Both new Directors were busy in their departments, but were useful to Margaret. With the majority of the Board now in the office, they had been given certain powers of action on behalf of the Company without a full meeting being called. This, as intended, made for less cumbersome management.

Penelope's job reached its peak times with the advent of school holidays and back-to-school days, which saw the escort Aunts flooding the railway stations and airports, carrying out their instructions. By the '70s there was a wide variety on the basic model of the Aunt. Younger ones, bred in nannyless days and accustomed to helping with young brothers and sisters and babysitting around the family, now made trustworthy escorts and were popular with travelling children. The mature Aunt was more casual and relaxed than her earlier counterpart. Huskies and Barbours or ski trousers and jerkin had replaced hats and gloves. She was no longer a figure of awe but a friend who was not shocked if one roller-skated down the platform to meet her or confided about a girl- or boy-friend or divorced parents. Sometimes one felt the Aunt was a bit of a lark too, and told Mum and Dad so; it usually got back to the office.

Dear Miss Henshaw,

We earnestly request that the below-mentioned Aunt will not be dismissed the force, the lady obviously has considerable human qualities, though my wife and I have to register a small complaint.

Yesterday on the arrival home of George and Edward for the holidays, there was much discussion about their car journey across London from Waterloo to King's Cross in their Universal Aunt's super new car, what the super Aunt had pointed out to them en route and the goodies she had supplied, food and reading matter for the long journey. With no doubt in my mind that all had been managed to perfection for two excited eleven-year-olds by this paragon, I idly threw in an enquiry, 'And she made you fasten your seat-belts in the car, I hope, George?' 'Oh no, Daddy, she had her jolly nice retriever dog with her and he was in the front seat with the seat-belt on, and Edward and I were in the back, where there weren't any seat-belts at all.

Yours etc.

The office corridor was not usually alive with the sounds of music, but there it was, very pop and very loud. Investigating heads came out of rooms and with her telephone to one ear, Jean threw her hand over the other as she tried to hear the caller on the switchboard. 'For goodness sake, fetch Penelope!' she called out to anyone within earshot. It was an 'in-the-middle-of-meetings' day; some 500 schoolchildren and a web of Universal Aunts would, in the ensuing three or four days, be passing in and out of the doors to and from their various planes and trains for the school holidays. Mountainous piles of bulging cases and holdalls, tons of strapped wooden and metal trunks, together with loose cricket bats, tennis racquets, coats, caps, and small personal battered packages, adorned reception, while the overall scent of the schoolroom pervaded the offices, a bit muddy and wet-woolly, with the added ingredient of the ripening Camembert collected from Paxtons and being taken home for Dad.

Out of the neatly stacked mountain was issuing the pop music, and a number of boys, girls and assorted Aunts appeared rooted and un-certain. Penelope appeared on the trot, her experienced eye sweeping the scene – well in command, no panic to be allowed – to locate the source.

'It's coming from there; come along, boys, let's move some of these cases,' she commanded as she led the onslaught. It proved not to be a simple problem. One small boy had packed his transistor in the middle of all his clothes, for safety, in the biggest and strongest of the school trunks standing there. The humps and bumps of the journey had turned it on.

'Here we are,' said Penelope. 'Where's your key, John? We'll soon have it out!'

Not so simple.

'Oh, Daddy doesn't let me carry keys because I'm always losing them, so we keep one at school for when my trunk is there, and he keeps the other at home himself,' replied John, pink with importance. Penelope, not for the first time, silently endorsed her conviction that parents weren't fit to have children.

'Oh dear, that's difficult. We can't have all that noise in here and we can't have it disturbing everyone all the way to Edinburgh, which is surely how long it will take for the battery to run down.'

The next move came from an interested spectator, a bigger, freckled boy. 'I can pick a lock with a bit of wire.'

'Splendid fellow. Find him some wire.'

'Picture wire,' said Jean, removing one from the wall and unravelling the length. Within minutes the offending musical article was unearthed.

Penelope refrained from putting her foot on it, and returned briskly to her own room.

'Ah, hello Chris!' she greeted one of the most experienced escorts. 'Is all going well?'

'Yes, I've just put the Naylor child on her train and found a motherly passenger to keep an eye on her, as well as the guard. She's a nervous little girl. I'm off to Heathrow for my Air India one now.'

Penelope buzzed. 'Jean, now that Chris has gone, would you send up the one waiting for an interview – I have the form she filled in.'

A jolly-looking type came into the room – might she be a winner?

'Hello, Mrs Walker, I understand that you would like to help in our Meetings department. I see that you live round the corner and are a driver, which is good, so let me give you a brief outline of how we operate at meetings time. When all our background work and placings are done, I try and let you have at least one meeting for each of your available days. Your instructions are typed out on one of these yellow forms and given to you, then you come in for briefing and to cover any particular points. All is worked out beforehand to eliminate or cover any snags, so that one is left with only natural disasters – fog, flood, landslides and strikes causing train and aeroplane delays and re-organizing!'

'It sounds terrifying. Are there many mistakes?' Mrs Walker was still jolly, a good sign.

'Fortunately very few. New escorts are so anxious to get it right that they take the greatest care, and old escorts are so experienced they know every snag. Also, we give you a complete twenty-four-hour back-up here at the office, and airlines and stations have the list of our emergency escorts in case of problems or unexpected arrivals.'

'I'd very much like to join you.'

The phone buzzed.

'Penelope, one of the boys down here has got a pet gerbil and apparently it's hungry.'

'Would one of you pop down to reception for a moment with biscuits for a gerbil? Actually you'd better take the tin, I should think the children might like some too.'

Many a back-seat confidence would be exchanged while the Aunt was driving. 'Although we hear it so often,' reported Joss, 'it still never fails to amaze me how resilient children can be to circumstances.'

'Are you going out to your Mum and Dad?' said one of the boys to another.

'My Mummy's real but I've only got half a Daddy there,' said the other, and went on, 'My Dad and my half-Mummy have got a new baby and I'll see it next hols, but my real Dad and my real Mum had me. It's great, I have some hols in America and some in Spain.'

It was always the little ones who were the easiest. They would come looking like small grey parcels covered in badges, (as many as they could get hold of) and liked to be met and cared for when feeling homesick at night. With the fourteen- and fifteen-year-old girls one could expect anything. The last thing they would want was to be safely escorted across London and, though possibly addicted to badges of every other sort, certainly resented sporting a round orange disc with the black UA. Straight out of the barriers with the school train behind them, they dashed to the loo, making holes in the carefully planned travel timetable, while they changed into their own sophisticated clothes, painted their faces, and fluffed out their hair. When they emerged, it was clear that they were even more in need of care and protection! The slightly older ones, the students, were like the little ones – happy to share a confidence and seek advice or guidance while being escorted towards the new freedoms of college or bed-sitter land.

Jess, driving a Turkish student to her college in Devon, discovered that the terrified girl was convinced she was being kidnapped, and had almost no spoken English with which to communicate. Jess pulled the car off the road and persuaded the girl to make a telephone call to the college, who could explain. On the way home for the next holidays, Jess fetched her again. 'Hello, this is your old kidnapping friend,' she greeted her. By then the girl was happily able both to understand and to laugh.

Dozens of daily telephone calls went back and forth in the department, and as one Aunt arrived in the room she was surprised to hear, 'Hello, am I speaking to the Holy Family?'

'Don't worry,' explained Penelope, 'she's talking to the Convent, not the Almighty.'

Another head came round the door.

'When Penelope's free, tell her our overnighter left a small lizard under his pillow. I thought it was a toy at first, but it's alive. I'm dashing for my next meeting now but I'll liaise with you later about how to keep it until the child returns from school.'

'That's one to juggle with; rather you than me,' was the response. 'But then I so often feel that. I think you're all marvellous. I'd sooner be here safely at my desk than on your jobs.'

'Ah, but that goes for us too. We like the out-and-about variety, and wouldn't have your complicated background work and worry for anything.'

'Good, so we're all happy.'

A small word of praise makes everything worthwhile. A father wrote:

I do hope you can assist in this matter, as all I can get from the school is, 'If you use Universal Aunts, everything will sort itself out'.

In the meantime, Kate was managing her end of things. The card shown on the left was in the files of many legal firms throughout the country, offering a specialized service for replacement in monetary terms necessitated by cases of bereavement or injury. The specialized information available from an agency with long and first-hand knowledge of domestic placings had come to be much sought-after by solicitors and barristers, and was obviously acceptable for consideration by a judge. For instance, how much would it cost a husband to employ someone to run his house if his wife died? Could he get one person who would be wife and mother, nurse, nanny, teacher, housekeeper, cook, laundry-maid, waitress, shopper, driver, cleaner, gardener, painter and book-keeper? Alternatively, a husband's work might suffer because he had to take time off to attend to the needs of the children and household. His career prospects could, as a result, be seriously affected.

Kate therefore spent a certain amount of her time visiting solicitors' offices, barristers' chambers, or engaged for a day in Court, providing the relevant information on costs for the claimant, and replying to any questions from the opposing barrister. She would first set out the general advice in a preliminary letter.

Dear Sir,

Thank you for your enquiry. I am pleased to supply the attached evidence as requested, this being the usual form of statement required of me.

It is generally assumed that one woman, usually described as a housekeeper, will replace all the wife/mother services. This is seldom so, but should such a person be found her pay should be proportionate to the tasks.

From experience we would warn that the immediate compassion of friends and neighbours, that follows a tragedy, should not be relied upon as a permanent situation from which to obtain help.

The type of help and source of supply would be determined by the standards of life customary within the family background. However, from wherever the help is obtained, whether through an agency or privately, the rate for the job should be calculated as being a standard 'going rate'. These rates are recognized by all reputable agencies as a basis upon which they give their current quotations. I list below the present rates and terms of employment.

Housekeeper: No formal training, but experienced. Shopping, cooking, personal laundry and ironing, light cleaning. Would seldom drive. Some like light gardening but that is not an understood duty.

Daily help: which would be expected for some number of hours a week: hoovering, polishing, silver cleaning, window cleaning.

Gardener.

Nanny: Nursery nurse qualifications. Exclusive care and all training of the child. Decisions on and care of child's diet, clothing, rooms and transport. Most are drivers.

Yours faithfully.

It was great good fortune for her to have a lawyer son ('Anthony, what is the procedure in Court?'), so from her very first case she could be properly prepared.

An award did not ease the heartache of the claimant, but it could make life materially easier.

21

1970S

REMEMBERED WITH AFFECTION

Clementine Spencer Churchill – Miss Monica Dickens –
GI Gerry surfaces

UNIVERSAL AUNTS LTD – 1921–1976

55 years old and still a household name. Overseas guests and residents here will find a haven in our Special Services department. We book your concert, cup final and theatre tickets: do your personal shopping, packing, mailing (or give you guidelines), arrange your parties: and open a personal door to some of Britain's most charming private homes. Plus a special bonus for 1977 – if you want to enjoy our royal Silver Jubilee celebrations! To get the most out of Europe, call on us for a Proxy Parent and leave your family safely in the hands of 'another mother' while you forget yourselves in Paris, Perthshire or Provence.

36 Walpole Street
London SW3
Telephone:
(01)-730 9834

1976 was the year when it became clear that Eveleigh was not in the best of health, and by June she resigned. Frances temporarily stepped into the position of Chairman; but at her age did not wish to take it on permanently. Margaret was overwhelmingly elected one month later, and Penelope and Kate became the joint Managing Directors. There were ever-increasing responsibilities, more red tape, problems and paperwork, and a greater involvement with staff; on top of which they both still ran departments. In view of this, both they and the Board agreed that the task shared would be less arduous and less lonely.

For seventeen years Agnes had run her Babysitting department, the epitome of reliability and quiet efficiency. Her friends in the nursery world were legion. Her time of retirement had now come also; and flowers, cards and messages flowed in to her from nannies, nurses, hotel housekeepers, babysitters and mothers. The saying that no one is indispensable may be true, but the Babysitting department would never be quite the same again. Some of Agnes's older workers decided it was retirement time too, so her leaving party saw a number of farewells. It was not entirely good-bye to Agnes, who was always to be found at her pretty garden flat in Kensington, available for sewing commissions, and able to return to the Aunts on celebration days.

Before her departure, however, she shared with the rest of the office the keenly felt closing of a chapter when Emmie Faulder died in old age and peaceful retirement – that great personality in the history of the organization, that first Aunt envisaged by Gertie, with whom she had travelled side by side and long beyond. Very shortly afterwards the Aunts had gathered again, in the Church of St Jude, for the memorial service to Phyllis Johnson, another name that would be passed on in affectionate memory.

Missing her old friend of the switchboard, Agnes's sad sense of loss was brightened when Phyllis's daughter Jill provided her with a moment of delight. A request had come in for the Aunts to supply a reader for Lady Churchill. She too was an old lady now, and her eyesight no longer good. Several readers were tried, but most of all she liked the clear voice of the actress and Jill herself. The sessions continued and one day Lady Churchill presented Jill with a gift. That was the last reading session, for Lady Churchill became too ill and died a little while later. Jill brought her gift into the office for Agnes and all the others to see. She unwrapped a small, thick book, beautifully bound in red and tooled and edged in gold. The title was *Winston Churchill, His Wit and Wisdom*, and all eyes were on what was written on the flyleaf in quite a firm hand, '*Clementine Spencer Churchill 1977*'.

'Now Phyllis would have liked that,' smiled Agnes gently. Most particularly Jill, but all of the Aunts too, felt very proud to have been of service.

Kate's number buzzed and Jean's voice was low.

'Kate, strictly speaking this is Jobs Abroad but I think it needs a Director. Could you come to reception?'

There, rising to his feet, was a tall, slender Arab. His skin was palely tanned, and his eyes and short, neat beard were black. The immaculate robes were purest white and the headdress was corded round in black. Answering the smile of encouragement with a deep, unblinking gaze, he came stright to the point. 'Good afternoon. I have my card here which will describe me.' The small visiting card changed hands and Kate read the name of a sheik. 'I wish to take an English lady and for you to arrange this.'

'In what capacity do you wish to employ this lady, and where?'

'To marry – I already have her name and I will tell you what I wish to offer.'

He had seen her at a reception and was quite respectfully, and with determination, pursuing her. He had armed himself with information about the lady and wished Universal Aunts to negotiate on his behalf. To the completely unsuspecting and most respectable lawyer's widow he was offering houses, cars, aeroplanes, yachts, an island, a desert if she wished, a lot of barrels of oil, and an Aladdin's cave of jewels.

As one of the few services Universal Aunts had never offered was that of a marriage bureau, a careful and polite explanation of the fact sufficed. When in doubt, use the embassy; the suggestion that they might be the most reputable source to suggest a negotiator was well received. With graceful farewells and bows, the interview ended. The Aunts were not, of course, involved with the end of the story; but they did find out, at first hand, that the lady, if she received such a proposal, kept it between herself and the gentleman concerned, for she continued in her calm and pleasant life in London.

Amongst the routine of every day there were always the 'tales of the unexpected'.

Mary, in her Accommodation department, put down the telephone after a complaint from one of her landladies. 'The young American couple you've placed with me,' she began.

'I hope they're nice?' said Mary, sensing trouble.

'Oh, they're nice young people and I'm very *sorry* for them that the husband is over here for medical treatment, but I don't know if I can manage them for *seven* weeks, they seem so accident-prone. So far they have shorted the electrical system with their travelling iron, on arrival they tore a piece of wallpaper off the staircase going up with their suitcases, and they disconnected the fridge overnight by turning off the wrong plug. This morning, they have flooded the bath,' she ended wearily. 'The last paying guest you sent was perfect,' she sighed.

'Oh yes!' Mary laughed. 'The delightful Australian carpenter who spent his whole two weeks' visit to London in his room, with curtains drawn against the sun, watching Wimbledon, then left for home.'

Marion had arrived back from lunch. 'I have just seen William

Norcliffe Roberts almost blown to Kingdom Come,' she said. All ears
pricked up. William, a grey woolly miniature Schnauzer, lived further
down Walpole Street, his doctor master caring for the health of a
number of Universal Aunts and, in an emergency, the children in their
charge. Willie had popped out of his front door, down the steps, heading
for the nearest lamp post. Fortunately the electricity man from his hole
in the ground saw the dog and read his intentions. Quick off the mark
and none too gently, he diverted William from the open maintenance
box at the base, a drenching of which might have done him no good at
all!

Universal Aunts enjoyed their dogs as they came and went: Mary's
Boots, a biscuit-coloured imperious Imperial Peke, top dog in 'his'
office and watchful for interlopers; Catherine's Galaxy, a long-haired
dachshund with silky bronze coat and flowing tail, who out of office
hours liked the best restaurants; Sue's Digger, a perky blue and tan
Australian terrier, now and again visiting the office for a quick inspection; Samantha's Rupert, an elegant white-and-gold cocker spaniel
prone to getting lost in Chelsea if out of her sight for a moment; and
Maria's troupe of tiny Yorkies, two spry girls and a frailer boy, with pink
or blue bows on their topnots, scattering about like leaves in a breeze.

At that moment Maria, an alluring young Aunt with tight pink jeans
and flowing blonde hair, rushed in. 'I'm double-parked and have just
had a crisis,' she announced.

Marion groaned. 'You haven't bumped another Rolls?' The other
Aunts swore that Maria spent more in fines and parking tickets than she
earned. 'No, but I *did* have to *persuade* a warden not to book me. Well,
there I was, early this morning, driving down Park Lane and there *it* was
in the *middle* of the road.'

'What?'

'The sweetest green and yellow budgie! *Naturally* I screeched to a
stop, got out and *crept* towards him but he fluttered further into the road.
Back to the car I rushed and had just snatched up my purple cardigan to
throw over him, all the other cars were driving well round us, when there
appeared this warden and asked what I thought I was doing.'

Marion felt every sympathy for the warden.

'I showed him,' continued Maria, 'by throwing my cardigan over the
bird, scooping him up and putting him into my car. I said to the warden,
"I should think some poor child is sobbing her heart out; don't you think
we'd better phone the police?" I gave him my name and address because

I thought he would have more time than I, because, as I told him, "If I don't get these passports to the embassy, Universal Aunts will have a *fit*."'

'What *did* he do?' Marion sounded exhausted.

'He seemed a bit limp and just said, "Drive on."' Maria paused. '"Bless you," I said to him. I was *just* about to go when I had a thought, so I opened the window a crack and told him, "They are often trained to talk, you know. I'll *ask* him, he might give his name and address." So there he is in my car outside.'

Lola Lumb Inglis' silver-blonde curls and stunning marshmallow prettiness was made elegant by her tallness. This morning her excellent figure was clad in dress and jacket of blue, matching her eyes. The rest of them always likened her to *Vogue*'s mature 'Mrs Exeter'. They were all very aware of the value of Lola as their public relations personality, for her bubbling and sincere friendliness, coupled with the fact that it never occurred to her that she would not have an entrée, always got her a hearing if not a commission. Undaunted, she never thought any the worse of anyone for not realizing how useful the Aunts could be to them. She really liked people and next time would greet them as charmingly and enthusiastically as ever. It was also her job for part of each day to continue in the Letting department finding the right house or flat to fit the client, having begun at 8 a.m. by opening the post.

'Good morning, Marion, one of your letters this morning is in Spanish, quite a long one, so I've put it on your desk and when you're ready, I'll come and translate it.' Her Spanish was perfect. 'Now, the rest of you girls, do you have up your sleeve a typically British old-worlde cottage, with log fires, new-fangled plumbing, dishwasher and freezer, to house six, with a rose garden and heated swimming pool, all in a perfect village between here and Brighton, for those super Americans from California for two months from June?'

'No, Lola,' was the chorus.

'Now come along, think of all your contacts please. I'm going to have a cup of coffee before I start and I'll make one for you too. Just watch the warden, the meter's empty, but I'm going in half an hour to view a house in Richmond.'

Before the coffee was made, Lola was called back to the telephone. She always smiled into the receiver when it was one of her favourites.

'Hello, good morning Mrs Jenkins, how nice to –' She gasped. 'Oh, how horrific, how terrible, heavens.' The listeners were riveted as Lola

plumped down in a chair and her voice rose. '*All* the legs?' She paused.
'Yes, if the money isn't instantly handed over, hadn't you better get on to
your solicitor or the police? You know one hears that once people get
away into diplomatic immunity or some such thing, they disappear and
there is no redress. I can't tell you how ghastly I feel that we introduced
them to you. How could we guess, after all these years of sending you
dozens of guests – nothing so dreadful. Well, it is kind of you to say so,
but what a shocker this is. I'll get off the telephone now and do please let
me know what happens.'

She clattered the receiver back and explained.

'We had a letter from Dubai asking for hotel accommodation for a
month – husband, wife, nanny and three children. We arranged for two
large suites at Ethelbury House; they arrived last week. Apparently after
taking the children shopping for toys yesterday, the parents went out for
the evening and the so-called nanny sat and watched while the boys
practised with their new carpentry sets. They sawed *every* leg off *every*
chair and table. *Nothing* is left standing – and the parents are quite
unperturbed.'

'Different standards. Look at last year when you let the flat to a newly
oil-rich husband of four wives and they lit a small fire, for some kind of
purpose, in the middle of the drawing-room carpet,' said someone sadly.

In Kate's post was a letter of great interest. Monica Dickens was a
household name and a lady who, through her delightful books, had given
pleasure to thousands of people around the world. She wrote from her
home in North Falmouth, Massachusetts, to say that,

> Long, long ago, in about 1937, I got my first job as a cook general at
> Universal Aunts, which led two years later to my first book, which was
> called *One Pair of Hands*.

Miss Dickens, engaged in writing her current book, wanted a bit of
information about those far-off days. The ensuing correspondence,
revealing that Universal Aunts was approaching its Diamond Jubilee,
resulted in the first thoughts and attempts to write its story more fully
than just as anecdotes for the archives.

> How marvellous it is [wrote Miss Dickens] that the agency has
> developed and grown like that over the years. It must have been quite
> small when I first went there, but since it represented adventure to

me, it seemed efficient and frightening, until I got to know the lady
who helped me get jobs. She was indeed more like an aunt than an
agent.

Yours sincerely,

Monica Dickens

And so it continued to be, more adventure, more surprise. Another
contact with the past came in the shape of GI Elmer – the wartime Elmer
Pope of Staten Island, New York. Quite rightly expecting that none of
the Aunts who knew him then were still in the office, he re-introduced
himself and went on to beseech the present Aunts to trace his English
friends.

Unfortunately, my modest pension forbids the payment of a high fee.
However, if you can do this I will pay, if necessary, up to a maximum of
five hundred dollars for the address of and/or a letter from, this lady.
This is all the pertinent information I can give you: Miss Nona Holly,
present age about fifty, quite probably married, formerly of 21
Morton Road, Crouch End, London N8. At the same address were
her mother and father, Edith and Ted Holly, and maternal aunt and
her family, Mick and Gladys Jennson, with their children John, now
about forty-five, and Chris, about forty-two. Other relatives were
Alec and Judith Reeves of Coghill Street, and their son David, at that
time in the Royal English Navy.

I will appreciate any help you can give. The fee that I can pay in no
way reflects the very high regard I have for these people, especially for
Miss Holly. When I was lonely, homesick, and sorely in need of
friendship, they provided that friendship, wholeheartedly and un-
selfishly. Having recently retired, I had hoped to revisit London, but
though I learned to love your city very much in the three years that I

spent there, unless I can find these good friends I fear that the trip
would not be worth while.

> Very sincerely yours
> Elmer Pope,
> Staten Island,
> New York,
> USA.

Jos, an experienced 'beaver Aunt', was put on to the job of outside
investigation. A request was also made to Michael Aspel of 'Where Are
You Now?' on Capital Radio to broadcast the details. Jos inspected the
electoral roll for the area, but there was neither a Holly nor a Jennson
there. She drove down to N8 and found number 21 Morton Road
unoccupied, looking very derelict and boarded up. There was a small
shop on the corner; when she enquired, they were polite but hadn't
heard the names thereabout. As she was leaving, Jos asked, 'How long
has number 21 been empty?'

'Since a year ago come last March when there was the fire. The old
lady was got out but the landlord never repaired it and she never came
back.'

'Who was the old lady?'

'Oh, that was Mrs Reeves, Judith Reeves,' was the magic answer – the
aunt from Coghill Street, realized Jos. After a quick explanation Jos
was directed to the next street where 'Mrs Allen lives at number 7,
she used to be friendly to the old lady and might know where she's
gone'.

In answer to her knock at number 7, the door opened a crack.

'You from the council?' was the fairly belligerent enquiry.

'No,' answered Jos, mounting the last step towards the pinny and
headscarf-encased occupant. 'I have been told at the shop that you may
be able to tell me the whereabouts of Mrs Judith Reeves.' After a small
explanation, with well-placed words like 'war-time' and 'American',
curiosity prevailed and produced an invitation to 'come in'. Soon she
was sipping a cup of tea.

'Snoopers I can't abide,' declared Mrs Allen. 'But I can tell now
you're not one of *them*.' Having decided that, Mrs Allen was happy to
relate as many details of the fire as she could recall.

'And do you know where Mrs Reeves went?' asked Jos.

'Yes, she was took to the Walbeck Hospital a mile down the road, but she was all right and I know her son David took her out of there, but I don't rightly know where he lives.'

They parted friends, Jos took the information back to the office and the rest was done from there. The Walbeck, though unable to divulge any information about a patient, willingly forwarded Universal Aunts' letter to Mrs Reeves, and a copy of the letter from Elmer Pope. Within a fortnight the delighted gentleman wrote:

My dear Ladies,
I have received both a telephone call and a letter from my friends in England. Mere words cannot express my gratitude. Without your help I would probably never have seen them again. Many, many thanks for a job well done.

He did see them again; he also came in to see the Aunts, bringing Mrs Nona Dilkes, formerly Holly, with him, and they all lunched on smoked salmon sandwiches and a bottle of wine and listened to fascinating reminiscences of an England most of them could not really have known.

Joy glided in from Accounts – porcelain skin, slender hands tipped with pastel, almond nails, and dressed in a smart sage-green hopsack coat and skirt, a gold Victorian brooch and small string of pearls. She was well aware of the reluctance of departments to understand anything financial beyond their own billing sheets, and dealt with this by imparting information in gentle, low tones, thereby preventing anyone getting het-up by 'figures'. In the same way, but with determination, she extracted from the departments exactly what she needed to know and, in spite of their sluggish response, without delay. Her Accounts department was run with efficiency and she was always there with a dependable explanation to a query. 'I think, Marion, this comes under Special Services rather than Accounts,' she said. 'There is a charming old lady in reception who has come in to enquire what terms are offered to decayed gentlefolk.'

Marion went along to cope and reported back.

'She had paid Universal Aunts a fee of ten guineas in 1927 and wondered whether that still entitled her to use the agency,' Marion laughed.

'I expect she's very rich,' answered Joy briskly.

'I wouldn't be surprised, but I've made a nice compromise,' Marion went on. 'We decided that she did not need the expensive service of someone to change her library book. But as she needs a cleaner for her flat a couple of mornings a week, the cleaner can pop round to the library and change it, and the cleaning agency fee is much lower.'

'Well done,' said Joy. 'Just look at this.' She handed Marion an airmail envelope she had just opened. 'We placed a boy in holiday accommodation in September last year; his father in Columbus, Ohio, has needed three reminders to pay and at last he has. Now look what he's written on the back of the *envelope!*' she said, enraged. Marion read, in capital letters: SORRY IT'S LATE, BUT WHEN YOU HAVEN'T GOT IT YOU HAVEN'T GOT IT.

'What a *sauce*,' snorted Marion.

As she got back to her office, two of the young Universal Uncles had arrived for a briefing. Having recently left school, they were quite smart young men about town when they weren't doing cleaning jobs for the Aunts!

'So, how's life?' Marion enquired merrily.

Both standing lankily dignified, one replied, nonchalant but slightly indignant, 'We thought we'd have afternoon tea at the Bunny Club on Park Lane yesterday afternoon, but the chap there said they didn't serve tea. Extraordinary, but he was quite nice about it.'

'What did you do?'

'We went to the Ritz.'

'How wise,' said Marion, without batting an eyelid. As she also said, after their departure, '*Men Only*, hidden under *Horse and Hound* in the downstairs loo, has much to answer for!'

'What is Mark up to?' asked Mary about another of the young Uncles.

'Enjoying his work,' was the reply. He's been placed with Lady Mulligan, whose cleaning woman has threatened to leave if she doesn't get someone else to polish the acres of parquet. Mark arrives, puts cloth bags on his feet and *skates* away all over it. No newfangled Bissel there. While this goes on, Lady M sits on the staircase and they discuss greyhound form, he being a devotee and she, in past days, a considerable breeder of the dogs on her Irish estate. This happy arrangement makes housework a joy for both.'

Shopping commissions were as brisk as ever. One yearly repeat order to Paris caused a certain amount of speculation. 'Hello, hello – La Tante Universale – Madame Pellerin? London here, Special Services. Is your mother, Madame Adamian, in good health, Madame? You will be pleased to hear that our postal strike is over and we wish to thank you for arranging the collections of Paris mail which we brought over to Le

Touquet during these last weeks. May I now tell you the shopping list for Mr X of Colchester? All as usual from Victoire, and the sizes unchanged.

'One full length nightdress, the bodice to be lace and sleeveless, and please choose a flesh tint. One short nightdress with tie-ribbon shoulder-straps in white, pure silk. One full-length nightdress and matching negligée with a full sleeve in pale coffee satin. The same in peach silk. Also from Victoire's catalogue, the new evening cardigan in baby-blue angora with the giant pearl button fastening, size 36. All as before to be sent to us here, from where we shall arrange the usual collection.'

The high French voice echoed the repeat of the order – and a sentence or two more.

'Yes, I do agree, we too are intrigued . . . five years of these orders, telephoned in by a nondescript female voice and a good deposit of cash to cover the bill in advance. All under the name of Mr X of Colchester, and the collection from our office made by a silent, drab woman who could be a maid. We all think *he*, whatever his real identity, must be someone's rich lover. Or a rich lady, ordering for herself, for assignations.'

Less intriguing, but more exciting for the office, were the regular instructions of Mr O'Callaghan of New Jersey to purchase Christmas gifts to be sent to the staff and families of his British associate companies – thirty or forty people to shop for. One Aunt would have a gorgeous time spending lots of lovely American money. First a trip around the shops to view, then a telex to New Jersey, with suggestions: china, glass, leather, books. One year the shopper had given a strong recommendation for a particular item; Mr O'Callaghan had liked the idea; and forty were bought and delivered to the office.

Walking into Room 3, one saw an array of small boxes, pillbox-size to snuffbox-size, in jewel-like colours with engaging drawings and designs, round, square and oval. Halcyon Days had revived the craft of enamelling on copper which had flourished in the late eighteenth century. No doubt one day these might be treasures, if not perhaps in the league of Georgian Battersea and Bilston boxes. There were hunting, shooting and fishing scenes, garlands of flowers, shepherdesses and little animal miniatures, with a surprise depicted on the inside of each lid – one tiny object plucked from the main theme. For girls and boys, there were nursery rhymes and children's joys, a snowman or a ladybird.

Some celebrated the seasons or commemorated a painter, writer or composer. One depicted a great moment in history. The more personal ones, for wives and mothers and lovers, had not of course been chosen on this occasion. They were all packed and ribboned in the office and on each small, pale-blue card was written, '*Wishing you a Happy Christmas from Joe O'Callaghan, New Jersey.*' Then off they went in the Christmas post to the lucky recipients.

Those were the happy aspects of the Aunt's work. On the same day, amongst other calls of distress, Jenny had one from a grandmother begging help for her son. His wife had just died, leaving children of twelve, eight, six and six weeks, the eldest a Downs Syndrome child. It was no good just feeling sad; it was Jenny's job to get the best possible person to them as fast as she could.

22

1980s

A DIAMOND JUBILEE

A Royal engagement – Goodbye Walpole Street –
Personalities – Sir John Betjeman – Aage Tharup

Universal Aunt's Jubilee Year began with world-wide joy and celebration – not for them, but for a future royal lady whom they knew. On that
morning, when the news broke, everyone had something to say, wanting
to share the great occasion. Maria's father, Anthony Garton, an old
friend, telephoned the office: 'I have to congratulate you on the
engagement of one of your Universal Aunts,' he said. A charming bit of
fun – for in June of 1979 Lady Diana Spencer had become one of the
young part-time Aunts to help with the care of children. At the time of
her engagement, as all the world knows, her chosen work was in a
nursery school, immersed in even more children.

In 1962 the Mayor and Mayoress of the Royal Borough of Kensington and Chelsea had honoured Universal Aunts' arrival in Walpole
Street with a visit. The present Mayor and Mayoress did so again on the
occasion of the Company's Diamond Jubilee.

It was a happy occasion on a sparkingly hot summer evening, held in
rooms whose windows overlooked that first little office of sixty years
before. Cars unloaded women in pretty frocks and handsome men, then
parked nose to tail all over Lowndes Square or in Charles Hammonds'
premises. The Member of Parliament, Nicholas Scott came, looking, as
always, suave and affable. 'Jennifer' made a stunning, sweeping entrance
in pale sweet-pea blue chiffon with the famous bow in her hair, and
immediately spied 'friends' and others she knew. Frances, in splendid
old age, was transported by car and borne up the stairs in her wheelchair
by two strong Universal Uncles. She was placed where all could go and
pay homage and, frail though she was, she undertook two special duties
of the evening: the presentation of a gift to Margaret to mark her Silver
Jubilee with the Aunts, and a gift to Mrs Hacker, who had announced
her retirement from caring for the comfort of the staff. The Aunts super

'couple', Ron Morris and *his* (Spanish) Maria butled and waitressed
with their customary finesse, unbothered by the crush and the warmest
night of the summer. Flowers and hugs and kisses and congratulations
saw the Aunts hopefully on the way to their hundred years!

The immediate days went on as usual.

Mrs Hacker's departure was imminent. For an unbelievable fifty-
three years out of the sixty, mother and daughter had cared for the
domestic arrangements and orderliness of the office. Mrs Hacker had
overtaken her mother's service by completing thirty-three of those
years. Who would take over? Certainly not Lilly Moggs, a cleaner on the
books, who had informed the office that she took her husband with her
to work because the hoover was too heavy for her!

Molly was still upright and trim, economy her watchword over the
stationery cupboard. Like Pooh, she preceded activity with a tuneful
hum, a warning sign which cleared desk tops of excess pens, staples, and
clips. For rumour had it that with a sweep of her gaze, she registered just
what she could raid at an opportune moment, put back into store and
redistribute as new!

Muriel had a brief encounter with the Aunts. She and one of them,
being members of the same club, had struck up a conversation there
while lunching, during which it transpired that Muriel was looking for
office space in which to work. 'Much paper-work, and such a small flat
that I need a desk somewhere else for three months,' she explained.
Back at Walpole Street the problem was discussed – perhaps the
temporarily empty little room 3 could be put to use to the benefit of both?
Negotiations were soon completed and Muriel installed.

She humped through the swing doors each morning with her grey
Irish wolfhound, Geraint, almost as tall as herself, a vast carpet-bag, and
several plastic bags stuffed with books and papers. Muriel was short and
round as a pudding, with a pleasant scrubbed face and pale eyes that
gazed trustingly from behind thick spectacles, all topped by short,
springy curls, faded in middle age from ginger to sandy. Her dress was
interesting, loose and ill-assorted, and mostly covered by a tapestry coat
of many-coloured squares. Pinned among the layers were large jewelled
brooches, much too valuable to be left in an empty London flat all day; a
string of pearls made little bumps under her jersey and each of her
chubby fingers sported a beautiful ring.

'Might you not get mugged?' enquired the Aunts.

'Oh no, Geraint wouldn't let me be.'

'He's so huge – aren't you afraid he might be too strong for you or get into a fight?'

'He's well trained and good natured. But in case of trouble I carry this.' From a pocket Muriel produced a plastic squeezy lemon. 'It has water inside. When sprayed in the face of fighting dogs it doesn't harm them but gives them such a surprise that they stop.' Happily and confidently she ambled away to her room and, with door closed, got on with whatever she did there.

Muriel was quite happy to stop for a chat, but seldom sought one. She seemed to be vaguely surprised by the incidents of daily life, and now and again paused to relate one. 'Do you know, on my way here I saw an extraordinary thing. Two policemen were coming out of a house down the road, carrying large suitcases and followed by a man. I thought, how kind of them to help that man with his cases, and I said so to a nice-looking person who was passing and had also noticed. "Madam," he said to me, "the man is handcuffed to them!"'

A somewhat private person, she seldom expressed her views, but when she did so they were very black and white; and her mildness evaporated when faced with cruelty and injustice. She clearly found London an unhappy place. Seeing the report of a rape in the morning paper in reception, she announced, 'The man should be hounded down and castrated.' Mid-morning she was caught up in a discussion on the changing face of London. 'We ought to be repairing old streets of houses, not building tower blocks,' was Muriel's opinion. 'People were meant to have contact with the earth beneath their feet and feel they belong there, not to live disorientated in lonely space.' During Muriel's short stay in the city, Battersea Dogs' Home must have got used to her delivering stray animals there.

At the end of the three months she removed her piles of papers and books, herself and Geraint, and bade the Aunts a charming goodbye for the moment. Her last gesture was an invitation to Rebecca, an elderly, rather lonely Aunt, to spend the coming Easter holiday 'with us in the country'. After the holiday, Rebecca reported back.

'I knew her house was in north Wales, and we set off early on Good Friday,' she began. 'After Shrewsbury we saw the Welsh mountains ahead and Muriel said, "Almost home." About an hour later we passed through a small grey village, went over a river bridge and through large iron gates.' Rebecca paused for effect, knowing that they had all been intrigued by their remote office lodger. '"Home",' she said, 'was a beautiful little Welsh castle, a perfectly delightful large and adoring husband who farmed a famous pedigree flock of sheep there, and three grown-up married children who arrived with their families for the weekend.'

'*Whatever* was she doing in London for three months?' asked the stunned audience.

'She's M.B-H., the writer,' said Rebecca. 'She always gets right away and lives alone to research her next book, and goes back home to write it. I had a marvellous Easter in a lovely family.'

'Now I know why I thought I'd seen her face before,' said Marion. 'It's on the back of her books.'

Margaret attended to big matters and small. There were the businessmen who took it upon themselves to do a 'search' and propose improving Universal Aunts' image, it being the era of takeovers. Their presumptuous offers were briskly refused; 'The Company would settle its own future'. But other approaches were dealt with more gently.

A small, brown, woolly figure came into reception on a grey and chilly afternoon. Jean's was an end-of-the-day smile. 'Can I help you?'

The answering tone was commanding. 'Yes, I wish to see your Director on a matter of some local importance.' Margaret sallied forth, following Jean's low summons. A few quiet words with the visitor and they both disappeared into the outside dusk, where they could be seen in earnest discussion and contemplating the skyline. Margaret tottered back and explained: 'That was Lady Calthrop. She has had from the agents of the building she lives in a letter stating the landlord's intention to build several penthouses on top, and she has come to us.' Margaret was by now thawing out on Jean's radiator. 'We supplied her mother with a cook in 1922 and her with a finishing school. Miss Leith taught her sister to fly in the '30s, and we escorted Lady Calthrop's own children on their school journeys in the '40s. She feels that the prevention of this '80s outrage can safely be left in our hands.'

A day or two later, a very typical lunch-time session took place. Jenny puffed in, and tossed a packet of sandwiches on her desk. 'Oh, hello Peggy,' she greeted one of the Aunts who was seated by Marion's desk being briefed for a job. Jenny went on, 'I should think every senior citizen is riding round on British Rail's cheap ticket offer. I've just heard the saddest thing. A little old man was just in front of me in the queue, standing and reading the menu-board on the wall, and when his turn came he said to Blondie, "I've just come up on my £1 sponsored ticket so I'll have the lot – egg, bacon, sausage, tomatoes, fried." "Sorry, love, it's orf – cook's gone on *her* £1 away-day!"' she told him.

'Let me tell you a conversation I've just had and you tell me *who* you think it might have been,' said Marion. 'Over the telephone came a charming male voice enquiring, "Could you tell me where to get trouser repairs done?" "Well, yes," I said, "we do have someone who does sewing. But trousers need tailoring. Do you know you can get the service at any good cleaner?" "Really! I knew Universal Aunts would have the answer." "May I ask what repair you need?" "I want them narrowing." "Well, I recently took some to Sketchley, and they were very good." "I expect it varies from place to place," he said. "I'm just looking through the Yellow Pages, and I think Horseferry Road may be the nearest to me." "I took mine to Stag Place. Where do you live?" I said. "Buckingham Palace!"' he answered.

Peggy was a long-standing Aunt and friend, experienced and reliable, so they all paused when she said, 'I have to tell you I've let the name of the Aunts down badly,' – with a small grimace.

'Oh yes? What on earth have you done?' said Marion disbelievingly.

'Well,' Peggy said, 'I went by train to collect a boy from Eastbourne at the end of term last week. A woman came into the carriage and I thought I knew her face, so we exchanged a smile. I glanced at her several times and was certain that I knew her, so I leant across and said, "Are you on the job, too?" She looked a bit startled, and picked up her bag and left!'

'Oh, *Peggy*!' they all laughed.

The autumn and winter of 1982 brought the weddings of two very important young Aunts. Mary left the Accommodation department she had run so well and, as a beautiful, stately bride, dressed by Hardy Amies, married Ian. The Aunts travelled up to Yorkshire to see this take place in the lovely country setting of her home there. Maria soon after became an almost-Christmas bride to Michael, a blonde fairytale princess, the icy diamonds in her grand tiara blazing into a myriad of colours in the hundreds of tiny flames of the candlelit ceremony in St James's, Spanish Place, late on a dark winter afternoon.

June of 1983 came round and the Company told their friend and landlord Peter Martin that after twenty-one years they wished to restyle their administration and move to an open-plan office. He showed them the same kindly consideration as he had over other matters, and rescued them from the remainder of their lease. The move was made to premises only a few minutes away, the old Register Office in King's Road at number 250.

It all seemed very new and unestablished, but the aura of a place is soon built up by the occupants and happenings therein, and the Aunts had never been short of these! The photograph of Gertie was hung and those of the Aunts, old and new, placed round the walls.

Margaret decided that her days of coming up from the country now seemed arduous. She, as Emmie had done, became Consultant Director, a fund of knowledge and a wise counsellor when needed. She passed her role of Company Secretary to Penelope, and Kate became sole Managing Director, jobs which had to take them away from running their own departments. No problem with Special Services: Marion was there already. But, once again, after so long, there were gaps to be filled, and even in the '80s, the old grapevine brought forth exactly the right recruits.

Catherine had been, on and off, a young Universal Aunt since her schooldays had ended. In between doing public relations for her vast acquaintance of young people who were 'going places', her writing, her selling, her travelling and socializing, this bright, enthusiastic and head-turning redhead had taken over Accommodation when Mary married. Catherine's methods involved a lot of new, shiny, plastic folders, and much marking of day books and forms with brilliant pink and green highlighter pens. All of this proved to be not only an attractive bit of up-dating but also a serious method of efficiency, and the department sailed along in capable and sensible hands.

As Penelope stepped out of Meetings, Maureen arrived to take over. Like Marion some twelve years earlier, she had retired from a former career, in her case seventeen years in publishing with Heinemann. A well-read and articulate addition to any conversation, she did everything with quick, dancing movements. No one was surprised to learn that the young Maureen had indeed assisted the famous Madame Marguerite Vacani to teach the bevies of tots with noble names their first steps, curtsey and bows. Maureen's style fitted a life in the arts. An attractive gamin-shaped haircut curled round her mobile, smiling face; and her clothes, often of her own making, encouraged one to look up as she entered each morning to see what she was wearing – good cut and colour, expensive fabrics, and a store of belts and buckles, beads and pendants. Most importantly for the job in hand, Maureen had spent a lifetime dealing with *people* of all ages. In a soft, low voice, with clear diction, she was not slow to make her mark with Aunts, clients, airlines and railway officials.

The ideal 'escort' Aunt was brought in from her outside duties and became Maureen's number two. Army wives had always made good escorts to the travelling children, being reliable and knowledgeable, and having spent their married lives *en route*. Rosemary was typical: a tall, smart, affable redhead, with an Army husband and three grown-up sons well on their way, she managed two houses, a brisk social life, and was willing to add to it all a part-time job. She settled in in the same confident and orderly way that she had always undertaken the Aunt's assignments. Now the vital checking of information and briefing of escorts replaced her former work for the Aunts, which had relied on those instructions and carried them out. The Meetings partnership soon established itself in mutual respect and liking, a good enough omen.

The Aunts acquired another of their 'outside' Aunts in a closed partnership. On arrival at the new offices they decided that the low rate of agency fee for babysitting services did not warrant employment of one member of staff to run it at the current salary level. No other head of department had enough time on her hands to absorb it, and the list of babysitters on the books was informed accordingly that the department would close.

One of the babysitters, Rhonda Hughes, telephoned to ask for an appointment to see the Managing Director. Kate had not met this particular worker, but on checking, found that she had been a reliable stalwart for some five years. A tall, slim, unsmiling blonde arrived dead on time: well-cut hair, smartly belted long fawn riding-style raincoat over trousers, expensive flat shoes and shoulder bag.

'I had your notice that you are closing the Babysitting department,' she began, without any hedging. 'I want to know if you will let me take it over.'

'In what way would you propose to do that?' Kate questioned her.

'I would buy out your list of babysitters and clients.'

'What is your job? Our evening babysitting is, I imagine, just an extra for you?'

'I'm with an estate agent, but I want to run my own business now, house- and flat-letting. It might take time to get off the ground and a babysitting service would help on the side. I've had enough experience with you to know how it works,' she replied honestly. She was earnest, anxious and utterly sincere.

Kate liked her directness and dealt with her similarly. 'I shall consider your proposal, discuss it with my partner, Miss Henshaw, and contact you tomorrow, if that is convenient to you.' She brought the interview to an end, another possibility forming in her mind. Like all the older members of the Board, Lola, too, now wanted to return to her private family life. Who would replace her to run her House-letting department, what salary would a newcomer expect – and would *that* department be viable, either?

The new administration of the Company required the services of an accountant who could personally supervise that department within the office on a regular basis. Obviously a busy city accountant such as Philip Strode could not encompass this commitment. Contacts had produced a nice friendly accountant, partly retired from his busy Essex practice. Peter Collins now spent his days with his golf-champion wife on the best courses, combining it with 'accounting for the few'. He had agreed to make the business of the Aunts one of his 'few'. As he enigmatically put it, he had never undertaken anything quite like it!

Peter was now telephoned and gave his blessing to the proposed venture. A call to the Company solicitor, Aubrey Roberts of the original firm, and he could find no reason why not either. Twenty-four hours later, as promised, Kate telephoned the general outline of the deal and Rhonda Hughes accepted.

A franchise was arranged and Rhonda formed her own company, applied for and was granted her own licence, and on 1 December 1983 took up her own desk in the open plan scheme of things.

The Aunts discovered they had a winner. A most hard-working, loyal and honest girl was very soon a part of their lives. Then she thawed and smiled, and they had also got themselves an extraordinarily attractive, shrewd young asset, who was to their advantage as much as their experience and backing was to hers.

The trouble with pretty young Aunts was always that charming young men discovered them. But, to the Aunts, that was part of the circle. So it was when Christopher swept Catherine off her feet. Once again silk frocks were donned, but not hats, it being an early summer wedding in a garden under bowers of flowering laburnum. Aunts greeted and engaged in conversation, passed round plates of Welsh sea-salmon from the waters that lapped the shores of the bride's father's castle there, having first helped her mother with great spreads of flowers and blossoming shrubs from the gardens. A new generation in the network was on the scene: Kate's little grand-daughter Polly, calling herself the 'petal girl', strewed roses, silver horse-shoes and bells, walking backwards before the bride and groom.

This happiness had followed a sad good-bye. The Aunts had for some time served an enchantingly teddy-bearlike gentleman, who was tall, but frail in stature and great in distinction, – Sir John Betjeman. Even a brief visit to him in nearby Radnor Walk was a remembrance to treasure. By ten a.m. or thereabouts he would be ensconsed, spruce but ailing, in a chair in his small book-lined drawing-room, ready to receive. Not able to rise alone, he extended a hand and slightly bowed his head. 'A little glass of champagne?' His invitation sparkled with naughty wit, it being not yet mid-day. His twinkling eyes awaited one's reply.

'Oh, Sir John, I have to get back to the office and *work*.'

With or without the champagne, the day was made special. To work for *him* the Aunts were proud.

Sir John went to visit the Cornwall he so loved, and died while there. At his memorial service in Westminster Abbey, everyone had his or her own memories. The Aunts who were present had theirs.

yours sincerely

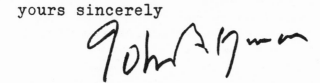

To Sue, like many Aunts before her, becoming a serious working girl was a bit of a shock. She bounced in to take over Catherine's Accommodation department. Dark, glossy hair flowing, with merry, loud voice and quick wit, her exuberant and friendly personality was soon put to good use in getting to know her landladies. Sue liked people and this was apparent to the clients who arrived to seek some kind of accommodation. They felt that she cared and tried to place the right guest in the right house, which was the essence of her job. One day it dawned on Sue that she was doing it all rather well, and that office life was not too bad after all! Another Aunt had come to stay.

Binky only came into the office to register as a temporary Aunt for six months. The following June she was to leave for Crete to photograph the hundreds of species of wild flowers there. Having done so, her commission was then to write a simple accompanying text, which would be produced as a guide for tourists. When offered the job on the staff to run a trial Day Jobs department to cope with the flow of clients needing non-resident domestic help, she gave up Crete. The new department began well under her super efficiency, and photography was confined to British flora for the time being.

Behind the smooth running of the departments was another team, the 'Floaters': Peg, Julia, American Maria (third of the Aunts' Marias), Joan, Susie, Patsy, Della, Alice, Peggy, and the newest, Cynthia and Veryan. They were part-timers, all with their own homes to run; flexible, calm and enormously valuable, with the agility of mind to slip into a department, take over for a while, handle clients and workers with tact, and hand back the department in good order. Most importantly, never to re-organize!

Samantha came on a more regular basis and worked for months in departments that suddenly needed extra force of staff. Fred, as she was called by her nearest and dearest, was a wizard on her electric typewriter, and being Montessori-trained was lovely with the children and those needing special help. A sight for sore eyes when she wished to be, she was young and thin, with long, loopy fair hair and often swathed in red fox. Frequently she would disrupt the entire office by bringing in her 'floating' goldfish to see if 'you think he's going to die!'

The domestic comfort of the Aunts in their new premises passed into the hands of John, grey-haired and dapper in his spotless blue boiler-suit, moving in at 5.30 p.m. to empty the baskets. 'Good evening, ladies.' Come each day, John was one of the early-morning brigade and he would dust and polish and open windows or put on fires so that the days might begin well. The only domestic sighting, by the time the offices came to life, might be of Amy, having attended to the building's common parts, disappearing into their cubbyhole with her dustpan and brushes.

Way down in reception, Sylvie, having cleared the mountain of post, would be there to direct those valuable callers upstairs to their business with the Aunts.

Now, nearly sixty-five years later, a word of praise from a client is still as exciting as the very first must have been to Gertie.

Dear Jo,   17 SEP 1995
        I just want to say a big THANK YOU
for your delightful service which was really a
great welcome when I arrived in London.
You were very helpful and your friendliness
simply warmed my heart.
        My hosts are equally nice people and
the home is perfect.
        THANKS for your concern
                and
        God Bless you!
                        Love,
                        Leong Kok Fong
                        (the chinese boy from malaysia)

Only the other day, Kate was invited to meet that most famous Royal
Hatter, Aage Thaarup. 'Kate is a Universal Aunt,' said her hostess, Jay.
    The gentleman responded, 'Universal Aunts! I first heard that name
in Poona in 1921!'

INDEX